The John Lardner Reader

A Press Box Legend's Classic Sportswriting

Edited and with an
introduction by John Schulian

FOREWORD BY DAN JENKINS

UNIVERSITY OF NEBRASKA PRESS | LINCOLN & LONDON

© 2010 by John Schulian
Foreword © 2010
by the Board of Regents
of the University of Nebraska

John Lardner's essays are reprinted
here by permission of Susan Lardner.

Library of Congress
Cataloging-in-Publication Data
Lardner, John, 1912–1960.
The John Lardner reader: a press box legend's classic sportswriting / John Lardner;
edited and with an introduction by John
Schulian; foreword by Dan Jenkins.
p. cm.
ISBN 978-0-8032-3047-7 (pbk.: alk. paper)
1. Lardner, John, 1912–1960. 2. Sportswriters—United States. 3. Sports journalism—United States. 4. Sports journalism—Authorship. I. Schulian, John.
II. Title.
GV742.42.L34A3
2010
070.449796—dc22
2010006345

Set in Janson Text by Kim Essman.
Designed by Ray Boeche.

Contents

Foreword

It's my strenuous opinion that any newspaper or magazine sports scribe over the last fifty years who is worth his weight in typewriter ribbons—or delete keys nowadays, I should say—has studied the works of John Lardner, the greatest sportswriter who ever lived, although he was more of an essayist than a sportswriter. No, that's not right either. Literary giant is more accurate.

Reading Lardner in the late forties and throughout the fifties in his weekly *Newsweek* column as well as in the other magazines for which he occasionally toiled—the *New Yorker, Saturday Evening Post, True*—was the finest creative writing class in the world.

Who but John Lardner could have written this lead in 1954?

"Stanley Ketchel was twenty-four years old when he was fatally shot in the back by the common-law husband of the lady who was cooking his breakfast."

Slit my wrist was what this aspiring young typist wanted to do when I read that, thinking I could never come close to being that good—might as well look for a job in janitorial services.

Red Smith, another icon in our lodge and as nice a man as any of us ever knew, once called that lead on the Ketchel piece in *True* "the greatest novel ever written in one sentence."

But there were hundreds of Lardner gems. We used to fondle them, memorize them, argue about the best of them, and steal from them in those carefree days at the *Fort Worth Press* when my guru and godfather Blackie Sherrod constructed a young, adventurous sports staff out of yours truly and Bud Shrake and Gary Cartwright, and armed us with clanking Royals and Remingtons and what we referred to as the publication's isosceles-triangle copy paper.

Every week there was always an urgent dash to a newsstand to grab *Newsweek* and desperately search out Lardner's column. The one that came to the office was Sherrod's, and if any of us dared touch it we might be sentenced to cover a high school football game between the Itasca Wampus Cats and the Trent Gorillas.

Maybe it would be the day that Lardner wrote:

"In 1951, which was the last time Leo Durocher's license to think was extended beyond September, the N.Y. Giants made a good, rousing fight of the World Series, against the Yankees. They came up to the Series tired and emotionally ragged from three playoff games. Their pitchers were overworked and disorganized. Willie Mays—this was Willie in his early days, before he was eight feet tall—was lunging and missing at the plate."

If so, I would be the one who stuck it on our cork bulletin board in the sports department next to the old metal cabinet where the photos, negatives, and mats were filed in mysterious order, with a note attached that said:

"Let Tolstoy or Dostoyevsky try to go up against this, by god!"

We all owned the Lardner bibles, his three hardcover collections—*It Beats Working, Strong Cigars and Lovely Women,* and *White Hopes and Other Tigers.* They were a guide to life itself, not just sports typing. I guarded mine closely, consulted them often for inspiration, and at times felt more love for them than any date I could lure into the back seat of my Bel-Air hardtop.

Also, Sherrod and I formed our own private collections by clipping out and storing up hordes of Lardner's other *Newsweek* columns for fear that they might not make it to hardcover someday.

The above Durocher piece comes from my private stock, as does this old favorite:

"It is hard to estimate, as yet, just what percentage of the burden of national and international affairs was taken off the shoulders of D. D. Eisenhower, game, crowd-pleasing President, when Charlie Dressen went down to Washington to manage."

One of Lardner's greatest abilities was his talent to amuse, tease, correct, and criticize without drawing blood.

I suppose if you struck a match to my private parts and made me select another all-time Lardner lead, something to rank up there with Ketchel, it would be this one:

"Take yacht racing, now. Why does it fascinate the sporting public so much that crowds will stand all night outside a newspaper office in Terre Haute or Des Moines waiting to hear the result of a regatta for F-Class Butterfly Sloops off Throg's Neck, L.I.? For that matter, who was Throg?"

Without benefit of that classic literary paragraph, I doubt that I would ever have been able to write one morning on deadline at the *Fort Worth Press*:

"Take the Southwest Conference track meet, please."

So I stand before you today without embarrassment to say I continue to worship the work of John Lardner, and I eagerly look forward to placing this book among my treasures, and within handy reach. All he did was give me a career.

Dan Jenkins

Acknowledgments

The foundation for this book comes from four earlier collections of John Lardner's essays: *It Beats Working, Strong Cigars and Lovely Women, White Hopes and Other Tigers*, and the volume that opened my eyes to his genius nearly four decades ago, *The World of John Lardner*. As the years passed, I kept telling myself that someone would come along to revive his work for both old admirers and curious young readers who deserve to know about him. Wonder of wonders, it turned out to be me. I am honored to have had the opportunity, but I hasten to add that I would never have succeeded if I hadn't been aided, abetted, and inspired by:

Rob Taylor, who instantly embraced the idea for the book and championed its cause until his colleagues at the University of Nebraska Press just couldn't say no;

the advocates of great writing at *Newsweek* and the *New Yorker* who gave Lardner a forum lo those many years ago and their successors who wanted nothing more than to see his prose in print again;

the editors who made *True* and *Sport* magazines so vital and memorable in an era when reading was truly a democratic pastime;

Irving T. Marsh and Edward Ehre (may they both rest in peace), the guiding lights of the old *Best Sports Stories* series, who leaned so heavily on Lardner when they came out of the starting gate in 1944;

Robin McMillan, of *Golf* magazine;

Martha Briggs and Helen Long, of the Newberry Library, in Chicago, who proved that Lardner's papers couldn't be in more caring or competent hands;

Dan Jenkins, most definitely;

Sally Jenkins, facilitator;

Alex Belth, indefatigable student of American sportswriting;

Jane Shay Wald, the queen of intellectual property law;

Steve Kelly, son of Walt, who wanted this book to become a reality as much as I did;

and most of all, John Lardner's daughter Susan, who gave the book her blessing without hesitation, pitched in to help wherever she could, served as a trusted sounding board, and became a better ally than I could ever have imagined.

J. S.

Introduction

JOHN SCHULIAN

Since TV and talk radio started throwing crazy money at them, more and more otherwise admirable sportswriters have been only too happy to install whoopee cushions where their regard for the language used to be. It's a natural reaction, I suppose, like realizing that the only way to be heard in a noisy bar is to shout louder than everybody else. But sly humor and high style have taken a drubbing everywhere sports are written. Worse yet, John Lardner has been forgotten. That's as wrong as wearing white socks at a funeral.

In a perfect world, there would be lessons in Lardner wherever sportswriting is taught, although I suspect the man himself would have used them as fodder for one of his laugh-out-loud columns for *Newsweek*. He had a fondness for the sublimely ridiculous, and there was plenty of it going around in the benign era when he was hammering away at his typewriter. Not that he wouldn't have feasted on such contemporary targets as steroids, overindulged athletes, bloated contracts, conniving agents, and soulless team-owning corporations. But he must have had a hell of a lot more fun writing about characters who are a hell of a lot more fun to read about: gamblers and golf hustlers, fight racket exotics, screwball ballplayers, and the occasional Roller Derby queen.

Consider this:

"When Ezzard Charles won the heavyweight championship by licking J. J. Walcott, two years ago, Ezzard's manager, Jake (Madman) Mintz, passed out in the ring. Last July, when Walcott won the title, it was Charles who fell, while Jake remained on his feet throughout. That is my idea of a perfect partnership—always one man conscious, to count the house."

The amazing thing about Lardner—well, one of them, anyway—was his ability to shift from seven-hundred-word sprints for *Newsweek* to quirky rambles five and ten times that long for magazines like *True*, *Sport*, and the *New Yorker*. He never dropped so much as a semicolon. So it was that he wound up atop the same mountain with Red Smith and Jimmy Cannon, the giants of the newspaper game, and W. C. Heinz, who abandoned a daily column to apply the techniques of fiction writing to magazine journalism. Whether they knew it or not—and it's likely that even the pugnacious, streetwise Cannon didn't—they were revolutionaries.

They put a hammerlock on American sportswriting after World War II and marched it right up to the edge of literature. No longer would the business be the province of cliché-spewing hacks and old drunks waiting to be paid off by wrestling promoters. Suddenly the most talented and perceptive men chronicling fun and games (women would come later) aspired to do more than get the score in the first paragraph. There were full-blooded personalities to be written about, earthy vernacular to be captured, sacred cows to be tipped. And there was always the debate about who was the heaviest hitter: Smith, Cannon, Heinz, or Lardner.

Fate cheated Lardner out of his just due when he died too young, at forty-seven, in 1960. The others lived to write another day and then some. There were anthologies of their best work too, the last of

Cannon's posthumous, Heinz's while he was still living, and Smith's both before and after he drew his final breath. Roger Kahn did what he could for his favorite sportswriter in '61 by compiling a splendid collection called *The World of John Lardner*. But there hasn't been another such book until the one you hold in your hands.

For way too long, only true believers like Dan Jenkins, Jim Murray, and Rick Reilly have honored Lardner's sportswriting legacy. The civilian populace simply forgot about him, starting with the fact that he was the eldest son of Ring Lardner, the legendary American humorist who was the first writer to poke holes in the notion of the ballplayer as demigod. And this too was forgotten: that Ring's boy John handled whimsy and satire with a deft touch unmatched by anyone in the press box before or since. "John was funny, but not like his old man," Red Smith wrote when Lardner died. "He wasn't funny like anybody else. He was funny like John Lardner, a bonafide original."

The laughter his prose evoked made it easy, too easy perhaps, to forget that he was also a scrupulous reporter, a digger with an archaeologist's instincts and a poet's love of the language. Nobody was more impressed by what Lardner unearthed than Bill Heinz, himself a no-bull reporter of the first order. Despite his inherent modesty, I never doubted that Heinz relished being called the champion of the press box, but a year or so before he died, in 2008, he sent me a note in which he cast his vote for Lardner. "He was," Heinz wrote, "the best of all."

I wonder how Lardner would have handled such praise, for he was, by all accounts, the quietest man at every bar he ever stepped up to. Tall and solemn, with a cigar in hand as he looked at the world through dark-rimmed glasses, he likely would have just blown a smoke ring. If there was a twinkle in his eyes, the one place his emotions showed, it didn't matter if nobody noticed. My guess is he preferred it that way.

Whatever he shared of himself with the public came via the printed word. The grace and precision of his sentences seems geared for readers who know their way around every writer from Shakespeare to Hemingway. But to think Lardner's appeal stopped there is to underestimate the power of prose that doesn't have its nose in the air. I imagine lunch-bucket guys of his generation trying not to drip mustard on his latest column while reading it as ravenously as they did such paperback favorites as Raymond Chandler, Max Brand, and Ray Bradbury. Lardner touched something in everyday people not just because he wrote about sports—it was because he wrote in their voice, the American voice.

No great leap is required to imagine that he developed an ear for it by growing up in a home where his father evolved from *Chicago Tribune* baseball writer to book world sensation. The stories that carried Ring Lardner into the big time were based on a fictional bush league pitcher's letters to a buddy back home. Gathered in a volume called *You Know Me Al*, they proved rich in truths the half-bright pitcher had stumbled upon: "That's the hell of it, in baseball; it costs too much to take your wife on a trip with you, and it ain't safe to leave them at home."

At the risk of making Ring sound like a literary stud horse, he produced one son after another with a gift for putting words on paper. Ring Jr. wrote the screenplays for *M*A*S*H* and *The Cincinnati Kid* and won an Oscar for *Woman of the Year*. He also had a capacity for longevity that eluded his brothers. Jim left his job as a reporter for the *New York Herald Tribune* to fight for the Republican cause in the Spanish Civil War and became, at twenty-four, the last American volunteer killed. David was twenty-five when he died while covering World War II in Europe for the *New Yorker*.

Though John lived long enough to die in peacetime, he tempted fate for the same magazine by covering battles in North Africa and Italy and then moving on to the Pacific for the invasion of Okinawa. A. J. Liebling, who was on some of the same battlefields with Lardner, wrote, "John was naturally brave; when he saw blinding bomb flashes at night, he used to walk *toward* them to see better."

It is possible Lardner was even braver when he came home to carry on what he had begun by publishing his first piece in the *New Yorker* when he was nineteen and writing a syndicated column for the North American Newspaper Alliance at twenty-three. The prodigy was now a man with a sense of purpose. He turned down an offer to write a column for the *Herald Tribune* and denied the world what would have been a tandem of himself and Red Smith, the sportswriting equivalent of Babe Ruth and Willie Mays in the same outfield. Lardner preferred the flexibility afforded by *Newsweek*, where he took up residence in 1939; he could break away and write about the theater and TV for the *New Yorker* as well as sports for every magazine that wanted him—and they all did. No matter what the subject, though, he proved as funny and generous of spirit as ever, so much so that readers couldn't have imagined the burdens growing increasingly heavy on him. He wrote, as Walt Kelly, the comic-strip genius who created *Pogo*, said, "against a background of tuberculosis, the pain of heart disease, multiple sclerosis, personal troubles too private for anyone else to reveal, and a gnawing, understandable premonition that he would not live to be forty-eight years of age. He had just about a month to go."

When he had his fatal heart attack, Lardner was at home writing *Newsweek*'s obituary of Franklin P. Adams, a columnist and humorist with a seat at the Algonquin Round Table. An MD who had become Lardner's friend rushed to his side and desperately massaged his chest. "John," the doctor said in a choked voice, "you can't die,

John, you're a noble human being." Lardner looked up and said, "Oh, Lou, that sounds like a quotation." And then he was gone.

It was a family tradition to keep emotions reined in. Lardner never betrayed it, no matter how gloomy his predictions for himself. There are in this book, for example, only two pieces with a whiff of melancholy, "Battling Siki" and "No Scar, No Memory," and Lardner handles them so exquisitely that a reader doesn't leave either with the blues. In everything else, he is his usual self, embracing the eccentric and the unappreciated, celebrating scamps and scoundrels, deflating the pompous but never drawing blood. The Lardner way was to skewer with laughter.

I'm tempted, as always, to offer proof by quoting more of his great lines, but the time for that has passed. By now, you've most likely jumped ahead and started reading the master already. Maybe you've even found his nonpareil lead about hell-raising Stanley Ketchel, the twenty-five most perfect words ever written in the name of journalism. If for some inexplicable reason you haven't begun exploring, it's time to get your priorities in order. I'm just the guy who's opening the door. It's John Lardner you're here for, and you've kept him waiting for this showcase long enough, nearly fifty years to be exact. He was too great to be put in a holding pattern, too great to be forgotten. The proof awaits you.

In a Class by Themselves

Down Great Purple Valleys
from *True*

Stanley Ketchel was twenty-four years old when he was fatally shot in the back by the common-law husband of the lady who was cooking his breakfast.

That was in 1910. Up to 1907 the world at large had never heard of Ketchel. In the three years between his first fame and his murder, he made an impression on the public mind such as few men before or after him have made. When he died, he was already a folk hero and a legend. At once, his friends, followers, and biographers began to speak of his squalid end, not as a shooting or a killing, but as an assassination—as though Ketchel were Lincoln. The thought is blasphemous, maybe, but not entirely cockeyed. The crude, brawling, low-living, wild-eyed, sentimental, dissipated, almost illiterate hobo, who broke every Commandment at his disposal, had this in common with a handful of presidents, generals, athletes, and soul-savers, as well as with fabled characters like Paul Bunyan and Johnny Appleseed: he was the stuff of myth. He entered mythology at a younger age than most of the others, and he still holds stoutly to his place there.

There's a story by Ernest Hemingway, "The Light of the World," in which a couple of boys on the road sit listening to a pair of seedy harlots as they trade lies about how they loved the late Steve Ketchel in person. This is the mythology of the hustler—the shiniest lie the girls can manage, the invocation of the top name in the folklore of sporting life. Ketchel is also an article of barroom faith. Francis Albertanti, a boxing press agent, likes to tell about the fight fan who was spitting beer and adulation at Mickey Walker one night in a saloon soon after Mickey had won a big fight.

"Kid," said the fan to Walker, "you're the greatest middleweight that ever came down the road. The greatest. And don't let anybody tell you different."

"What about Ketchel?" said Albertanti in the background, stirring up trouble.

"Ketchel?" screamed the barfly, galvanized by the name. He grabbed Walker's coat. "Listen, bum!" he said to Walker. "You couldn't lick one side of Steve Ketchel on the best day you ever saw!"

Thousands of stories have been told about Ketchel. As befits a figure of myth, they are half truth—at best—and half lies. He was lied about in his lifetime by those who knew him best, including himself. Ketchel had a lurid pulp-fiction writer's mind. He loved the clichés of melodrama. His own story of his life, as he told it to Nat Fleischer, his official biographer, is full of naïve trimmings about bullies twice his size whom he licked as a boy, about people who saved him from certain death in his youth and whom he later visited in a limousine to repay a hundredfold. These tall tales weren't necessary. The truth was strong enough. Ketchel was champion of the world, perhaps the best fist fighter of his weight in history, a genuine wild man in private life, a legitimate all-around meteor, who needed no faking of his passport to legend. But he couldn't resist stringing his saga with tinsel. And it's something more than coincidence that his three closest friends toward the end of his life were three of the greatest Munchausens in America: Willus Britt, a fight manager; Wilson Mizner, a wit and literary con man; and Hype Igoe, a romantic journalist. They are all dead now. In their time, they juiced up Ketchel's imagination, and he juiced up theirs.

Mizner, who managed Ketchel for a short time, would tell of a day when he went looking for the fighter and found him in bed, smoking opium, with a blonde and a brunette. Well, the story is possible. It has often been said that Ketchel smoked hop, and he knew brunettes by the carload, and blondes by the platoon. But it's more likely that Mizner manufactured the tale to hang one of his own lines on: "What did I do?" he would say. "What could I do? I told them to move over."

Ketchel had the same effect on Willus Britt's fictional impulse. When Britt, Mizner's predecessor as manager, brought Ketchel east for the first time from California, where he won his fame, he couldn't help gilding the lily. Willus put him in chaps and spurs and billed him as a cowboy. Ketchel was never a cowboy, though he would have loved to have been one. He was a semi-retired hobo (even after he had money, he sometimes rode the rods from choice) and an ex-bouncer of lushes in bagnio.

"He had the soul of a bouncer," says Dumb Dan Morgan, one of the few surviving boxing men who knew him well, "but a bouncer who enjoyed the work."

One of Bill Mizner's best bons mots was the one he uttered when he heard of Ketchel's death: "Tell 'em to start counting to ten, and he'll get up." Ketchel would have lapped it up. He would have liked even better such things as Igoe used to write after Ketchel's murder—"the assassin's bullet that sent Steve down into the great purple valley." The great purple valley was to Ketchel's taste. It would have made him weep. He wept when he saw a painting, on a wall of a room in a whorehouse, of little sheep lost in a storm. He wept late at night in Joey Adams's nook on Forty-third Street just off Broadway when songwriters and singers like Harry Tiernery and Violinsky played ballads on the piano. "Mother" songs tore Ketchel's heart out. He had a voice like a crow's, but he used to dream of building a big house someday in Belmont, Michigan, near his hometown of Grand Rapids. In it there would be a music room where he would gather with hundreds of old friends and sing all night.

The record of his life is soaked in fable and sentiment. The bare facts are these:

Ketchel was born Stanislaus Kiecal on September 14, 1886. His father was a native from Russia, of Polish stock. His mother, Polish-American, was fourteen when Ketchel was born. His friends called him Steve. He won the world's middleweight championship in California at the age of twenty-one. He lost it to Billy Papke by a knockout and won it back by a knockout. He was champion when he died by the gun. He stood five feet nine. He had a strong, clean-cut Polish face. His hair was blondish and his eyes were blue-gray.

When you come to the statement made by many who knew him that they were "devil's eyes," you border the land of fancy in which Ketchel and his admirers lived. But there was a true fiendishness in the way he fought. Like Jack Dempsey, he always gave the impression of wanting to kill his man. Philadelphia Jack O'Brien, a rhetoric-lover whom he twice knocked unconscious, called Ketchel "an example of tumultuous ferocity." He could hit powerfully with each hand, and he had the stamina to fight at full speed through twenty- and thirty-round fights. He knocked down Jack Johnson, the finest heavyweight of his time, perhaps of any time, who outweighed him by thirty to forty pounds. He had a savagery of temperament to match his strength. From a combination of ham and hot temper, and to make things tougher on the world around him, he carried a Colt .44—Hype Igoe always spoke of it dramatically as the "blue gun"—which was at his side when he slept and in his lap when he sat down to eat. At his training camp at the Woodlawn

Inn near Woodlawn Cemetery in the Bronx, New York, Ketchel once fired the gun through his bedroom door and shot his faithful trainer Pete (Pete the Goat) Stone in the leg when Pete came to wake him up for work. Ketchel then leaped into his big red Lozier car and drove Stone to the hospital for treatment.

"He sobbed all the way," said Igoe, "driving with one hand and propping up Pete's head with the other."

The great moments of Ketchel's life were divided among three cities: San Francisco, New York, and Butte, Montana. Each city was at its romantic best when Ketchel came upon it.

Ketchel was a kid off the road, looking for jobs or handouts, when he hit Butte in 1902 at the age of sixteen. He had run away from Grand Rapids by freight when he was fourteen. In Chicago, as Ketchel used to tell it, a kindly saloonkeeper named Socker Flanagan (whose name and function came straight from Horatio Alger) saw him lick the usual Algeresque bully twice his size and gave him a job. It was Flanagan, according to Ketchel, who taught him to wear boxing gloves and who gave him the name of Ketchel. After a time the tough Polish boy moved west. He worked as a field hand in North Dakota. He went over the Canadian line to Winnipeg, and from there he described a great westering arc, through mining camps, sawmills, and machine shops, riding the rods of the Canadian National and the Canadian Pacific through rugged north-country settlements like Revelstoke, Kamloops, and Arrowhead, in British Columbia, till he fetched up on the West Coast at Victoria. He had a .22 rifle, he used to recall, that he carried like a hunter as he walked the roads. In Victoria, he sold the .22 for boat fare down across the straits and Puget Sound to Seattle. In Seattle he jumped a Northern Pacific freight to Montana. A railway dick threw him off the train in Silver Bow, and he walked the remaining few miles of cinders to Butte.

Butte was a bona fide dime-novel town in 1902. It was made for Ketchel. Built on what they called "the richest hill in the world," it mined half the country's copper. The town looked sooty and grim by day, but it was red and beautiful by night, a patch of fire and light in the Continental Divide. As the biggest city on the northwest line between Minneapolis and Spokane, it had saloons, theaters, hotels, honky-tonks, and fight clubs by the score. Name actors and name boxers played the town. When Ketchel struck the state, artillery was as common as collar buttons.

Ketch caught on as a bellhop at the hotel and place of amusement named the Copper Queen. One day, he licked the bouncer—and became a bouncer. As Dan Morgan says, he enjoyed the work; so much so that he expanded it, fighting all comers for $20 a week for the operator of the Casino Theater, when he was not bulldogging drunks at the Copper Queen. If Butte was made for Ketchel, so was the fight game. He used to say that he had 250 fights around this time that do not show in the record book. In 1903 he was already a welterweight, well grown and well muscled.

All hands, including Ketchel, agree that his first fight of record, with Jack (Kid) Tracy, May 2, 1903, was a "gimmick" fight, a sample of a larcenous tradition older than the Marquis of Queensberry. The gimmick was a sandbag. Tracy's manager, Texas Joe Halliday, who offered $10 to anyone who could go ten rounds with his boy, would stand behind a thin curtain at the rear of the stages on which Tracy fought. When Tracy maneuvered the victim against the curtain, Texas Joe would sandbag him. Ketchel, tipped off, reversed the maneuver. He backed Tracy against the curtain, and he and the manager hit the Kid at the same time. The book says, KO, 1 round.

The book also says that Ketchel lost a fight to Maurice Thompson in 1904. This calls for explanation, and, as always, the Ketchel legend has one ready. A true folk hero does not get beat, unless, as sometimes happened to Hercules, Samson, and Ketchel, he is jobbed. At the start of the Thompson fight a section of balcony seats broke down. Ketchel turned, laughing, to watch—and Thompson rabbit-punched him so hard from behind that Ketch never fully recovered. In the main, the young tiger from Michigan needed no excuses. He fought like a demon. He piled one knockout on top of another. He would ride the freights as far as northern California, to towns like Redding and Marysville, carrying his trunks and gloves in a bundle, and win fights there. In 1907, after he knocked out George Brown, a fighter with a good Coast reputation, in Sacramento, he decided to stay in California. It was the right move. In later years, when Ketchel had become mythological, hundreds of storytellers "remembered" his Butte adventures, but in 1907 no one had yet thought to mention them. In California the climate was golden, romantic, and right for fame. And overnight Ketchel became famous.

When minstrels sing of Ketch's fights with Joe Thomas, they like to call Thomas a veteran, a seasoned, wise old hand, a man fighting a boy. The fact is, Thomas was two weeks older than Ketchel. But he had reputation and experience. When Ketchel fought him a twenty-round draw in Marysville—and then on Labor Day 1907, knocked him out in thirty-two rounds in the San Francisco suburb of Colma—Ketchel burst into glory as suddenly as a rocket.

Now there was nothing left between him and the middleweight title but Jack Twin Sullivan. The Sullivans from Boston, Jack and Mike, were big on the Coast. Jack had as good a claim to the championship (vacated by Tommy Ryan the year before) as any middleweight in the world. But he told Ketchel, "You have to lick my brother Mike first." Ketchel knocked out Mike Twin Sullivan, a welter, in one round, as he had fully expected to do. Before the fight he saw one of Mike's handlers carrying a pail of oranges and asked what they were for. "Mike likes an orange between rounds," said the handler.

"He should have saved the money," said Ketchel.

Mike Twin needed no fruit; Jack Twin was tougher. Jack speared Ketchel with many a good left before Ketchel, after a long body campaign, went up to the head and knocked his man cold in the twentieth round. On that day, May 9, 1908, the Michigan freight-stiff became the recognized world champion.

His two historic fights with Billy Papke came in the same year. Papke, the Illinois Thunderbolt from Spring Valley, Illinois, was a rugged counterpuncher with pale, pompadoured hair and great hitting power. Earlier in 1908 Ketchel had won a decision from him in Milwaukee. The first of their two big ones took place in Vernon, on the fringe of Los Angeles, on September 7. Jim Jeffries, the re-tired undefeated heavyweight champion—Ketchel's only rival as a national idol—was the referee. The legend-makers do not have to look far to find an excuse for what happened to Ketchel in this one. It happened at the start, and in plain sight. In those days it was cus-tomary for fighters to shake hands—not just touch gloves—when the first round began. Ketchel held out his hand. Papke hit him a left on the jaw and a stunning right between his eyes. Ketchel's eyes were shut almost tight from then on; his brain was dazed through-out the twelve rounds it took Papke to beat him down and win the championship.

Friends of Ketchel used to say that to work himself into the mur-derous mood he wanted for every fight he would tell himself sto-ries about his opponents: "The sonofabitch insulted my mother. I'll kill the sonofabitch!" No self-whipping was needed for the re-turn bout with Papke. The fight took place in San Francisco on November 26, eleven weeks after Papke's treacherous coup d'état in Los Angeles. It lasted longer than it might have—eleven rounds; but this, they tell you, was pure sadism on Ketchel's part. Time after time Ketchel battered the Thunderbolt to the edge of coma; time after time he let him go, for the sake of doing it over again. It was wonderful to the crowd that Papke came out of it alive. At that, he survived Ketchel by twenty-six years, though he died just as abruptly. In 1936, Billy killed himself and his wife at Newport Beach, California.

It was around this time that Willus Britt brought his imagination to bear on Ketchel—that is, he moved in. Willus was a man who lived by piecework. An ex-Yukon pirate, he was San Francisco's leading fight manager and sport, wearing the brightest clothes in town and smoking the biggest cigars. He once had a piece of San Francisco itself—a block of flats that was knocked out by the 1906 earthquake. When Willus sued the city for damages, the city said the quake was an act of God. Willus pointed out that churches had been destroyed. Was that an act of God? The city said it didn't know, and would Willus please shut the door on the way out?

Britt won Ketchel over during some tour of San Francisco night life by his shining haberdashery and his easy access to champagne and showgirls. In this parlay, champagne ran second with Ketchel. He did drink, some, and the chances are that he smoked a little opium. But he didn't need either—he was one of those people who are born with half a load on. "His genes were drunk" is the way one barroom biologist puts it. His chief weaknesses were women, bright clothes, sad music, guns, fast cars, and candy.

Once, in 1909, after Britt had taken him in high style (Pullman, not freight) from the Coast to New York, Ketchel was seen driving on Fifth Avenue in an open carriage, wearing a red kimono and eating peanuts and candy, some of which he tossed to bystanders along the way. The kimono, gift of a lady friend, was a historical part of Ketchel's equipment. A present-day manager remembers riding up to Woodlawn Inn, Ketch's New York "training" quarters, with Britt one day, in Willus's big car with locomotive sound effects. As they approached the Inn, the guest saw a figure in red negligee emerge from the cemetery nearby.

"What's that?" he asked, startled.

"That's Steve," said Britt, chewing his cigar defiantly.

Britt had looked up Wilson Mizner as soon as he and Ketchel reached New York. Mizner, a fellow Californian and Yukon gold-rusher, was supposed to know "the New York angle"; Britt signed him on as an unsalaried assistant manager. Free of charge, Mizner taught Ketchel the theory of evolution one evening (or so the legend developed by Mizner runs). Much later the same night Mizner and Britt found Ketchel at home, studying a bowl of goldfish and cursing softly.

"What's the matter?" said Mizner.

"I've been watching these ———— fish for nine hours," snarled Ketchel, "and they haven't changed a bit."

Mizner, a part-time playwright at this time and a full-time deadbeat and Broadway night watchman, was a focus of New York life in 1909–10, the gay, brash, sentimental life of sad ballads and corny melodrama, of late hours and high spending, in which Ketchel passed the last years of his life. Living at the old Bartholdi Hotel at Broadway and Twenty-third Street, playing the cabarets, brothels, and gambling joints, Ketchel was gayer and wilder than ever before. He still fought. He had to, for he, Britt, and Mizner (unsalaried or not) were a costly team to support. Physically the champion was going downhill in a handcar, but he had the old savagery in the ring. His 1909 fight with Philadelphia Jack O'Brien ended in a riddle. O'Brien, a master, stabbed Ketchel foolish for seven rounds. In the eighth, O'Brien began to tire. In the ninth, Ketchel knocked him down for nine. In the tenth and last round, with seven seconds to go, Ketchel knocked O'Brien unconscious. Jack's head landed in a square flat box of sawdust just outside the ropes near his own corner, which he and his handlers used for a spittoon.

"Get up, old man!" yelled Major A. J. Drexel Biddle, Jack's society rooter from Philadelphia. "Get up, and the fight is yours!"

But Jack, in the sawdust, was dead to the world. The bout ended before he could be counted out. By New York boxing law at the time, it was a no-decision fight. O'Brien had clearly won it on points; just as clearly, Ketchel had knocked him out. Connoisseurs are still arguing the issue today. Win or lose, it was a big one for Ketchel, for O'Brien was a man with a great record, who had fought and beaten heavyweights. The next goal was obvious. Jack Johnson, the colored genius, held the heavyweight championship which Jim Jeffries had resigned. To hear the managers, promoters, and race patriots of the time tell it, the white race was in jeopardy—Johnson had to be beaten. Ketchel had no more than a normal share of the race patriotism of that era; but he was hungry, as always, for blood and cash, and he thought he could beat the big fellow. Britt signed him for the heavyweight title match late in the summer of 1909, the place to be Sunny Jim Coffroth's arena in Colma, California, the date, October 16.

"At the pace he's living, I can whip him," Ketch told a newspaperman one day. He himself had crawled in, pale and shaky, at 5 a.m. the previous morning. Johnson—on whom, at thirty-one, years of devotion to booze and women had had no noticeable effect whatever—called around to visit Ketchel in New York one afternoon in his own big car. He was wearing his twenty-pound driving coat, and he offered to split a bottle of grape with the challenger.

"I wish I'd asked him to bet that coat on the fight," said Ketchel afterward. "I could use it to scare the crows on my farm."

Ketchel was still dreaming of the farm, the big house in Belmont, Michigan, where he would live with his family and friends when he retired. He had a little less than one year of dreams left to him. One of them almost came true—or so the legend-makers tell you—in the bright sunshine of Colma on October 16. Actually, legends about the Ketchel-Johnson fight must compete with facts, for the motion pictures of the fight—very good ones they are, too—are still accessible to anyone who wants to see them. But tales of all kinds continue to flourish. It's said that there was a two-way agreement to go easy for ten rounds, to make the films more saleable. It's also said, by Johnson (in print) and his friends, that the whole bout was meant to be in the nature of exhibition, with no damage done, and that Ketchel tried a double cross. It's also said, by the Ketchel faction, that it was a shooting match all the way and that Steve almost beat the big man fairly and squarely. Ketchel fans say Ketchel weighed 160; neutrals say 170; the official announcement said 180¼. Officially, Johnson weighed 205½; Ketchel's fans say 210 or 220.

There's no way of checking the tonnage today. About the fight, the films show this: Johnson, almost never using his right hand, carried his man for eleven rounds. "Carried" is almost literally the right word, for Johnson several times propped up the smaller fighter to keep him from falling. Once or twice he wrestled or threw him across the ring. Jack did not go "easy"; he did ruthless, if restrained, work with his left. One side of Ketchel's face looked dark as hamburger after a few rounds. But in the twelfth round all parties threw the book away, and what followed was pure melodrama.

Ketchel walked out for the twelfth looking frail and desperate, his long hair horse-tailed by sweat, his long, dark trunks clinging to his legs. Pitiful or not to look at, he had murder in his mind. He feinted with his left, and drove a short right to Johnson's head. No one had ever hit Li'l Artha squarely with a right before, though the best artists had tried. Ketchel had the power of a heavyweight; and Johnson went down. Then, pivoting on his left arm on the canvas, he rolled himself across the ring and onto his knees. In the film you can almost see thoughts racing through his brain—and they are not going any faster than referee Jack Welch's count. Perhaps it was the speed of this toll that made up his mind. Johnson, a cocky fellow, always figured he had the whole world, not just one boxer, to beat, and he was always prepared to take care of himself. He scrambled to his feet at what Welch said was eight seconds. Ketchel, savage and dedicated, came at him. The big guy drove his right to Steve's mouth, and it was over.

No fighter has ever looked more wholly out than Ketchel did, flat on his back in the middle of the ring—though once, just before the count reached ten, he gave a lunge, like a troubled dreamer, that brought his shoulders off the floor. This spasmodic effort to rise while unconscious is enough to make the Ketchel legend real, without trimmings. It was an hour before Ketchel recovered his senses. Two of his teeth impaled his lip, and a couple more, knocked off at the gum, were caught in Johnson's glove.

Ketchel recuperated from the Johnson fight at Hot Springs, Arkansas. Sightseers saw him leading the grand ball there one night, dressed like the aurora borealis, with a queen of the spa on his arm. A few months later he was back in New York, touching matches to what was left of the candle. He kept on fighting, for his blonde-champagne-and-candy fund. They tell you that Mizner (Britt had died soon after the Johnson bout) once or twice paid money to see that Steve got home free in a fight—like the one with the mighty Sam Langford in April 1910, which came out "No decision-6." Dan Morgan says a "safety-first" deal was cooked up for Ketchel's second-to-last fight, a New York bout with a tough old hand named Willie Lewis. Dan's partner, and Willie's manager, was Dan McKetrick. On the night before the fight the two Daniels went to mass; and Morgan heard McKetrick breathe a prayer for victory (which startled him) and saw him drop a quarter in the contribution box. In the fight, Willie threw a dangerous punch at Ketchel, and Ketchel, alerted to treachery, stiffened Willie.

"You're the first man," said Morgan to McKetrick afterward, "that ever tried to buy a title with a two-bit piece."

"Tut, tut," said McKetrick. "Let us go see Ketchel, and maybe adopt him. If you can't beat 'em, join 'em."

McKetrick's hijacker's eye had been caught the night before by the sight of Mizner, nonchalant and dapper, sitting in a ringside seat drawing up plans for a new apartment for himself and Ketchel, instead of working in his fighter's corner. Maybe Ketch could be pried loose from that kind of management. Morgan and McKetrick called on Ketchel at the Bartholdi Hotel. They offered to take him off Mizner's hands. Ketchel, who respected Mizner's culture but not his ring wisdom, was receptive. The two flesh-shoppers went to see Mizner, to break the news to him.

"Why, boys, you can have the thug with pleasure," said Mizner. "But did he remember to tell you that I owe him three thousand dollars? How can I pay him unless I manage him?"

They saw his point. Mizner would need money from Ketchel to settle with Ketchel. Ketchel saw it, too, when they reported back to him. He turned white and paced the floor like a panther at the thought of being caged in this left-handed way. But he stayed under Mizner management.

Hype Igoe was Ketchel's closest crony in the final months that followed. To Hype, the supreme mythmaker, whatever Steve did was bigger than life. He used to tell and write of Ketchel's hand being swollen after a fight "to FIVE TIMES normal size!" He wrote of a visit Ketchel made, incognito, to a boxing booth at a carnival one time, when he called himself Kid Glutz and "knocked out SIX HEAVYWEIGHTS IN A ROW!" He told a story about a palooka who sobbed in Ketchel's arms in the clinches in a fight one night. "What's the matter, kid?" asked Ketchel. Between sobs and short jolts to the body, his opponent explained that he was being paid $10 a round, and feared he would not last long enough to make the $60 he needed to buy a pawnshop violin for his musical child. Ketchel carried him six rounds, and they went to the pawnshop together, in tears, with the money. The next time Hype wrote it, the fiddle cost $200. Ketchel made up the difference out of his pocket, and he and the musician's father bailed out the Stradivarius, got drunk on champagne, and went home singing together.

There was a grimmer, wilder side of Ketchel's mind that affected the faithful little sportswriter deeply. Ketchel used to tell Hype—he told many people—that he was sure he would die young. The prediction made a special impression on Igoe on nights when the two went driving together in the Lozier, with Ketchel at the wheel. As the car whipped around curves on two tires and Igoe yelped with fear, Ketchel would say, "It's got to happen, Hype. I'll die before I'm thirty. And I'll die in a fast car." Luckily for Hype and other friends, it happened in a different way when it happened, and Ketchel took nobody with him. The world was shocked by the Michigan Tiger's death, but on second thought found it natural that he should pass into the great purple valley by violence. To Igoe's mind it was the "blue gun" that Steve romantically took with him everywhere that was responsible.

Ketchel had knocked out a heavyweight, Jim Smith, in what proved to be the last fight of his life, in June 1910. Though he could fight, he was in bad shape, like a fine engine abused and over-driven. To get back his health he went to live on a ranch in Conway, Missouri, in the Ozarks, not far from Springfield. His host, Colonel R. P. Dickerson, was an old friend who had taken a fatherly interest in Ketchel for two or three years. Ketchel ate some of his meals at the ranch's cookhouse—he took an unfatherly interest in Goldie, the cook. Goldie was not much to look at. She was plain and dumpy. But because she was the only woman on the premises, Ketchel ignored this, as well as the fact that Walter Dipley, a new hand on the ranch, was thought to be her husband.

On the morning of October 16, as Ketchel sat at the breakfast table, Dipley shot him in the back with a .38 revolver. Ketchel was hit in the lung. He lived for only a few hours afterward.

Igoe used to say that it was because Ketchel had his own .44 in his lap, as always at meals, that he was shot from behind, and that he was shot at all. There was evidence later, after Dipley had been found by a posse with Ketchel's wallet in his possession, that husband and wife had played a badger game with money as a motive. Goldie, it turned out, was a wife in name only. Dipley, whose right name was Hurtz, had a police record. They were both sent to jail; Dipley, sentenced to life, did not get out on parole till twenty-four years later.

Ketchel's grave is in the Polish Cemetery in Grand Rapids. Visitors will find a monument over it, built by Colonel Dickerson—a slab of marble twelve and a half feet high, topped by a cross and showing these words:

STANLEY KETCHEL
BORN SEPT. 14, 1886
DIED OCT. 16, 1910
A Good Son and Faithful Friend

Legend had built an even more durable monument to Ketchel. Of the one in stone, a neighbor with a few drinks in him once said, "Steve could have put his hand through that slab with one punch."

"The Haig"

Rowdy Rebel of the Fairways
from *True*

Once, a man named Walter Hagen had a date to play a morning round of golf in Tokyo with Prince Konoye, of the royal blood of Japan. Hagen appeared at the clubhouse at noon.

"The Prince has been waiting since ten o'clock," he was told.

"Well," said Hagen, "he wasn't going anywhere, was he?"

There you hear the voice of one who succeeded, as few members of our meekly desperate species have done, in adjusting the shape, speed, and social laws of the world to his own tastes. Hagen was especially fearless of time; and, maybe for that reason, time has been respectful to Hagen. It's now more than a dozen years since the Haig quit playing even friendly golf. (It was no fun anymore; the finest putting touch in the history of the game had been fatally marred by, he said, a "whisky jerk.")

That's a long while to be out of action, out of the hot news, and still to be constantly remembered. But Hagen, rusticating in a house on a hill by a lake in Michigan where the water is cold enough to chase Scotch without ice, remains a living force in sport. They still talk about him with an awe and wonder as fresh as in the days when he had the golf world in a bottle, as the old song goes, and the stopper in his hand.

"Golf never had a showman like him," Gene Sarazen said two or three years ago. "All the professionals who have a chance to go after the big money today should say a silent thanks to Walter Hagen each time they stretch a check between their fingers. It was Hagen who made professional golf what it is."

By land and sea, in airplanes and in Wall Street, the age of Walter Hagen was the age of gorgeous individualism and golden soloists. In sports, the champions were Ruth, Dempsey, Tilden, Jones, Grange—and this fellow with sleek black hair, a full-moon face, and hooded, oddly Oriental eyes, who dressed himself to shine like the Milky Way on a clear night, and who used to say, by way of explaining how life should be lived: "Don't hurry. Don't worry. You're only here on a short visit, so be sure you get a smell of the flowers."

Seemingly, Hagen lived by that rule. In earning more than a million dollars at golf, he spent money as fast as he made it and often a little faster. Once, after winning the Canadian Open, he wired ahead to a Montreal hotel, as the first step in a victory party: "Fill one bathtub with champagne." The cost of the party eventually came to $200 more than the prize money he'd won in the tournament.

But, like other things about Hagen, the gay, hedonistic code was deceptive. If he had the philosophy of a butterfly and the appetites of a pasha, he had a brain like a pair of barber's shears.

In fact, he was full of contradictions:

1. "In swinging," said Mike King Brady, the old pro who first took him on the road in 1914, "Hagen was like a rocking horse."

But, says Ben Hogan, in speaking of golf technique, there is a fundamental kind of rhythm which "could also be described as the *order of procedure*. Walter Hagen was probably the greatest exponent of this kind of rhythm ever to play golf."

2. Hagen was prodigal with cash, a high spender and tipper, a compulsive check-grabber, a plunger on long, bright motor cars and soft, bright clothing.

But—he took care years ago to fix things so that he lives in perfect security today, on royalties and commissions from golf equipment.

3. Hagen was a loner and an egotist at golf, a pitiless competitor. He used every trick in the book of psychology to trim his friends and fellow pros.

But—he raised the living standards and promoted the independence of all professional athletes as did no one else, even Babe Ruth. By sheer force of his own love of comfort and freedom, he carried his profession onward and upward on his back. He revolutionized the status of the golf pro—from janitor to social hero.

Hagen's first job as a club pro, in 1912, paid him $1,200 for eight months, and this was not unusual. For several years after that, few pros averaged better than $50 a week. Socially, club members treated them in a friendly but patronizing way, like a chauffeur or a valuable cook. In 1914, $75 was a pro's standard charge for an exhibition match. By 1915, Hagen was asking and getting $200 and $300 for an exhibition, and he was mixing freely with millionaires and needling them into $500 nassaus in private games. They took it and loved it. By the time he had planted his full, democratic, do-it-my-way-or-to-hell-with-you brand on golf and on society, the American pro was a big shot, with a limitless earning capacity—and the European pro had come out of the servants' entrance and knew himself to be a man, as good as his talent could make him.

4. Hagen was a party guy, a nightbird, a wrecker of training rules.

But—he was also a sure-handed, clear-eyed all-around athlete, a winner at the top level for thirty years. (He won the croquet championship of Florida in his first try at the game. And once he outshot the whole field at a national live-bird shooting tournament.) Hagen didn't smoke or drink till he was twenty-six. Then he became a chain-smoker and went on winning. And when he discovered prohibition liquor, his luck stayed with him. It turned out that the man had a head like an old oaken bucket.

Take a look at him early on a hot summer morning in 1929. A golf fan stood in front of the Garden City Hotel on Long Island, admiring the dawn and thinking what a fine day it would be for the final round of the national PGA championship, when he noticed a dapper figure in a tuxedo approaching the hotel from out of the sunrise. It was Hagen—scheduled that afternoon to play Leo Diegel for the highest prize in professional golf. He had been training for the match by making a tour of Manhattan speakeasies. "Good morning," said Hagen, civilly.

"Good morning," said the startled fan. "Do you know Diegel has been in bed since ten o'clock?"

"No doubt he has, no doubt he has," said Hagen, as he walked on into the hotel. "But he hasn't been sleeping."

That was an accurate analysis—not only of Diegel, but of all Hagen opponents. A few hours later, Hagen won the championship by a score of 5 to 3.

The game with Diegel was one of a string of twenty-nine PGA matches in a row that Hagen won, over a period of five years, from the best and smartest golfers in the world. In his time, he captured eleven national American and British titles, including the British Open four times and the U.S. Open twice. When he gave up the game at the age of fifty, he had, in fact, proved everything.

Was he the greatest? His fellow pros said so in 1938, when they voted for him by two to one over Bobby Jones as the greatest tournament golfer they had ever seen. But "great" and "greatest" have become loose, flabby words in the sporting vocabulary. There were some who tried to describe Hagen more exactly, by calling him "the world's best bad golfer." Bob Jones himself once expressed the special, mortifying essence of Hagen even better, in something he said a few years ago, during the heyday of Ben Hogan.

In a way, Jones observed, a steady, consistent, mechanized player like Hogan makes an "easy" opponent at golf. Nothing he does surprises you; you can focus your mind on your own work. "But," Jones said, "when the other fellow misses his drive, and then misses his second shot, and then beats you out of the hole with a birdie, it gets your goat!"

He was speaking of Hagen—and Hagen had an answer to every criticism of this kind in one of his maxims: "The object of the game is to get the ball into the hole."

"Get your goat" is a gentle way of stating what Hagen did to Jones in a seventy-two-hole match they played in Florida in 1926 for "the championship of the world" (and also, as will be noted again later, for the purpose of selling real estate). Hagen went from stump to bush to sand, and, in the end, beat Jones by the whopping margin of 12 and 11. His purse, the biggest ever paid a golfer for one match, was $7,600. Off the top of this sum, he peeled $800 and bought Jones a pair of diamond-and-platinum cufflinks.

"We must encourage the breed of amateur," Hagen explained sweetly. "They draw their share of customers, and we take their share of the gravy."

So saying, he leaped aboard his Madame X Cadillac (a deluxe model of the period, of which Hagen owned the first specimen ever produced), and rode to his office to see how things were doing in the business (Florida golf promotion) which at that time paid him $30,000 a year and included, among other things, a blonde secretary who played the ukulele. The automobile was the latest in a line of flamboyant, Hagen-bearing vehicles that went well back into motor car history: a Chalmers, a Stephens-Duryea, a Chandler with an orange and black check, a red Lozier, a Pierce-Arrow, and in England, chartered Rolls-Royces and Austin-Daimlers.

This was the good life—the life toward which the Haig had begun to move a long time before, on the spring day when he climbed out the window of his seventh-grade classroom in Rochester, never to return to the field of formal education; at least, not regularly.

The schoolroom window commanded an irresistible view of the country club of Rochester. There, Hagen had first broken 80 in the year 1904, at the age of eleven. As a caddie at the country club, he made ten cents an hour, plus tips. His father, William Hagen, as a blacksmith in the railroad-car shops, made $18 a week. Once the younger Hagen had put the distractions of school behind him, he passed his father economically. A little later, he passed Andy Christy, the club pro, artistically. It cannot be said that Christy enjoyed this. In 1912, Andy went to the National Open in Buffalo with another pro and took Hagen, who had become his assistant, along. In a practice round, Hagen shot the course in 73.

"I'm thinking," said Christy, who was shooting much higher, "that someone should be home minding the shop. You can catch a train at 5:45."

The quick trip to Buffalo was not, however, a complete blank for Hagen: a whole new world was unfolded to him there. He was struck half blind with inspiration by the sight of a golfer named Tom Anderson, who wore a white silk shirt with blue, red, black, and yellow stripes, white flannel pants, a red bandanna around his neck, a loud plaid cap, and white buckskin shoes with wide laces and red soles.

By the time of the 1913 Open, at Brookline, Massachusetts, Hagen had reproduced the entire costume for his own use, except that he replaced the bandanna with an Ascot tie imported from London. This conservative touch was to be typical of his own evolving taste in clothes-horsemanship. He became a rainbow, but a smooth, sophisticated rainbow.

The 1913 U.S. Open at Brookline, which Hagen played in candy-striped shirt and red-soled shoes, was his first big tournament. It is famous today for the playoff in which a young American named Francis Ouimet beat out the British masters Vardon and Ray; few remember that Hagen finished fourth behind those three, narrowly missing the playoff. The next year, at twenty-one, he took the title, tying the tournament record with 290.

The win was crucial—it saved Hagen from becoming a Philadelphia Phillie. The Phils had tried him out both as a right-handed pitcher and as a left-hand-hitting outfielder. Having tasted top money in golf, Hagen evaded their snares. The signs of ambidexterity, however, stayed with him for life. There was no right-hander in golf who could play the rare and occasionally vital left-handed shot better, from a tree or a wall or a water bank. Sometimes Hagen played it with a putter or the heel of a right-handed iron, sometimes with a left-handed club he carried for emergencies.

He had eighty-five other ways of beating you, as the pros of the old balloon-ball era discovered. The pros were, in the main, a dour, cautious, Scotsmanly lot. Once, in Florida, on the morning of a one-day $500 tournament, a group of them agreed to eliminate cab fare by accepting Hagen's invitation to drive them to the course in his new open-top car. Hagen appeared at the rendezvous a half hour late. "We must go like hell, men!" he cried, with a look at his watch. They did. It was several months before they recovered fully from the ride. Hagen won the $500.

The Al Jolson musical show *Sinbad* was playing Boston in 1919 at the time Hagen acquired his second U.S. Open title, at the Brae Burn course near there. Hagen had recently learned how to oil his metabolism with occasional "hoots." ("Hoot" was one of his favorite words for a drink of whisky. Another was "hyposonica.") He saw a good deal of the Jolson troupe, after showtime, during the tournament. A gala getaway party was arranged for the night following the last round of the Open. As things turned out, the last round left Hagen tied for first place with Mike Brady. This called for a playoff next day, but Hagen did not see his way clear to passing up the party.

In the dawn that followed the revels, he left the flower and the chivalry of *Sinbad*, took a shower at his hotel, proceeded to the course by Pierce-Arrow, had two quick double Scotches in the clubhouse bar, and joined Brady at the first tee. Hagen, who did not feel entirely in the pink, decided that a dose of strategy was in order. Brady, prepared to do a man's work, had his shirt sleeves rolled well up toward the shoulders. "Listen, Mike," said Hagen, as they reached the second tee, "hadn't you better roll down those sleeves?" "What for?" Brady asked. "The gallery can see your muscles twitching," Hagen said. Brady hooked his tee shot violently, and lost the hole by two strokes. Hagen's margin at the end, as he won the championship again, was one stroke.

This, it should be noted, was medal play. Hagen's favorite style was match play, in which he could bring all the resources of his erratic long game, his murderous pitching and putting, his aggressive coolness, his concentration, and his sharp personal tactics to bear against one man. In the medal style of the open game, he was never happier than when he could reduce a tournament to man-to-man combat. The record shows—and it shows it of no one else in history—that in thirty years of big-league golf, Hagen never lost a playoff.

In private golf, in exhibitions, he tried always to introduce the personal element, the head-on gambling touch, that brought out his best. After the First World War, Hagen became the first important professional golfer to cut loose completely with the normal pro's life, a shop-and-lessons contract with a single country club. This led to endless exhibition tours. On tour, he always reached for the extra gamble.

At one strange club, he heard that the course record was 67, and offered to bet he would tie it. A member of the reception committee was willing to stake $50 against him. "Well," Hagen said, "the sun is high, and we have lots of time. Maybe we can do better than fifty." Eventually, a pool of $3,000 was raised among members, which Hagen faded.

The membership then followed Hagen around the course in a body. On the last green, he needed to sink a twelve-foot putt to tie the record. He tapped the ball, and yelled "Pay me, suckers!" before it dropped. It dropped.

A time was to arrive, and soon, when Hagen came to consider the British Open—especially on the seaside courses, lashed by wind and rain, with their shaggy rough and bony greens—as the truest test in golf, and a nagging challenge to himself personally. He was the first American-born golfer to win the British championship, at Deal in 1922. Before that, before he learned to throw away the effete book of American golf, with its high driving, pitching, and exploding, and its controllable greens, and to master the British technique of the low shot and the pitch-and-run, he was tossed back violently on the seat of his pants. On his first trip abroad, in 1920, British golf overpowered Hagen.

His playing partner on the last round was a civil old gentleman of sixty-two, who became the only player Hagen beat in the tournament. The old gentleman finished fifty-fourth, Hagen fifty-third. The American champion's golf gave the British many a dry chuckle. But Hagen startled the press by obtaining a printed retraction of one slightly nasty piece by the simple but unprecedented method of telephoning the paper's owner, Lord Northcliffe. Hagen followed this step by carrying the social revolution to France—a traditional spot for revolutions.

He traveled to the French Open at La Boulie, near Paris, with the British stars George Duncan and Abe Mitchell. The dressing room for pros was a stable, with nails for the players' clothes and stalls for the livestock. "If they don't let us use the clubhouse," Hagen told Duncan and Mitchell, appointing himself chairman of a committee of three, "we will pull out."

The British pros, limp with class consciousness, followed him into the president's office. The president finally yielded the point—though the three foreigners were the only ones to get into the clubhouse. Hagen won the tournament in a playoff with the French champion Eugene Lafitte.

Within the next few years, as the Haig made Europe and England his playground and the British Open title almost his private property, the force of his golf and his brash and gaudy independence knocked over the remaining social barriers one by one. Britain was shaken by a habit Hagen had of using first-prize money in the Open (it ran to about $300) to tip his caddy with.

The Prince of Wales, later the Duke of Windsor, followed Hagen around when he played, and automatically picked locks for him socially. (There's a story that on a green in Bermuda Hagen once said to the duke, "Hold the pin, Eddie." This is apocryphal, according to Hagen. "What I told him was, 'Hold the pin, caddie.'")

And while he removed the shackles from his fellow tradesmen, the Haig went on stealing their shirts and watches on the field of play. At La Boulie in 1920, striking a blow for liberty in France, he also ran Lafitte, his playoff opponent, dizzy. Hagen had heard that Lafitte hated to hurry his game. Hagen practically galloped around the course. At one hole, he climbed an uphill tee and drove before Lafitte had reached the top. Lafitte, panting after him, hurried his shot, and drove into the rough. The Frenchman lost the playoff by four strokes.

On the way to the playoff, Hagen used one of his favorite dodges, the wrong-club feint, to shake off Abe Mitchell. On a long hole, with his drive slightly ahead of Mitchell's, Hagen took his brassie from the bag as though to use it on his next shot. Big Abe went for the brassie too, and banged his ball into a row of trees that crossed the fairway. The Haig at once switched to his 2-iron and hooked around the trees to a point just short of the green. The stroke he gained on this hole shut the Englishman out of the playoff.

The same ruse tricked Al Watrous out of a vital hole one day in the PGA. Hagen's tee shot fetched up against the foot of a tree. He saw where it went, but Watrous didn't. "You're away, Al," Hagen said, nonchalantly hefting his brassie. Watrous could see Hagen's club, if not Hagen's ball. He grabbed his own brassie, though what he needed was a control club for a deliberate slice. His ball bounced off a tree and into a brook. Hagen swiftly replaced the wood with a niblick, backhanded his own ball out of trouble, and won the hole and match.

It was a finesse, too, that started Bobby Jones off to disaster in their great "world championship" match in Florida in 1926. The first hole was a par 4. All its nastiness lay just beyond the green. Hagen, for his second shot, ostentatiously chose a 4-iron and hit the ball a little softly—on purpose, critics have said. He landed short of the green. Jones, noting the shortness, used a 2-iron, overshot the carpet, had to struggle back, and lost the hole. From there on, Hagen never looked back as he marched to glory and a bag of gold and rubbed the great amateur's nose in the dirt.

It was heavily inflated dirt. The Florida land boom was on, and both Jones and Hagen had an interest in it. Hagen was president of the Pasadena Golf Club at St. Petersburg at $30,000 a year (plus a bonus of a couple of "hot lots"). Friends of the Jones family were anxious to glorify the real estate at Sarasota, down the line. The match consisted of thirty-six holes of golf at Jones's course, Sarasota, and thirty-six more a week later at Hagen's course. The region was crawling with butter-and-egg men, promoters, suckers, and other golf fans, and the air was charged with the rich flavor of gambling and excitement that Hagen loved.

The two players were clearly the world's best: Jones was American amateur and past Open champion, Hagen held the PGA and British Open titles.

Hagen took only fifty-three putts for the first thirty-six holes and was eight up at the end of them. On one green, after their second shots, Jones lay forty feet from the cup and Hagen twenty. Jones, using painstaking care, sank the ball—his finest putt of the match. "Whaddya know," shouted Hagen gaily, "he gets a half!" And while the meaning of these words was just coming home to his victim, he holed his own twenty-footer with a quick slap. It was a gesture that Jones never forgot.

In the second half of their Florida "world series," the Hagen-Jones match went downhill in a rout. It ended at the twenty-fifth green. In one history-making stretch of nine holes, Hagen needed only seven putts—he got by on seven long ones and two chip-ins. If the feat has ever been equaled, it was not done in the glare of the spotlight that bathed Hagen that day. The Haig agreed with other experts, as a general thing, that he always played his best golf with the 7- and 8-irons and the putter—the quick-death shots that can wipe out all past sins and break an opponent's heart. "I expect to make seven mistakes a round," Hagen used to say. "I always do. Why worry when I make them?" The short game always bailed him out.

He had an artist's passion for putting and an engineer's skill at judging the roll and grain of a green. There was a putt in the PGA in 1925 that stopped Leo Diegel as though he had been shot with a gun. Diegel had Hagen two down with two to go in their quarterfinal match. A forty-foot putt gave Diegel a four for the seventeenth hole; Hagen's second shot had left him fifteen feet to the left of the cup on a fast downhill green with a double roll. Hagen plotted the putt with the help of a small leaf that lay uphill from the hole to the right. The ball had to stop at the leaf, catch the momentum of the green there, and roll downhill at an angle to find the cup. It did all of that. As it dropped, Diegel fell flat on his face on the green. Hagen won the next hole easily, squaring the match, and ended it on the fourth extra hole. Or, it might be said, he won it on the third extra hole. There, an intricate putt put Hagen down in four. Diegel had a curving thirty-inch putt to tie. It was a tricky one, as both men knew in their hearts. Suddenly, Hagen knocked Diegel's ball aside. "I'll give you that one, Leo," he said. "Let's play another hole." The surprise of the gesture wrecked what was left of Diegel's nerves. Overwrought, he blooped his next drive into a hayfield, and Hagen marched grandly on to the title.

Though he gave up normal pro-shop duties when he was twenty-six, Hagen was a master club maker and club valet. Back in his early days, to earn a few extra dollars, he had worked as a mandolin maker and as a wood finisher in a piano factory. However, he had never made mandolins or finished pianos in the Deep South, where conditions are a little different. In Florida, in the 1920s, the Haig launched a golf club factory that he figured would make him rich for life. In a roundabout way, it did. The clubs he produced were like poems by Keats—in Florida. When they were shipped north, however, the colder weather warped and shrank their shafts till they rattled like a spoon in a cup of coffee.

Hagen was in the red for some $200,000 at the point where another rich friend, L. A. Young, Detroit's leading auto spring tycoon, put up his bail. The plant was shifted to Michigan. Under Young's management and later under the Wilson Co.'s, it has provided the royalties that have kept Hagen in comfort, bright plumage, fast cars, and "hoots" for the rest of his life.

The adventure proved what every golf pro in the world came to be convinced of in time: that you cannot top a man who has God and the angels on his side. At the Inwood course, where he won the first PGA title in 1921, Hagen liked to play the seventeenth hole by driving down the eighteenth fairway—it gave him a more open shot at the green. During the night after the first round of the PGA, Jock Mackie, the home pro, with the backing of a group of local comedians, set up a big willow tree between the two fairways in such a position as to block Hagen's drive. The sudden sight of the tree, as he teed up his ball, gave the Haig a start. At almost the same moment, a gust of wind shook loose the tree's wiring and knocked the willow over on its side. "Excellent timing," said Hagen smugly, and made his usual drive.

Even the spectators, as time went on, became infected by a sense of the fellow's omnipotence. There was a one-day tournament at Catalina Island, in the 1920s, for which Hagen showed up late—he had been shooting goats in the mountains all morning with William Wrigley, the island's owner. Hagen raced around the course to finish before dark. With three holes to go, he learned of a low score by Horton Smith which led the field at the moment, with everyone in but Hagen. Seeing Smith in the gallery, Hagen called out genially, "Well, kid, I can tie you with a three-two-one!" He got the three, then got the two, and then announced to the crowd, winking one inscrutable eye, "Now for the hole-in-one!" The hole was 190 yards. Hagen's tee shot hit the flag gently and stopped a foot from the cup.

Few mortal men can call a hole-in-one. And yet, Hagen once bet $10 even money at a short hole, in an exhibition match, that he would sink his tee shot, and then sank it. "The idea, when betting even money on a 100,000 to 1 shot," Hagen said mysteriously, as he pocketed the sawbuck, "is to recognize the one time when it comes along. It is done by clean living."

As noted, the U.S. PGA tournament was Hagen's special oyster for five straight years. It had to be. A cup went to the winner—and Hagen, unknown to everyone, had mislaid the cup. The name of this object was the Rodman Wanamaker Trophy, valued at $1,500. One day in 1925, Hagen, the temporary owner, left it in a taxicab in New York. He was always careless with silver. In 1926, he won the championship again. "You already have the cup, Walter," the officials told him, "so keep it."

The same thing happened in 1927. In 1928, however, the patient Leo Diegel broke through and won the title. Hagen was asked to turn over the cup. "Well, I would like to," he said, "but I haven't got the slightest idea where it is." The pros themselves saved the situation by chipping in for another cup for Diegel.

Hazy or not as to certain kinds of detail, the old brain continued to perform like a shears in one way and like an oaken bucket in another as the Haig's golfing years drew to an end. They tell of a day in Belleair, Florida, in the West Coast Open, which followed a long, hard night. Hagen groped his way to the course and took three practice shots. He topped a spoon shot, which traveled forty feet. He topped a 5-iron shot, which traveled six feet. "Okay, I'm ready to play," Hagen said. He toured the course in 62.

And the Haig himself tells in his breezy book, *The Walter Hagen Story*, of another morning after when his practice shots did the same kind of tricks, and the bright sun cut into his eyeballs like a knife. It was in Tampa, in 1935, when Hagen was forty-two. With a final hooker of corn liquor in him, he moved out from the soothing shadows of the locker room into the shimmering heat of the morning. Near the first tee, he saw three old friends from the Philadelphia Athletics ball club, Jimmy Foxx, Mickey Cochrane, and Cy Perkins, waiting with the gallery to watch him tee off in the tournament. Hagen tottered over to them and shook their hands with loving enthusiasm. "Hiya, Jimmy. Hiya, Mike. Hiya, Cy," he said. "Haven't seen you in a hell of a long time." "Good luck, Haig," said Mr. Foxx, Mr. Cochrane, and Mr. Perkins.

Hagen played the first nine holes more or less by instinct—and on the ninth green found himself needing a short putt for a 30. Looking up at the gallery, he noted with surprise and pleasure the presence of three old friends, Jimmy Foxx, Mickey Cochrane, and Cy Perkins. The Haig beamed, and walked over to shake hands. "Hiya, Jimmy. Hiya, Mike. Hiya, Cy," he yelled. "Haven't seen you in a hell of a long time."

The three Athletics were convulsed by this second ceremony. Their laugher faded into awe when they heard Hagen's score. He sank the putt, took a 64 for the day, and won the tournament with 280. It was to be Hagen's last big win in any big tournament.

But once in a while, in the few golfing years that were left to him, the magic of his bold, sudden-death touch came back again. Hagen was in his forties when he broke the course record at Inverness, Scotland, with a 64. In 1943, at the age of fifty, he captained a pickup team against the American Ryder Cup team and shot a 71 in his first match. Thus, his career overlapped to a degree those of the stars of the next generation. He saw them all—and, with the cheerful arrogance of a giant of the days when men were men, he gave them nothing. If they were brought together in their respective primes, he says, he, Jones, and Sarazen could beat Snead, Hogan, and Middlecoff, match or medal, for money, chalk, or marbles. Modern equipment and golf course engineering have lowered scores. But the fewer, cruder clubs of the old days increased the skill of the players. And by playing in all weathers, dirty and clean, they acquired a strength and wisdom, down to the marrows of their bones, that the new men cannot equal.

Until he settled in the house he lives in today—on Long Lake, near Traverse City, Michigan, with big fish to the right of him and tall highballs to the left and a sleek paunch like a Mongol chieftain's—the Haig never had a permanent home. The need of crowds, new crowds, with new faces and tastes (and new money), kept him tramping about the world for years, to England, Ireland, France, Scotland, Germany, Africa, Hawaii, Australia, New Zealand, China, the Philippines, Japan.

Even when he wasn't playing, the crowds still came to him. Johnny Farrell, himself a U.S. Open champion of the 1920s, was playing a major tournament one day, and burning up the course. Al Watrous walked over from a nearby tee to pass the time of day. "How's it going, Johnny?" he asked. "Terrific!" Farrell said. "I can't miss. Looks like I may break the course record."

"That's fine," Watrous said. He looked around. "Where's your gallery?" Farrell smiled philosophically. "Over behind the caddie house," he said, "watching Hagen play mumblety-peg."

The new men cannot hope to equal Hagen as a showman—but they play for big money today chiefly because Hagen boosted the price scale by his showmanship. The Haig used to say: "Make the hard ones look easy, and the easy ones look hard." He did, and for thirty years, hard and easy, he made them all.

2

Bats and Brawls

Babe Herman

from *Sport*

Floyd Caves Herman, known as Babe, did not always catch fly balls on the top of his head, but he could do it in a pinch. He never tripled into a triple play, but he once doubled into a double play, which is the next best thing. For seven long years, from 1926 through 1932, he was the spirit of Brooklyn baseball. He spent the best part of his life upholding the mighty tradition that anything can happen at Ebbets Field, the mother temple of daffiness in the national game.

Then he went away from there. He rolled and bounced from town to town and ball club to ball club. Thirteen years went by before he appeared in a Brooklyn uniform again. That was in the wartime summer of 1945, when manpower was so sparse that the desperate Dodger scouts were snatching beardless shortstops from the cradle and dropping their butterfly nets over Spanish War veterans who had played the outfield alongside Willie Keeler. In the course of the great famine Branch Rickey and Leo Durocher lured Babe Herman, then forty-two, from his turkey farm in Glendale, California, to hit a few more for the honor of Flatbush. A fine crowd turned out to watch the ancient hero on the first day of his reincarnation.

"It looks like they haven't forgotten you here, Babe," said one of the players, glancing around the grandstand.

Mr. Herman shook his head. "How could they?" he said with simple dignity.

And he went on to show what he meant. In his first time at bat he was almost thrown out at first base on a single to right field. The Babe rounded the bag at a high, senile prance, fell flat on his face on the baseline, and barely scrambled back to safety ahead of the throw from the outfield. The crowd roared with approval. Fifteen years earlier they would have booed themselves into the state of apoplexy, for that was a civic ritual at Ebbets Field—booing Herman. But this was 1945. You don't boo a legend from out of the past, a man who made history.

Before he went to California to stay, a few weeks later, the Babe gathered the younger players around his knee and filled them with bloodcurdling stories about his terrible past.

"You know that screen on top of the right-field fence," he said. "They put that there on account of me. I was breaking all the windows on the other side of Bedford Avenue."

Looking around to see if this had sunk in, he added, "There used to be a traffic tower on Bedford Avenue there. Once I hit one over the wall that broke a window in the tower and cut a cop's hand all to pieces. Wasn't my fault," said the Babe philosophically. "When I busted 'em, there was no telling where they'd go."

It's beyond question that Mr. Herman could bust them. He always admitted it. He used to be irritated, though, by the rumor that he was the world's worst outfielder and a constant danger to his own life. He was also sensitive about his base running.

"Don't write fresh cracks about my running," he once told an interviewer, "or I won't give you no story. I'm a great runner."

He proceeded to tell why he stole no bases in 1926, his first year with Brooklyn, until the very end of the season. It seems that the late Uncle Wilbert Robinson, then managing the Dodgers, came up to Mr. Herman one day and said sourly, "What's the matter, can't you steal?"

"Steal?" said the Babe. "Why, hell, you never asked me to."

So then he stole a couple of bases, to prove he could do everything.

One talent for which Babe never gave himself enough public credit was making money. He was one of the highest-salaried players of his time, year after year. He got these salaries by holding out all through the training season. Other players, starting slowly on the ball club's regular bill of fare in southern hotels, used to go down the street to the restaurants where Herman, the holdout, ate, and press their noses against the window like small boys, watching the Babe cut huge sirloin steaks to ribbons. It wasn't just the food that kept Babe from signing early. Holding out is a common practice with good-hit-no-field men like Herman, Zeke Bonura, and Rudy York in his outfielding days. The reason is obvious. The longer they postpone playing ball in the spring (for nothing), the less chance there is of getting killed by a fly ball.

Mr. Herman had such ambitious ideas about money that one year, returning his first contract to the Brooklyn office unsigned, he enclosed an unpaid bill from the dentist for treatment during the winter. The ball club ignored the bill. After all, Herman didn't hit with his teeth.

The Babe, as a player, was a gangling fellow with spacious ears who walked with a slouch that made him look less than his true height, six feet four inches. He was born in Buffalo in 1903. Leaving there for the professional baseball wars in 1921, Mr. Herman worked for eighteen different managers before he met up with Uncle Robbie, and for nine more after that. It is said that he broke the hearts of 45 percent of these gentlemen. The rest avoided cardiac trouble by getting rid of Babe as fast as they could.

He came up from Edmonton, in the Western Canada League, to Detroit, in the year 1922, and was promptly fired by Ty Cobb, the Tigers' idealistic manager.

"The Detroit club," said the Babe, his feelings wounded, "has undoubtedly made some bad mistakes in its time, but this is the worst they ever made."

He was fired from the Omaha club later in the same year while batting .416. A pop fly hit him on the head one day, and the Omaha owner lost his temper. The owner and the manager began to argue.

"Much as I would like to," said the manager, "I can't send away a man who is hitting four-sixteen."

"I don't care if he's hitting four thousand!" yelled the owner. "I am not going to have players who field the ball with their skulls. Fire him!"

The Babe explained later that the incident was greatly exaggerated.

"It was a foul ball," he said, "that started to go into the stands. The minute I turned my back, though, the wind caught the ball and blew it out again, and it conked me. It could happen to anybody."

Just the same, Mr. Herman was fired.

The Babe tried baseball in Boston briefly, when Lee Fohl managed the Red Sox. He never played an inning there. Studying his form on the bench, Mr. Fohl fired him. The Babe was just as well pleased. He said the Boston climate did not suit him. He went to Atlanta, where Otto Miller, later a Brooklyn coach, managed the team. Every morning for five days in a row Mr. Miller resolved to fire Mr. Herman. Every afternoon of those five days Mr. Herman got a hit that drove in runs and changed Mr. Miller's mind for the night. On the fifth day, playing against Nashville, he had four hits in his first four times at bat. He was robbed of a fifth hit by a sensational catch by Kiki Cuyler. After the game Mr. Miller told the Babe that they might have won the game but for Cuyler's catch. He meant it kindly, but Mr. Herman took it as a personal criticism of himself. He was hurt. He began a loud quarrel with Otto, and was traded to Memphis on one bounce.

The Brooklyn club bought the Babe for $15,000 a couple of years later, while he was causing nervous breakdowns and busting up ball games in Seattle. Then Brooklyn tried to get rid of him for nothing, and failed. This gross insult to the name of Herman occurred as follows: The Dodgers wanted a Minneapolis player, of no subsequent consequence, named Johnny Butler. They traded Herman and eight other men to Minneapolis for Butler. Minneapolis took the eight other men but refused to take Herman. Brooklyn was stuck with the Babe, and history began to be made.

Jacques Fournier, the Dodger first baseman, hurt his leg one day in the summer of 1926. Herman replaced him. He had a good season at bat that year and the Brooklyn fans began to take to the Babe, wide ears, chewing tobacco, and all. Uncle Robbie took to him some days. Other days gave him pause, like the day famous in ballad and prose when Mr. Herman smote a two-base hit that ended in a double play.

The bases were full of Brooklyns, with one out, when the Babe strode to the plate on that occasion, swinging his bat like a cane in his right hand. Physically, he was a phenomenon, a left-handed hitter with most of his power in his right arm. Scattered around the landscape before him were Hank DeBerry, the Brooklyn catcher, on third base; Dazzy Vance, the Dodger fireball pitcher, on second; and Chick Fewster, an outfielder, on first. Mr. Herman swung ferociously and the ball hit the right-field wall on a line. DeBerry scored. Vance, however, being a man who did not care to use his large dogs unnecessarily, hovered between second and third for a moment on the theory that the ball might be caught. When it rebounded off the wall, he set sail again, lumbered to third base, and made a tentative turn toward home. Then, deciding he couldn't score, he stepped back to third. This move confounded Fewster, who was hard on Vance's heels. Fewster started back toward second base. At that moment, a new character, with blond hair and flapping ears, came into their lives.

Mr. Herman has described himself as a great runner. What he meant was, he was a hard runner. He forgot to mention that he ran with blinkers on, as they say at the racetrack. He concentrated on running and ignored the human and animal life around and ahead of him. Passing Fewster like the Limited passing a whistle stop, the Babe slid into third just as Vance returned there from the opposite direction. Herman was automatically out for passing Fewster on the baseline, though nobody realized it at once but the umpire, who made an "out" sign. The third baseman, not knowing who was out, began frantically to tag Herman, who was already dead, and Vance, who stood perfectly safe on third base.

"What a spectacle!" observed Vance nonchalantly to Herman, as the third baseman looked in vain to the umpire for the sign of another out. Fewster, confused, stood a little distance away. His proper move was to go back to second and stay there, but Herman's slide had destroyed his powers of thought. Finally the third baseman caught on. He began to chase Fewster, who ran in a panic and did not even stop at second, where he would have been safe. He was tagged in the outfield for the third out of the inning.

Cheap detractors may say what they like about Herman's merely doubling into a double play. It's obvious that what he really did—the rule book to the contrary—was triple into a double play.

It's also obvious that Vance and Fewster were as much at fault as Herman. That is the old, true spirit of Brooklyn cooperation. But

Vance regarded Herman as the star of the act. A few years afterward, when Chicago officials announced that they expected a Chicago pennant in 1933 to make things complete for the Century of Progress exposition, Vance announced his counterplan for that year in Brooklyn. Instead of a Century of Progress, said Dazzy, they would feature "A Cavalcade of Chaos; or, the Headless Horsemen of Ebbets Field." Herman was to be the star. Unfortunately, by the time the year 1933 rolled into Brooklyn, Herman had rolled out of there to quieter pastures.

Uncle Robbie's comment on the celebrated double play of 1926 was "————." However, that was Robbie's comment on practically everything, and he meant it in a friendly way. He was tolerant of Herman, for he understood that criticism or scolding drove the Babe crazy. When 30,000 people booed him in unison—and that happened often enough in 1927, when his batting average slipped to .272, and in 1929, when he led the league's outfielders in errors—the Babe would sulk for days. It took Robbie a little while, at that, to learn patience with Herman. He asked waivers on him in 1927 but changed his mind and kept the Babe when John McGraw, of the New York Giants, refused to waive.

"If that crafty blank-blank McGraw wants him," reasoned Mr. Robinson, "there must be something in him."

As time went on, the Brooklyn crowds became more sympathetic, too. That's understandable. After 1927, Herman hit for averages of .340, .381, .393, .313, and .326. In 1930 he had 241 hits for a total of 426 bases, including 35 home runs. He scored 143 runs and batted in 130. The fans barbecued him one moment and cheered him the next.

"Not only is that fellow a funny-looking blank-blank-blank," said the manager, "but he is blankety-blank unlucky. Other men, when they're on third base, can sometimes beat the outfielder's catch when they start home on a fly ball. But not this blankety-blank Herman. He always gets called for it."

The wailing and the keening were great in Brooklyn when the Babe, called by Rogers Hornsby "the perfect free-swinger," was traded to Cincinnati in December 1932 in a six-player deal. It was not a bad deal for Brooklyn, in a strictly practical way. Herman never hit in high figures again after that year, while some of the players from Cincinnati helped the Dodgers into the first division. But the fans, in the main, never forgave Max Carey, who had replaced Uncle Robbie as manager, for sending Herman away. They didn't care about being practical. They wanted salt in their stew.

Removed from the choice Brooklyn atmosphere where he had flourished, the Babe began to bounce from place to place again as he had in the days of his youth. Managers resumed the practice of firing him to save their health. He went from Cincinnati to Chicago to Pittsburgh to Cincinnati to Detroit to Toledo to Syracuse to Jersey City, and finally, with a strong tailwind, clear out to the Pacific Coast. The slower he got as a player, the more money he asked, and the more loudly he asked for it. The Babe, however, did not like the word "holdout." Once, in the early spring of 1934, he denounced the press of Los Angeles, near his home, for using that term to describe him.

"You got the wrong idea entirely," he told the reporters sternly. "I am not holding out. I just don't want to sign this ———— contract the Cubs have sent me, because the dough ain't big enough."

On his second time around in Cincinnati, in 1936, Mr. Herman came into contact with baseball's leading genius, Leland Stanford MacPhail, who was the Reds' general manager. They were bound to get together sometime, even though the Babe left Brooklyn before MacPhail was ripe for that city. It was also inevitable that MacPhail should someday fine Herman, and someday fire him. They were not made to be soul mates. MacPhail fined him and Paul Derringer, the pitcher, $200 each one day in July. It was a true Herman episode. With hostile runners on first and third, Derringer made a balk, the runner on third went home, and the runner on first went to second. Herman, communing with nature in the outfield, missed the play completely. He thought there were still men on first and third. When the next hitter singled to the Babe on one bounce, he studied the stitches on the ball and lobbed it back to the infield. The runner on second scored standing up. MacPhail turned purple and levied his fines on both the pitcher and the Babe.

It's a matter of record that Derringer got his fine canceled by throwing an inkwell at MacPhail, which impressed the great man. Mr. Herman was less direct, and therefore less successful. He waited a few weeks after being fined; then he demanded from MacPhail a cash bonus over and above his salary. It was an ill-timed request.

"A bonus!" yelled the genius. "Why you aren't even good enough to play on the team!" He added that Herman was fired. And he was.

Right to the end of his playing days the Babe retained his fresh young affection for cash money. He was farming turkeys at his home in Glendale by the time he landed with the Hollywood club of the Pacific Coast League in the twilight of his career. One day in 1942—just a short while before that final, nostalgic, wartime bow in Brooklyn—he arranged to have his turkeys advertised on the scorecards in the Hollywood ball park. He then announced that he was holding out. The holdout kept him home in comfort among the turkeys, but not so far away from Hollywood that he couldn't drive over from time to time to negotiate. When he finally got his price and signed up to play ball, the Babe was fat and his reflexes were slow. So he made his season's debut at a disadvantage.

Hollywood was playing a game with Seattle. The score was tied going into the tenth inning. Seattle's young pitcher, a kid named

Soriano, had already struck out ten men. Hollywood filled the bases on him, with two out, in the last of the tenth, but the boy was still strong and fast. The manager asked Mr. Herman if he was in shape to go in and pinch hit.

"I may not be sharp," said the Babe, reaching for his bat, "and maybe I can't hit him. But I won't have to. I'll paralyze him."

He walked to the plate. He glowered at the pitcher and held his bat at a menacing angle. He never swung it. Five pitches went by—three of them balls, two of them strikes. Then Mr. Herman pounded the plate, assumed a fearful scowl, and made as though his next move would tear a hole in the outfield wall. The last pitch from the nervous Soriano hit the ground in front of the Babe's feet for ball four. A run was forced in, and the ball game was over.

"That's a boy with an education," said the Babe, as he threw away his bat. "I see he's heard of Herman."

Good-by to All That

from *Newsweek*

Your correspondent spent most of the 1950 World Series musing on the irony of life as it applies in the case of an old acquaintance, Charles Dillon Stengel. It was plain that whether his Yankees won or lost in the Series, this man, once gay and happy on the wrong side of the railroad tracks, had taken sudden success very hard. The year 1949, which elevated him socially, had filigreed his face with five new wrinkles and added 68.5 gray hairs to his crown.

What was most striking, he talked and acted just like the president of a bank. Conservative and solemn, if you know what I mean. On bank presidents such traits look fine. On C. D. Stengel they make you stop and think.

This is a man who once emerged from a manhole with the cover in his hand to catch a fly ball. This is the personality who once, responding to the public's snarls, removed his cap and released an English sparrow (*Passer domesticus*) from beneath it. This is the light-hearted (though heavy-footed) athlete who once ran out a home run with his thumb to his nose. Asked one day why he had failed to slide on a close play, he replied that capitalism had unmanned him.

"On what they pay me," said Casey, "I'm so empty that if I hit the ground I would bust like a light bulb."

On moving from labor to management he remained skeptical, because of what they gave him to manage. "Don't cut my throat," he told the barber one day. "I may want to do that later myself." However, Mr. Stengel never truly contemplated self-surgery in those days. He preferred satire.

While managing one team that was a little worse than most, back in the time of the stock-market boom, he heard his men speaking eagerly of their investments one afternoon.

"I've got a tip for you, boys," he said. "Buy all the Pennsylvania Railroad stock you can lay hold of. You'll all be riding back to the bush next week, and you might as well cash in on it."

Casey remained a merry fellow until the day the Yanks fired Bucky Harris and hired him. As a man of the world, he knew what he was letting himself in for. He knew the penalty of failure on the big time—Mr. Harris barely had time to reach for his hat—and the penalties of success. He knew he was kissing his life of gaiety in the lower brackets good-by. However, baseball men, no matter how disillusioned, are so constituted that when offered a team with a pennant chance, they grab it. They can't help it. Casey couldn't. And in a wan and haggard way he probably thinks he is happy.

Mr. Stengel has been so impressed by contact with the first good ballplayers he ever managed that he finds he cannot even kid them.

Casey is never flippant at the expense of his rich and dignified new ball club. He is downright respectful to persons like Tommy Henrich, a solid businessman who would not dream of thumbing his nose while running out the same kind of home run Mr. Stengel hit for the Giants in the 1923 World Series.

The Dodgers tried to recall Casey's past to him in 1949 by exhibiting a lot of his old teammates from the Brooklyn club of 1916. The old teammates gazed with astonishment and awe at Casey's solemn bearing. They probably never heard one of the last remarks he made while still a free philosopher, after telling a story of how he had outwitted the late John McGraw and his detectives and broken McGraw's curfew law.

"I was quite a rascal," said Mr. Stengel complacently. "But don't tell my boys about that," he added at once. "If they ever pulled the stuff I pulled, I would have to fine their ears off. There's no room on my ball club for a man like Stengel."

He meant the old Stengel, not the new one.

Memoirs of Old Satch

from *Newsweek*

I listened with interest to some remarks delivered not long ago by Mr. Satchel Paige, wealthiest and most famous of Negro baseball players, beginning with the statement, in answer to a question, that he is thirty-nine years old. Satch always utters this vital statistic with a deadpan, in a firm, crisp tone of voice which suggests that if you want to argue your point you will do him a favor by arguing it with someone else. As far as he is concerned, thirty-nine is official, and may continue to be so for some years to come.

Mr. Paige went on to say that a top-flight colored team is apt to have at least four ballplayers who could make the major leagues. He then let his memory rove at will, and touched on the great hitters he has faced in his long and prosperous career of throwing the ball past enemy batsmen.

Satchel is not a man who lets diplomacy deflect his judgment. He has pitched to famous white hitters, including Joe DiMaggio, as well as dark ones, and calls the field as he sees it.

"The greatest hitter I ever pitched to," he said decisively, "was Josh Gibson. No one else in the same class."

Gibson, who died early in 1947 and was in his prime the celebrated catcher for the Homestead Grays, held the distance record for slugging in more than one major league ball park. His feats were phenomenal, and there could be no more reliable witness on this score than Mr. Paige.

"The next best hitter I pitched to," added Satchel, "was Babe Herman. And Charlie Gehringer, he had a good eye too."

As I listened to this lean historian, I reflected that his solemn manner and terse way of speech are deceptive. Satchel can be frivolous when he wants to, in action, in the ironic style to which players in Negro baseball sometimes give way and which makes much better entertainment than the jeeps, bands, and gyrationists lined up by major league promoters like Bill Veeck of Cleveland and L. S. MacPhail of New York. No other players can make an exhibition game so much fun for the audience and for themselves.

En route to the Okinawa landing during the war, your correspondent shared meals now and then with Colonel Alan Shapley, commanding the Fourth Marine Regiment on that operation, who was a gifted performer in football, baseball, and boxing at Navy in the 1920s. After he left Annapolis, Shapley captained a Marine baseball team that once played an exhibition game with a team for which Satchel Paige pitched and Josh Gibson caught. This distinguished battery, Shapley told me, was seized by a fit of flippancy halfway through the game. The pitcher and catcher exchanged a signal as Shapley came to bat.

"You the captain of this team?" asked Mr. Gibson.

Shapley, swinging his stick and eyeing the great pitcher on the mound with awe and misgiving, admitted that he was.

"All right, you're gonna be the hero," said Gibson blandly.

The Marine did not attach much importance to this remark, for he failed to see how anyone could be the hero of the blank end of an overwhelming shutout. A moment later, however, a pitch came up from Paige so slow, fat, and round that it looked like a captive balloon. Shapley's eyes popped for a split second. Then the startled Marine recovered in time to swing at the ball. He got himself a single.

The furthest thought from his mind, as he stood at first base, was to steal on the celebrated Mr. Paige and the distinguished Mr. Gibson. But Paige suddenly went into his full windup, and the steal was inescapable. Gibson, with a genial gesture toward catching the runner, broke the local throwing record for distance. The ball sailed over the center fielder's head. Shapley kept running, and Mr. Gibson gave him a grave wink as he crossed the plate.

"See what I said," the catcher observed. "You're the hero."

It was the only run the Marines scored that day, while the opposition ran up telephone numbers. Colonel Shapley has been a certified baseball hero ever since, courtesy of Paige & Gibson.

Most Blood for Your Money

from *Newsweek*

What with the rugged desperation of the Dodgers and ingratiating personality of their manager, Mr. Leo Durocher, owner of the foulest tongue in baseball, you will sometimes get amateur bouts at Ebbets Field which are the fight fan's best return for his money these days. For less than two bucks—Mike Jacobs, the fight promoter, has gone as high as $100 ringside, and Jack Solomons, of London, up to twenty guineas—the Brooklyn customer can see herds of stately athletes charging each other with fingernails bared, while the constabulary stands around and says, "Tch, tch!"

The last time I saw the Dodgers grow hostile, they put on informal fight programs for two days running and threw in a ball game each day for the same price. Miss Gladys Goodding, who is the house organist for Ebbets Field as well as Madison Square Garden, played battle music on her mighty console, and not far away Mr. Ford Christopher Frick, president of the National League, fingered a gay tune on his cash register. When the topsoil had settled again, it appeared that Mr. Frick's League was $650 richer for the proceedings, as follows:

A $150 fine and eight-day suspension for Len Merullo, Chicago Cub shortstop.

A $150 fine and five-day suspension for Dixie Walker, Dodger outfielder and left-handed idol.

A $150 fine and five-day suspension for Red Smith, Cub coach.

A $100 fine for Peewee Reese, Dodger shortstop.

A $100 fine for Phil Cavarretta, Cub first baseman.

Mr. Walker, the idol, also lost a tooth and a half, and the National League, which leaves no asset undeveloped, was still combing the grounds for same as we went to press. When you add up the $150, the 1.5 teeth, and the bulk of Mr. Walker's hair, which had disappeared over the years through normal processes of depreciation, you can see that Dixie is one of the nakedest idols ever to hold the Brooklyn franchise.

The Cubs and Dodgers had spent many seasons in building up to this crisis. Only a few years ago Mr. Hiram Bithorn, a sensitive fastball pitcher, pitched his specialty at the head of Mr. Durocher and missed by a millimeter, to the profound regret of uncounted millions. As far back as the early 1930s, Mickey Finn, Brooklyn, and Bill Jurges, Chicago, were lurching at each other in the inept but dignified way which signifies fighting in baseball.

The recent riots produced better fighting and sharper punching than you usually see in our national pastime. My only objection is that the Brooklyn management did not advertise them in advance. In Installment One, Edward Stanky of Brooklyn and Merullo of Chicago rolled on the ground for five minutes in a horizontal punching bee, while Mr. Peewee Reese attempted "to stop the fight"—I quote the next day's newspapers.

Now your correspondent, being a sharp observer, saw what Mr. Reese was actually doing, and so did several of the Cubs. They passed the information along to Mr. Merullo. The next day, at batting practice, the latter approached Mr. Reese and said he knew him now for the fiend who had struck him while he was down, engaged with Mr. Stanky, on the day before. He even had finger-prints. He offered Mr. Reese some of his own in return. It was at this point that Mr. Dixie Walker, the people's choice, stepped in and obtained Mr. Merullo's attention at the sacrifice of one and a half teeth, while Cavarretta clasped Reese to his bosom and Mr. Red Smith, an ex–Notre Dame star, deflected Stanky from the play with a body block.

There were swarms of cops on the scene, and they might have interfered had not Charles Grimm, the Cub manager, raised a majestic palm and shouted: "Don't lay a hand on my boys!" This new injunction, apparently superseding the ordinary code of criminal law, confused the cops and held them off till the battle died of exhaustion. As an extra feature, obtainable till now only at Ebbets Field, Mr. Walker's nine-year-old son danced on the outskirts crying: "Daddy!" This touch, which the baseball customers got for no further charge, will someday be adopted by boxing promoters at the added cost of $15 per ticket to their clientele.

The Home of the Bean and the Kid

from *Newsweek*

"Williams beat out a bunt yesterday," said Mr. Martin Marion, the prolonged shortstop of the St. Louis Cardinals, after a World Series game with the Boston Red Sox one day, "and the headlines almost knocked your eye out. This afternoon I got three hits. What'll you bet that anybody mentions it?"

Naturally, nobody offered to bet in support of the proposition outlined by Mr. Marion, and, naturally, Mr. Marion did not expect that anybody would. The scene of the conversation was Boston. By the time the press of Boston has completed its daily treatment of Theodore S. Williams—the Kid, the glory and bewilderment of the city—there is no room left in the papers for anything but two sticks of agate type about Truman and housing, and one column for the last Greater Boston girl to be murdered on a beach. As a matter of record, many Greater Boston girls decline to be murdered at all in the baseball season because of the poor press they will get while Mr. Williams, the great hitter, is swinging his bat or his epiglottis.

There was no rancor in Marion's remark, just the honest astonishment of anyone who is exposed to Boston's Williams complex for the first time. It is worth a journey there to behold it, provided you do not mind the risk of being from three to five days late in hearing about the declaration of the third world war or the first rocket flight to the planet Neptune.

The Boston-Williams affair is complicated as well as violent. That is to say, it is not just a plain case of athletic prowess and public adulation. The state of Williams's mind is the thing that grips the city's interest. How does the Kid feel this morning, the public asks itself as it climbs out of bed. I assume that is what the public asks itself, because the newspapers do practically nothing but try to answer the question. The answers fluctuate, and they also conflict. It depends, as they say at the newsstands, on what paper ya read. Or what page of what paper.

On page thirty-five of a Boston evening paper one afternoon, I read the following bulletin: "Ted is low." The writer added that Mr. Williams was not feeling jovial.

On page thirty-seven of the same paper my eye was caught by the headline: "Williams Happy."

These psychological flashes appeared in the sports section. The first thirty-four pages of the paper were devoted to facts and rumors which might explain why the Kid was (a) low and (b) high. His owner, Thomas Yawkey, was said to be selling him to Detroit for $8,000,000 and the Willow Run plant, but Yawkey denied it. L. S. MacPhail of New York was thought to have offered Joe DiMaggio, the Triboro Bridge, and a slightly damaged mutual ticket for Williams, but MacPhail denied it.

On Tuesday, Yawkey assured Williams that he would never be sold. On Wednesday, Joe Cronin, his manager, assured him that he would never be sold. On Thursday, Cronin and Yawkey both assured Williams that he would never be sold. On Friday, Yawkey assured Cronin that he would never sell Williams, and on Saturday, in the tallest type available, Yawkey assured Williams that he had just assured Cronin that Ted would never be sold.

This made Mr. Williams feel high, but at the same time he was feeling low because, as any child in Boston could tell you, he was worried about a sick friend in Peoria and another in Palos Verdes, and also whether it was a curve or a fastball that Brazle whiffed him with in the seventh inning.

Other things that every child in Boston knows are as follows: (1) whom Ted rooms with—he rooms with Charlie Wagner; (2) whom he sits with on trains—he sits with Bobby Doerr; (3) how he feels about booing—he doesn't like it; (4) how he feels about cheering—he likes it; (5) what the duty of every Boston citizen is—not to boo Williams.

The Kid has two ghost writers—one for use against left-handed pitching, they tell me, and one against right-handers—but the fact that a good deal of stuff about Williams in the Boston paper appears under Williams's byline does not deter the rest of the press at all. There is room enough in the story of the Kid for a couple of ghost writers and for everyone else with a typewriter.

How many push-ups does the Kid do every morning to keep himself in shape? I'm just in from Boston, and I'll tell you. Thirty push-ups.

The World's Richest Problem Child
from *Newsweek*

The St. Louis Browns have hired a professional psychologist for the spring training season to currycomb their inferiority complex. The Boston Red Sox, on the other hand, have chosen a simpler way of treating their own psychological problem, who goes by the name of Theodore S. Williams.

I am taking the word of certain experts for it that Williams has, or is, a psychological problem. Around the American League the pitchers tell you that if anything is wrong with Williams, they can only pray very earnestly that it's not catching. Give three or four other batsmen Theodore's disease and the pitching profession will be totally wrecked.

However, as I say, many students of human mentality (most of them play the same instrument that I do, the typewriter, and have learned psychology by close observation of the bartender at the water hole around the corner from the office) have been saying for years that Mr. Williams has a complex. They watch him with honest pity as he gropes his way through the shadowland between .340 and .406. They agree with a sigh that he is the strongest left-hand-hitting neurotic they have ever seen.

A few weeks ago Thomas A. Yawkey, the Red Sox owner, took cognizance of Ted's condition and tried the cure I spoke of above. It is a form of shock treatment. The subject is pelted softly but firmly with handfuls of green banknotes in large denominations. The size of the dose varies with the individual. Mr. Yawkey might still be showering his patient with engravings of General Grant had not Williams, rising from the couch when the total reached $125,000, remarked, by way of small talk, that he was satisfied.

Your correspondent inspected the convalescent athlete the other day. Mr. Williams was tying trout flies beside an indoor tank containing trout, all members of Actors Equity. Nearby stood a mermaid, wooing germs in a new-model bathing suit. Next to her was a gentleman who wrestles alligators, and next to him was an alligator, named Strangler Mississippiensis, formerly the catch-as-catch-can champion of the Everglades. I say formerly, for the reptile had been losing straight falls to the wrestler every day that week. It was absolutely clear by then that an alligator is no match for a human being under water. In a tank of orange juice it might be different. I throw out the suggestion for what it's worth.

The scene was the National Sportsmen's Show, where Mr. Williams tied and cast flies to tune up his arm for the baseball training season. In the circumstances he was not only the highest-paid ballplayer in the world, but the highest-paid flycaster, and I watched the results with interest.

If you have never seen professional trout at work, you have a treat in store. Many of these fellows have been playing melodrama since the old Ten-Twenty-Thirty days, and some, as I understand it, have trouped in vaudeville. They do not actually wear fur-collared overcoats and carry sticks, but you can see that they are fish with a flair.

The trout defense against Williams, judging by early indications, is the direct reverse of the Boudreau defense, in which the players shift to the right. Williams pulls a baseball to the right. He has a tendency to pull a trout fly in the same direction, and that is the explanation of the trout's strategy. As Williams begins his cast, the trout shift in unison to the left, like a Ziegfeld chorus line. I suspect that in an open stream, with no holds barred, this would not get them anywhere, but indoors, being a performer himself, Williams shows a happy tolerance for the right of Equity trout.

"Live and let live is my slogan," he states.

I regret to say that the policy does not apply to pitchers, nor will it apply to trout after Mr. Williams has hooked his fill of pitchers and called it a career. His ambition, he says, is to fish every lake, stream, and river in the world when he quits baseball. I advise the trout to start warming up three or four left-handers in the bullpen now.

Hard-way Bill on the Mississippi

from *Newsweek*

Back when William Veeck, the curly baseball genius, had the Cleveland Indians but did not have them very high up, your correspondent quoted an opinion on Veeck's methods from Prof. Milo Herringbone, the well-known Brooklyn psychologist. "Veeck," said the professor, "is behaving like a Roman empire. To distract the people, he gives them bread and soicuses."

I don't remember the bread, but he soitanly, I mean certainly, gave them circuses. There were fireworks, clowns, and a brass band in center field. The band was just fair, but so was the ball club. A ball hit into the bass horn was scored as a ground-rules double. Mr. Veeck, a strong writer (I understand he wrote a novel during his recent vacation from baseball), wrote me a letter saying that he was not trying to fool the people.

"Wait and see," he wrote, and sure enough, Cleveland suddenly won a pennant and a World Series, and Veeck got waivers on the clowns.

It's true that in baseball you have to start somewhere. While you are starting, you have to pay the rent. This Veeck is a dead-game guy. He has just bought the St. Louis Browns, and you cannot start any lower than that without drilling. Many critics were surprised to know that the Browns could be bought, because they didn't know that the Browns were owned. They'd forgotten that some folks—a Wall Street man here, a Metropolitan soprano there—save Brown stock in the same way that people used to save Gift of Heaven Gold Mine stock, for the sake of the scalloped margins and the illustrations.

As soon as he had the Browns, or vice versa, Bill went over to the ball park and ordered drinks for the house. Sure, it was a modest beginning. Sometimes you can buy a drink for every man and lady at a Brownie ball game and still get change for a dollar. But Veeck also had fireworks shot off for the throng. There had not been a firework seen in Sportsman's Park since the day when a salesman wandered into the place with a line of second-hand pinwheels and wound up playing first base for the home team.

Now in building the Browns, Bill first had to round up the fugitives. For instance, the Browns had an outfielder working for an Oklahoma oil company, Oklahoma being as far away from St. Louis as the man could get on short notice. Players for other teams have outside jobs during the winter, but a Brown player who lands a job somewhere else will go straight to it, summer or winter. This fellow, Frank Saucier, wasn't doing the team any good in Oklahoma, Veeck figured, so he waved a $20 bill under his nose and brought him back alive. I have a tip for Bill. There's a Brown pitcher living under an assumed name on an island in Hudson's Bay. He's been there six years. A sawbuck more a month, and car fare, might nail him.

In one of his first moves Veeck announced that he had brought Satchel Paige to St. Louis as the start of a new youth movement. It's a logical step. In Cleveland when things were tough, Bill shot Satchel into the Indians' bloodstream. Satch was then, and had been for some time, thirty-nine years old. Before the Indians let him go, still at the age of thirty-nine, Paige drew some big crowds. Today at thirty-nine, he is doing the same thing in St. Louis.

For men like Bill Veeck and the late Houdini, who prefer to begin the act at the bottom of a river tied up in a sealed box with a count to two strikes and three mortgages on them, the orthodox move is to fire the manager. Zack Taylor is the Browns' manager, or was when I wrote this. Possible successors are Rogers Hornsby, Joe Gordon, Happy Chandler, Eddie Stanky, Rita Hayworth, and Aly Khan.

But there is a better trick than changing managers that Bill can perform, if he wants to divert attention from the team for the moment. He can change towns. So far he has denied that the franchise will be switched to Los Angeles, San Francisco, Seattle, or Milwaukee. That leaves, as possibilities, Los Angeles, San Francisco, Seattle, or Milwaukee.

One place the Browns are sure to move, though, given Veeck and time, is up. They can't go nowheres else.

They Walked by Night
from *Sport*

One day in 1922 a large, convivial fellow from the South, Shufflin' Phil Douglas by name, was thrown out of baseball on a quick double play by John J. McGraw and Judge Kenesaw Mountain Landis. The event took place in Pittsburgh. Mournfully borrowing $100 from McGraw, the outlaw climbed on a train for New York to collect his wife and children and take them off into exile with him. Sharing the ride with him was his very own personal watchdog. It was their last ride together.

A dog is said to be man's best friend, and there were tears in the eyes of both parties as the train rolled east.

"Let's have a beer at the next stop, Jess," said Mr. Douglas to the watchdog, whose name was Jess Burkett. "I'm gonna miss you."

"I'm gonna miss you too, Phil," said Mr. Burkett with a manly catch in his throat. "Why, hell, I'm so used to following you from saloon to saloon, making notes, that I won't know what to do with myself."

It's a matter of record that the New York Giants didn't know exactly what to do with Burkett, either, once Douglas was kicked out of baseball. They finally sent him on the road as a scout. For many months before that, Jess's only task with the Giants had been to watch Douglas—watch him and report. He always had something to report, too, for in the company of Shufflin' Phil there was seldom a dull moment, or a dry one.

It may well be that the Shuffler was the only man in baseball history ever to have a detective all to himself for the whole season. The great Rube Waddell, one of the game's foremost night-walkers, could not make such a boast. Rube's boss, Connie Mack, was too frugal to waste a whole detective on one man. Casey Stengel, when he played for the Giants, had to share a detective with a teammate, Irish Meusel. When Casey stopped going out with Meusel at night, McGraw sold him to Boston rather than sign the check for an extra shadow at union rates. "If you think I'm going to pay to have you followed all alone, you're mistaken, my friend," said McGraw to Stengel. And he proved it.

But Shufflin' Phil Douglas was something else again. He had to be followed in a big, exclusive way.

The era of the night-walking ballplayer—the man with a single-minded thirst and feet that point away from home—is just about over and gone. So is the era of the detective in baseball. True, Bucky Harris, when he managed the New York Yankees in 1948, is said to have hired gumshoes to stalk a few of his players. The Yankees should have been easy to stalk because, belonging to a high-class ball club, they drank martinis and left a trail of olives. Groping from olive to olive, however, the cops were sidetracked by the onion in a Gibson-type martini one day and lost the scent. Nothing much came of the Harris hunt.

The last outstanding night-walkers in baseball were Rollicking Rollie Hemsley, until he joined Alcoholics Anonymous, and Baron Boots Poffenberger, until he joined the Marines. I rate them close behind Phil Douglas, though a case can be made out for Charles Flint Rhem of Rhems, South Carolina, as the most ingenious of all the night-walkers. It was Rhem, in 1930, after he had been missing from the sight of man for forty-eight hours, who reported back to his team, the St. Louis Cardinals, pale and shaken, with the story that he had been kidnapped by gangsters, locked in a hotel room, and forced to drink great quantities of liquor at the point of a gun.

With Poffenberger and Hemsley, the leading rebels of our own generation, detectives were seldom used. The owners of these two wandering pieces of merchandise resorted to the method of the straight cash fine, or plaster. Life was a race between owner and player to see which would come out ahead financially at the end of the season. There were times when Rollie and the Baron, fighting off drought in the desert sands of Chicago, Philadelphia, or Cincinnati, were fined to a point where their paychecks touched bottom, but they rallied strongly toward the end of each year and almost never failed to break even.

Phil Douglas, who will always be King of the AWOLs in your correspondent's book, was the largest man in baseball in his day, and thus had the most trouble keeping his tanks full, though he worked very hard at the job. The Shuffler, standing six feet four and weighing better than two hundred pounds, was a pitcher—and a great one. He had a spitball, a rubber arm, and a world of shrewdness, which he always left in the ball park after a day's work so as not to be bothered with excess baggage when he went out to the water holes at night.

Philip broke in with the Rome, Georgia, team, and in 1915 worked his way rapidly through the Cincinnati, Brooklyn, and Chicago clubs of the National League, where he attempted to introduce a labor routine that was far ahead of anything the CIO or the AFL has yet proposed. Mr. Douglas liked to consider his absences from duty as vacations, and he argued that he was entitled to a vacation after each pitching turn.

"So long as I win some ball games for the club, which is what I am paid to do," he used to say, "what difference does it make what I do between times? A fella like me has got to relax."

This sounds reasonable to the outside observer but it wore out the nerves of the patient Uncle Wilbert Robinson in Brooklyn, and several other managers. Relaxing in a subway car in Brooklyn one day in 1917, when he worked for the Cubs, Mr. Douglas put his pitching hand in an electric fan suspended from the ceiling. Both the hand and the fan were somewhat damaged, but since Phil could lift beer with his left hand in emergencies, he bore the subway company no ill will and took a pleasant unscheduled vacation. What with one thing and another, the Cubs decided to sell him to the Giants in the summer of 1919.

The date of the sale coincided with a Douglas vacation, so that the Giants did not see the Shuffler for several days after they had bought him. A little later, on the eve of an important series with Cincinnati, he disappeared again. This absence cost the Giants $40,000, which was the sum they sent to Boston to get Artie Nehf, the southpaw, to fill the hole in their pitching staff. It was a fine investment in the long run, since Nehf became a Giant hero, but at the moment McGraw felt that $40,000 apiece was too much to pay for Douglas vacations.

"You are through for life," he told Phil when the latter reappeared still vibrating slightly from the effects of his holiday. "I can't use you."

"There'll come a day when you'll be sorry, Mac," said Mr. Douglas reproachfully, borrowing an expression from 746 popular songs.

The day came in 1920, and Shufflin' Phil was reinstated. In a game with the Phillies in June of that year, Mr. Douglas began a vacation a little earlier than usual—while he was still pitching. The Phils got nineteen hits off him. Taking the pitcher aside after the game, McGraw called him four new names for each of the nineteen hits. Phil's feelings were hurt, and he disappeared. This time he was gone four days.

McGraw came to the conclusion that what Philip needed was someone to watch him twenty-four hours a day. The appointment of Jess Burkett as chief inspector in charge of Douglas followed soon afterward. Burkett found that Douglas, because of his size, was hard to lose in a crowd, but that the crowd was always standing around a bar. However, he kept the Shuffler out of important trouble throughout the season of 1921, which turned out to be Douglas's best and driest. Two one-hit games were pitched in the National League that year, both by Douglas. In the World Series against the Yankees he started three games, all against Carl Mays, and won two of them. He began the season of 1922 in high gear, with Burkett closer to him than his own undershirt.

That was, however, the year of the Shuffler's final binge—a beauty—and his final tragedy. On July 31, he won his eleventh game of the season. He felt an overpowering need for a vacation. He could move fast when he had to, and a few hours later Burkett lost him. Before they could get Douglas back in line again, he had washed himself out of baseball for good.

There are two stories of what went on in the first week of August 1922—the Douglas story and the Burkett-McGraw story—and they check pretty closely. Douglas, stopping here and there to take on the high-octane fuel of the Volstead age, came to a party at a friend's apartment in New York, where he passed out. Before he did so, however, there was a friendly argument, conducted two octaves above middle C, and the neighbors complained. Two detectives from the nearest police station came to investigate the complaint. When they returned to the station, they took the Shuffler with them in an ambulance. He was a large package to keep around the house, so the law telephoned Judge Francis X. McQuade, a Giant executive, to ask what should be done with him. The Judge got in touch with a snake pit, or sanitarium, on Central Park West, and booked Philip in.

Douglas could not get out of the sanitarium for several days. That, of course, was part of the rules of the treatment—unsolicited—that they were giving him. When he did get out, the Shuffler had several hypodermic holes in his arm and a wild idea in his head. On August 7 he went to the Giant clubhouse at the Polo Grounds, got some Giant stationery from the attendant, and wrote a letter to Leslie Mann, an outfielder working for the St. Louis Cardinals, who were playing in Boston. It was a letter that led to front-page stories a few days later. It ran:

> *Dear Leslie*
>
> I want to leave here. I don't want this guy [meaning McGraw] to win the pennant and I feel if I stay here I will win it for him. You know I can pitch and win. So you see the fellows, and if you want to send a man over here with the goods, and I will leave for home on the next train, send him to my house so nobody will know, and send him at night. I am living at 145 Wadsworth Avenue, Apartment 1R. Nobody will ever know. I will go down to fishing camp and stay there. I am asking you this way so there can't be any trouble for anyone. Call me up if you all are sending a man. Wadsworth 3210. Do this right away. Let me know. Regards to all.
>
> *Phil Douglas.*

It was McGraw whom Shufflin' Phil considered responsible for his troubles, and it was McGraw—before he knew about the letter—who bawled out Douglas for taking his last vacation but, to the Shuffler's surprise, did not fire him. According to Douglas, the pitcher then telephoned Mann in Boston and asked him to destroy the letter. It was too late. Mann had turned the hot potato over to his manager, Branch Rickey, fifteen minutes after he received it. Rickey sent the letter to McGraw.

On August 18, after a meeting with Judge Landis in a Pittsburgh hotel, McGraw announced that Douglas had been put on the permanently retired list. Douglas, who had just rejoined the club to go to work, was shuffling through the lobby that afternoon, when he met Landis.

"Is this true, Judge," he asked, "that I'm through with baseball?"

"Yes, Douglas, it is," said the Judge.

It was. The Shuffler and Jess Burkett made their last tearful trip back to New York together, and a few hours later Phil Douglas disappeared from the game forever. In 1934 a reporter found him raising hogs, dogs, and grandchildren, fairly happily, in a small town in Tennessee, where he also sang in the church choir. Some years afterward, however, he was found again, this time in Alabama, living in a shack on relief. No night-walker ever paid for his pleasure quite so stiffly as Douglas. On the other hand, the rest of them did not write the kind of letters Phil did. Most of them didn't write letters at all. They were too busy.

Of Rollicking Ralston Hemsley, the Brown, Indian, Cub, Pirate, Red, and Yankee catcher, it can be said that no one ever worked harder to make his paycheck come out ahead of his fines for the month. It was an uphill fight, for Rollie had a motion he used for throwing the ball down to second base which he often used in the soda fountains at night, with no ball in his hand. He could clean up a Pullman car, including the inmates, faster than any porter in the trade. Rollie was a serious fellow as well as a good catcher, so that when he decided to quit the sauce he did it in a thorough way, with the help of Alcoholics Anonymous. His gain was history's loss.

For a time, Cletus Elwood Poffenberger of Williamsport, Maryland, carried on the struggle for self-expression alone. Mr. Poffenberger, known to a narrow circle of admirers, which included himself, as Baron Boots, was perhaps the greatest night-walker of modern times. Disappearing was so strong an impulse in the Baron that it became a habit. Once, when fired by the Brooklyn Dodgers, he applied for unemployment compensation in Michigan. On the day his papers and cash were ready in Michigan, Mr. Poffenberger had disappeared. He hated to stand still long enough even to take free money.

The Baron was a man of culture who had broad views about curfews. The curfew—the deadline for getting to bed at night for ballplayers—was midnight among the Dodgers. Poffenberger was almost always in at midnight—by San Francisco time when the team was in Cincinnati, by Honolulu time when the team was in St. Louis.

Leo Durocher, who managed the Baron for Brooklyn, tells of sitting in the lobby of the Bellevue-Stratford Hotel in Philadelphia for three nights running, watching Boots come home. On the morning after the third night, he grabbed Mr. Poffenberger's buttonhole and charged him with kicking the curfew to pieces.

"You've come in after midnight for three nights," he snarled.

"Not by my calculations," said the Baron suavely. "You've noticed the clocks in the hotel lobby. I go by the second one from the top on the left-hand side, and I'm home by midnight every night."

The clocks in the hotel showed the time of day in all the great cities of the world. The clock the Baron went by showed standard time in Denver.

It may be that Mr. Durocher's stories about Poffenberger are not strictly reliable, for after Boots was fired, Leo denied he had ever wanted to hire him and laid the blame on Larry MacPhail. Other witnesses say it was Leo's idea, that he was sure beforehand that he could reform Mr. Poffenberger. He couldn't, so why should he dwell on his failures?

The Baron was a young right-handed pitcher with a great deal of stuff. "He drank a great deal of stuff, so why shouldn't he have it?" said a teammate one day.

Boots's first big-league club was Detroit, which he joined a few days late, saying that he had taken the wrong train in Chicago. There was no curfew rule on the Tigers when Poffenberger arrived, but there was soon afterward. In 1937 he was good enough to beat Bob Feller one day. In 1938 he was enterprising enough to leave the team in Washington and tour the world by himself. The next that manager Mickey Cochrane saw of Boots was in the Tiger clubhouse in Philadelphia, where the wanderer suddenly turned up in a card game.

On this occasion the Baron was fined $100 and suspended for seven weeks. Del Baker, the next Detroit manager, complained of Poffenberger's tendency toward fat, especially around the head. "We take two pounds off him every day and he puts on three every night," said Mr. Baker.

Brooklyn paid about $20,000 for Boots in 1939, and a few months later his big-league career came to an end. He missed the train out of New York to Boston one night, though he was thoughtful enough to leave a dummy in his berth for Durocher to talk to when he checked up. The Dodgers recovered $200 of Poffenberger's purchase price the next day, out of Poffenberger's pocket. In Cincinnati, soon afterward, they got back $400 more. Touring the hotel at midnight, Mr. Durocher found Boots absent from his bed. He was also absent from the clubhouse meeting at the ball park the next day.

"I saw Poffenberger at the hotel," said Dolph Camilli, the first baseman, to Durocher, "and he asked me to give you a message.

He said it was too hot to work today. He also said he didn't like the way you were treating him."

This cost Boots two fines of $200 each, but before the Baron could be reduced to bankruptcy he was sold to Montreal. He did not appear in Montreal. He appeared in Nashville in 1940. He behaved with great circumspection there until 1941, when he threw a ball at an umpire's head and was sold to San Diego. In the wartime year of 1943 the Baron joined the Marines. The Marines, at last report, have survived the impact.

One day, in the ripe wisdom of his advanced years, Mr. Dizzy Dean, commenting on night-walkers like Poffenberger, remarked that they were foolish men. "You stay in your room like I used to do," said Diz, "and you can't get in trouble."

Yet Mr. Dean, after a night in his room a few years ago, showed up in the morning with a black eye he attributed to the telephone on his night table. "I was trying to use the phone," he explained, "and it slipped in my hand and hit me."

That never happened to Baron Boots Poffenberger or to Shufflin' Phil Douglas. Maybe a man is safer in the streets, at that.

Baseball Eye

from *Newsweek*

I'm Jack Larkin, a private eye. You name it, I'll do it. Right now, I'm on a trick in Philly, tailing ballplayers.

You think I'm a lucky guy? Well, I've got to admit it looks that way. I'm six-two. I'm hard as nails. I'm beautiful. Dames follow me, and I follow ballplayers. If they don't get home by midnight (or 2 a.m. after night games) they're dead. I've sent many a left-handed hitter to the hot squat. That doesn't bother me. I see it this way: If a ballplayer gets in at 12:01 (or 2:01 after night games), he's not fit to live. He's a mad dog. In this game, society calls the shots.

But the assignment is not all steak and eggs. It's mean. It's murder. You probably read in the papers the other day where a private op, name of Charles Leland, was picked up by the cops while tailing Hamner, the Phillie infielder. What happened? This Hamner pulled the hidden-ball gimmick on him. He spotted the tail and phoned police headquarters.

Before the shamus knew what had happened, he was in the can, under $500 bail. He had to pretend he'd got Hamner mixed up with a divorce case, driving the same make and color heap.

Bob Carpenter, the Phillie president, finally took him off the hook. He said that all ball clubs put tails on their players. He said it's for the good of the game. Suppose Hamner got in at 2:02 some night? Suppose he took a beer? What do we want here, Russia?

Well, Mr. Carpenter was right. But that didn't do the dick any good. For him, it was tough. It was embarrassing. These ballplayers are mean as foxes.

I had a trick the same night. The Old Man said: "They want you to tail Robin Roberts. If you lose him, don't come back." I looked right at him. I figured I could do one of three things: Punch him, borrow $10, or do what he said. So I sneered, "OK," and drove to Philly.

I took a plant at the ball park. Pretty soon, out came Roberts, looking innocent. He climbed into his boiler and drove away. I followed, keeping two blocks between us all the way. Don't ask me which two blocks. Probably Walnut and Chestnut.

Suddenly, at the corner of Third and Peanut, crash! Bam! Another bucket, a blue-gray sedan, hit me from the side. The driver came out with his gun in his hand. I came out the same way.

But it was only Charlie Schultz, another op from our office. I recognized him before we'd exchanged more than half a dozen shots. I said: "What's the matter with you?" He said: "I'm tailing Richie Ashburn. He can fly." I told him to get lost and we went back to work.

For a few blocks, I still thought I had Roberts in front of me. But then he scratched his nose with his left hand, and I knew it was Simmons. Well, I thought, what's the difference? These pitchers are all alike. One of them is just as liable to get drunk, or sell our secrets to Hawaii, as the next one. And just then, sure enough, he parked his car across a sidewalk at Fifth and Coconut and went into a gin mill.

I followed and took a plant behind a cuspidor. I watched him drink six fast bourbon-and-waters in a row. I was ready to turn to the next page in my notebook—we average six drinks a page—when he took the glass away from his face for a split second, and I saw it wasn't Simmons. It was Charlie Gratz, another private eye.

"What's up?" I snapped at him. He said: "I was tailing Willie Jones. I had him in a rundown between Fourth and Betel-nut, but he got away." "Kicked the ball out of your hand, I suppose?" I sneered—and I meant it to hurt. But he wouldn't tell me any more. He was low—mighty low.

We left the joint together. There, walking down the street right in front of us, was Jim Konstanty. At least, it looked like him. We were on him like a couple of wildcats. I socked him in the pit of the stomach. Charlie kicked him in the knee. Then the guy socked, kicked, gouged, and butted us, tied us up, and threw us into the meat wagon. He turned out to be Sergeant Delehanty, the light-heavyweight champion of the riot squad.

As Mr. Carpenter says, if the players aren't watched, what will become of the game?

Passing of an Unlicensed Hero

from *Newsweek*

Big Bill Lange died in San Francisco last year, aged seventy-nine. The papers gave him as many inches of obit space, probably, as a sporting character of the 1890s can be expected to rate in these times. The word "immortal" was used here and there. As baseball meanings go, Bill was immortal, all right. But not officially immortal.

One of the things they do in Cooperstown, New York, besides pretend that baseball was invented there by the innocent General Abner Doubleday, is conduct a Hall of Fame, which is stocked from time to time with official immortals, old and new. Understandably, every ballplayer would like to have his name inscribed there. Bill Lange would have liked it, as I know from somewhat rueful personal experience.

Ten or twelve years ago, while Mr. Lange was minding his own business in San Francisco, a few people, including your correspondent, proposed him for the Hall of Fame. I am not as old as my sparse gray bangs would indicate, so I do not claim to have seen Lange play ball. But it doesn't even need the evidence of eyewitnesses like Clark Griffith or the late A. G. Spalding—the record is enough—to suggest that Big Bill, also known in his day as Little Eva, was very possibly the best outfielder of all time.

That's a large order, admittedly. I'll try to prop it up in a minute. Meanwhile, I regret to say that after poisoning Big Bill's honest mind with stray seeds of ambition, our movement failed. A handful of old immortals were inserted in the Hall of Fame. After that the voters concentrated on newer immortals as they became eligible. The category of ancient stars froze where it was. Even before he died, time ran out on Bill.

It would be silly to say that this matter of the Hall of Fame was the most important thing in a life as wide, full, and remarkable as Lange himself. It was just a small disappointment for a tall old man.

"It would be nice," he told me once on the Coast, "to be in there, but how would you expect people today to remember me?"

So this is a nudge, maybe a last one, at the memories of people today.

Griffith and Spalding have said that Lange was a better center fielder than Tris Speaker. He could go back for a fly ball as far and as fast as any fielder in history; he was unequaled at coming in for short line drives. His batting average, over a six-year period with a very dead ball, ranged from .324 to .388. And he ran the bases like an intelligent buffalo.

They say that in the 1890s there was no nobler and more stirring sight in nature, or in baseball, than Big Bill going down from first to second. The rules and distances of the game became "modern" in 1893, so that when Lange stole 100 bases in 1896, he was not only the last "modern" major leaguer to do so, but the first.

One of the things that put Ty Cobb into the Hall of Fame, where he deserves to be if any ballplayer does, was his base running. A fact known to all fans is that Cobb stole 96 bases one year (the year of 1915). A further item in the record says that he was thrown out stealing on 38 occasions that same year. There is an affidavit in my knapsack to the effect that in 1896 Lange attempted 101 steals. He got there safely 100 times. The other time he tripped and fell between first and second, where an infielder, after making sure that it was not a trap, timidly tagged him out.

For this department's money, though not necessarily for the Hall of Fame's, one of the most memorable things about Bill Lange is the fact that he was the only great player in the history of the game to quit while he was great. The Chicago Colts (they were no longer the White Stockings, as some of the obits said) paid Bill very well. That means, on the authority of Warren Brown, the historian, $3,000. So when he fell in love with a wealthy young lady and her father offered to take him into the real estate business, Mr. Lange got married and kissed Chicago's $3,000 good-by all in the same iconoclastic gesture.

He was a man of character as well as true athletic genius. May he rest in peace, if not in the Hall of Fame.

The All-American Rookie

from *Newsweek*

The All-American rookie was a young man, name of Lou Mandel, who used to go around the big-league baseball training camps in Florida offering managers a chance to sign up a new Walter Johnson, i.e., himself, for any reasonable sum in five figures. Mr. Mandel picked a good time for his joyous fantasy, for it was an era when many ball clubs were suspected of "covering up" players—retarding their advancement from the minor leagues—for their own selfish purposes. The managers figured that Mr. Mandel might be a star, at that, and he ate many a free breakfast.

Finally he awarded the honor to Casey Stengel, then managing the Brooklyn Dodgers.

"I'm ready to sign with your club," he announced, walking into Mr. Stengel's room one evening. "If your roster is full already, you better dispose of Mungo. I pitch."

"Check in," said Mr. Stengel, on the theory that you never can tell. "I'll look you over tomorrow."

Casey had trouble persuading Mr. Mandel to display his stuff next day, for Mandel was not in the mood, having eaten two breakfasts at the club's expense. Finally, however, he got out on the mound and demonstrated a fastball which would quite likely have broken an egg, two times out of five, if it happened to hit the egg.

"I can't use you, boy," said Mr. Stengel.

"You'll regret this," said Mr. Mandel.

"I'm sorry," said Mr. Stengel.

"You may well be sorry," said Mr. Mandel. "I am gonna jump to the Athletics."

Mr. Mandel lasted two days with the Athletics, dining meanwhile at the expense of Cornelius Mack. He then proceeded to the bivouac of the St. Louis Browns, where anybody who even looked like a ballplayer was welcome.

Rogers Hornsby had not been warned about Mr. Mandel.

"Show me what you got," said Hornsby, not unreasonably.

"I'll pitch when I'm good and ready," said Mandel. "Let's talk contract, kid."

This is the wrong way to approach Mr. Hornsby. Mandel left the Browns' camp two jumps in advance of a spiked shoe, hurled by the Rajah's good right arm.

It was Mr. Mandel's claim, in those days, that if some manager did not sign him quick he would go straight home and take a proposition of $25,000 which was waiting for him there. Mr. Casey Stengel thought he could guess Mandel's secret.

"What he means," said Casey, "is that he can go home and turn himself over to the cops and collect $25,000 reward. Especially if he brings himself in dead."

After that first year, the All-American rookie became a familiar figure in the Florida camps. He mingled with the players and lived for such moments as that memorable occasion a few years back when Pepper Martin obligingly gave him hook-sliding lessons in the lobby of the Princess Martha Hotel in St. Petersburg, Fla. Sometimes a ball club permitted Mandel to hang around and work with the boys just for luck. Such was the case this year with the St. Louis Cardinals, for whom Mandel promised to win thirty games.

The Cardinals began to lose, so Ray Blades, then their manager, administered the old heave-o, and Mr. Mandel landed on his feet somewhere in the neighborhood of Clearwater, Florida. Seeing a goodly hotel on his left, a princely inn, in fact the famous Belleview-Biltmore, he walked into the lobby and found himself face to face with Judge Kenesaw Mountain Landis, late high commissioner of baseball. The Judge had never seen or heard of Mandel, but Mandel knew the Judge.

"Hey, wait a minute!" he hollered. "I've been covered up!"

"What's that?" said the Judge, who was on his way to the golf course.

"I've been covered up illegally," explained Mr. Mandel. "Make me a free agent, kid, and I'll sign with a certain club for a bonus of $40,000."

The Judge studied Mr. Mandel closely and reached for his niblick.

"I'll cut you in for $5,000!" promised Mr. Mandel, backing away.

The Judge raised his niblick, and Mr. Mandel disappeared, threatening to take his case to the Supreme Court.

He may have got there. The Supreme Court went into a losing streak about that time.

Ball Fans and Other Primates

from *Newsweek*

You'll recall that in the closing days of the 1950 pennant race, when the Philadelphia Phillies were edging toward the championship with the red-blooded apathy characteristic of National League teams about to meet the Yankees in the World Series, there was a game in Brooklyn at which a subdebutante from Canarsie or Red Hook reached out from her box seat and touched a baseball lightly on its jowls. The umpires ruled interference and a Philadelphia run scored from third base.

Why a young girl would wish to pet a 1950 official league ball, which, for all its soft, dewy skin, contains more venom than a cottonmouth snake, I do not know. In this case retribution followed as the night the day. The maiden and a girlfriend were led weeping from the ball park by heavy-handed minions of the law like a couple of Anne Boleyns en route to the scaffold. Justice in Brooklyn is swift and terrible. It's getting so a girl can't even make book there, let alone reach out of bounds to fondle a ball in play.

Shortly afterward Mr. Red Barber, a radio announcer who is also the informal guardian of the city's morals, repeated his famous sermon on interfering with baseballs. It beats Billy Sunday all hollow. The ears of those girls must have burned, if they had a portable radio with them. Mr. Barber's attitude toward reaching into the cage to touch a ball is not, like a sign that says "Don't feed the tiger," humanitarian. He is not trying to protect fingers. He is trying to improve the manners of the public while supporting the by-laws of the gospel according to Happy Chandler. Often he seems on the point of despair and I don't blame him. The public is a very shocking institution.

I was thinking about this matter of dignified baseball vs. human nature a few days later during the World Series in Philadelphia. Philadelphia is a town where human nature is rampant up till closing hours. In the third inning of the first game of the Series, John Mize of the Yankees hoisted a foul fly to right field. While Del Ennis of the Phillies was waiting close by the grandstand for the ball to come down (which even the 1950 ball will do, if given enough time) a cash customer, probably a mad-dog type, lunged out and deflected the potato out of Ennis's reach.

What Mr. Barber would have said about that, if the air had been at his disposal, I hesitate to think. Fortunately, the guilty fan will be able to live with himself in future years, because (a) Mr. Barber was not at the microphone, and (b) Mize popped out on the next pitch. Otherwise, though the fan paid about $6.50 for his constitutional right to deflect baseballs hit to his neighborhood, he would have been a mighty miserable deflector.

Dignity and deportment are dear to a great many people besides Mr. Barber. So is fair play, a phenomenon, possibly contrary to nature, that was discovered in England in A.D. 923. But it seems to me that those who deplore the animal instincts of spectators at ball games (by Darwinian theory, the instinct to reach out for baseballs comes to us from the great anthropoids, who reach out for coconuts) are ignoring the facts of baseball.

Mr. Barber one day during the recent season made a remark that dripped with involuntary irony. Some of the fans booed a ballplayer—Cal Abrams, if memory serves me. The sound of their wild Greenpoint jungle cries disgusted Mr. Barber.

"Can you imagine that?" he said. "Booing a man who is just trying to make his living out there!"

The question arose and still arises: Where does the living of Abrams, and everyone else in baseball, come from? From those who pay their way into the ball park, to boo or not to boo, as suits their taste. It's a pretty public job. John Barrymore didn't like audiences to cough. They went on coughing. He went on taking their dough.

Memoirs of a Mild Fanatic

from *Newsweek*

On a recent big-game hunting expedition in Brooklyn (the biggest I could find was a twenty-cent limit game, with the one-eyed jacks wild) your correspondent heard a powerful humming sound and traced it to its source. It came, naturally, from the brain of Mr. Branch Rickey and indicated a little medium-deep thought. By the time it subsided, Roy Campanella, the best catcher in baseball, had been signed to a contract for 1950.

The sight of Campanella reminded me that I had neglected to write enough about him during the 1949 World Series. Too much was going on then, most of it in the nature of the Yankees showing their muscles. The Yanks themselves, though, did not overlook Campanella, even in the heat of their victory. In clubhouse talk they recognized him for what he is—the class of the field.

"The best catcher since Bill Dickey," said one of them, which is a Yankee way of looking at things.

I'd go farther. All season long in 1949 the art of Campanella put me in mind of something I used to see away back—'way, 'way back—when I was an urchin in Chicago. I mean the work of the catcher for the White Sox of those days. I would say that Campanella is the best since Ray Schalk.

This is not to disparage Dickey. Dickey and Gabby Hartnett

were both fine catchers and strong hitters. But they were big, heavy-footed men, and in the defensive part of their jobs they could not match the range, the speed, the mobility of Schalk. Mickey Cochrane came closer to it; considering his hitting, he was perhaps the best all-around catcher of this age. Mickey Owen for a few seasons was a defensive craftsman of a high order. But to find the like of Campanella, you have to go back to the subject of my childhood memories, Mr. Schalk.

There was a day I remember in the World Series of 1919. A Mr. Horace O. (Hod) Eller, a Cincinnati shine-ball pitcher, was on third base (how he got there is strictly the business of the Chicago pitcher, Mr. Lefty Williams, who had been influenced in the region of the wallet by certain gamblers). The next hitter hit one deep to the infield, and a throw was made to the plate. It was a high, late throw. Mr. Eller was thundering home as Schalk leaped in the air and got the ball in his mitt with his back to the runner. He did not have time to turn around, so he arched his back, threw his arm over his shoulder, and tagged Mr. Eller out.

There was an aspect of this and other plays in the same Series that did not become known till later. Schalk's team was the Black Sox of fragrant memory. Schalk was one of the few men on it who was trying to win. His effort was something to see, and so was his bitterness at the men around him who had sold the chance away.

"Do you think he'll be able to catch Ed Walsh?" said Charles A. Comiskey, the White Sox owner, when coach Kid Gleason introduced Schalk to him in 1912. Schalk was a small man, and Ed Walsh, with his fastball and spitball, was a murderous pitcher.

"He can catch Walsh sitting in a rocking chair," replied the Kid. Schalk could catch anyone and anything. He could throw harder and truer, and also quicker, than any catcher between his time and Campanella's. He handled the catcher's mitt like an infielder's glove.

The last gift is one shared by Campanella, and watching it is a true pleasure for people like me who are harmlessly nuts about the technical side of baseball.

While in Brooklyn, Mr. Rickey chanced to say that if his left-field grandstand were moved back thirty feet, Campanella would get fewer home runs.

"Are you going to move it back thirty feet?" asked your correspondent, grabbing up the notebook in which he records scoops.

"No," said Mr. Rickey, as he lit a fresh cigar.

Which leaves Campanella right where we found him, and a pretty good position, too.

Razor Blades Amok

from *Newsweek*

Charlie Dressen, manager of the National League's 1951 front-running Dodgers, would probably not deny under oath that he is a shade sharper mentally than Leo Durocher, manager of the contending Giants. Durocher, if pressed for a statement, would doubtless admit that he can outwit Dressen morning and night with half his brain tied behind him.

We have it on the authority of Durocher's autobiography that when Dressen worked for him, as he did for many years, Leo called the pitches from the bench, and Dressen, on the coaching line, relayed them to the hitters. In short there was one mastermind and one stooge. Dressen, however, said Durocher tenderly, in the same book, was "my right arm." He used that expression when Branch Rickey temporarily fired Dressen for horse playing.

Quite a few years later we find these two unabashed thinkers competing head-on for the pennant. If Dressen has the edge, it may well be because, as his admirers claim, he always was smarter than Durocher, or maybe because he just naturally had the better ball club. The reason is immaterial. No one cares but Dressen and Durocher (who care very deeply) which man is cuter than the other. The fun for us outsiders lies in watching their brains collide in action, like a couple of runaway razor blades.

Take the events of July 4, 1951, when the Dodgers and the Giants met twice in one day. Leo watched Charlie like an eagle. Charlie watched Leo like a hawk. The air was humid, if not downright stagnant, with strategy.

Dressen approached the umpires at one point in the first game with a new lineup studded with replacements. Durocher left the bench and landed in the middle of the conference with a single bound. He examined Dressen's lineup through a thick lens. He tested it for fingerprints. Transfixing his old assistant with a look of suspicion, he went, "Tsk, tsk!"

A bit later Durocher made as though to substitute a runner for Whitey Lockman. Then he changed his mind. At once Dressen lunged forward, yelling, "Is that legal?"

"Yep," said umpire Scotty Robb.

"Oh," said Charlie, quick as a flash. "I just thought I'd ask."

A crisis developed in the second game. Dressen and three of his henchmen lost their tempers at a call by umpire Robb. They pelted Mr. Robb with bouquets of Anglo-Saxon words and were all thrown off the field. Durocher followed Dressen's exit with a glance of such piercing intelligence that Sherlock Holmes would have been proud to own it. He was not deceived for an instant. When Dressen reappeared, attired in mufti, in a chair in the Brooklyn club box, Durocher grabbed umpire Robb by the arm.

"Look, there's Dressen," he snarled.

"I see him," said Mr. Robb. "Looks better than he did. Probably took a bath. I hoped he washed out his mouth with soap."

"He don't belong there," howled Leo. "He's supposed to be out of the game! I am playing the rest of this ill-conducted affair under protest."

Mr. Robb explained to no avail that the same situation had come up and been dealt with the month before. Dressen, he said, was within his rights in bobbing up like a cork, provided he stayed off the field and made no signals to the team. True, he might be emitting invisible brain waves, which would be in the worst possible taste, but—

"Never mind," said Mr. Durocher coldly. "I am playing the rest of this under protest." And he did so, until Dressen shrewdly withdrew from the box, on which Durocher craftily withdrew the protest. You have to get up very early to outsmart Leo—earlier, in fact, than seems really necessary. A better way, according to some experts, is to sleep late and then outscore him.

The chances are that Durocher and Dressen are roughly equal intellectually. It's a tribute to Dressen's brain that he uses Jackie Robinson every day, but, if he didn't, he'd be back in Oakland, Calif. It speaks well for Durocher that he pitches Sal Maglie whenever he can, but, if he didn't, a man from the state hospital would come and drop a net over him. Call it a good, clean draw.

The Space Revolution

from *Newsweek*

It never occurred to Commissioner Kenesaw M. Landis that he could see a ball game better at home than at the ball park. It never occurred to Commissioner Albert B. Chandler. To be fair to those boys, it never occurred to Commissioner Ford C. Frick either, until he came down with appendix trouble in the fall of 1958. Staying in his own diggings to recuperate from an appendectomy, Commissioner Frick caught the World Series by television, and a new and dazzling light broke over him. History, as they say, was made. Baseball space laws dating back to Abner Doubleday were officially reversed.

As you know if you read the science news last week, Frick, nine hundred miles away, was able to advise umpire Charles Berry that he had been insulted by pitcher Ryne Duren from a distance of approximately sixty feet. Frick's announcement of his discovery came two days after a rocket was fired one-third of the way to the moon. The two developments, though similar in purport, were by no means equal in weight. Frick's feat was more important to, for instance, pitcher Duren. As you know if you read the fines-and-assessment news, it cost Duren 250 clams, while the lunar rocket cost him nothing, except perhaps in taxes.

Probably some will say that Frick's discovery was a fluke. They will claim that the appendectomy was a chancy thing, like Newton's apple. Cynics will speak of "Frick's luck." Luck or not, you can bet that no commissioner will ever go near a World Series game again, when he can do a better and stronger job in his parlor.

Chancy or not, the experiment was performed under ideal conditions. In other words, it was "controlled," to use a scientific term. The control was Deputy Commissioner Charlie Segar, representing Frick's office at the scene of the crime.

"I'm not sure it happened," said Deputy Commissioner Segar, in reference to the outrage committed by pitcher Duren.

"It happened," said Commissioner Frick, reaching firmly for the $250. And the TV audience of 50 million (give or take 30 million) knew he was right. Like him, they had seen it whole and clear. Experts on the ball field and in the press box, who had been at a disadvantage, were still struggling last week to reconstruct the event. Some speculated that Duren had "clutched his Adam's apple." As any screen shepherd could have told them, Duren clutched nothing. He merely flicked two fingers toward his throat. The purpose of his unspeakable gesture was, of course, to suggest that umpire Berry had miscalled a pitch from lack of courage, which, according to baseball superstition, is located in the trachea.

Personally, I thought that Frick used his discovery with great restraint. Like Curie and Salk, he was humble in success. He might have called Duren's pitch, notifying Berry by telephone whether it was a ball or a strike. He might have made a ruling on whether a hit by Covington was or was not trapped by Mantle. Apparently he has elected to confine his new power to the administration of moral laws and to let the umpires do the rest, thus forestalling widespread unemployment. In the 1959 Series, as I see it, the officials, wearing headphones, will tune in on a flow of guidance from the commissioner in Bronxville, New York, as follows:

"Bauer is thumbing his nose out there, Jocko. Tell him it will cost him a hundred the next time he does it . . . Al, I wouldn't stand for the kind of language Logan is using behind your back . . . Did you see what Berra did when you called that last pitch a ball, Frank? . . . Oh, you called it a strike? . . . What's the trouble today, your sinuses bothering you? . . . Well, carry on, carry on . . . John, keep your eye on Herman in the dugout. He's starting to reach for a towel . . ."

As noted, the new baseball space laws were worth $250 to the commissioner's office in this year's Series. Commissioner Frick earned an additional $1,100 by fining twenty-two Braves for telling secrets to the press. You say this is unconstitutional? So is baseball unconstitutional. So is television. So is space, and so are rockets. It's too late to turn back now.

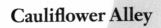

Cauliflower Alley

3

Morgan on Jaws

from *Newsweek*

The scarcity of good heavyweight fighters to meet Joe Louis is no mystery to Dumb Dan Morgan, who can find an answer to anything.

Dumb Daniel managed Jack Britton, world's welterweight champion, through twenty-eight (or was it thirty-one?) fights with Ted Kid Lewis, and back in the days of the white-hope panic of 1908–1915 Mr. Morgan was second to none at the business of luring farm boys out of their fathers' cowsheds to yell for the blood of Jack Johnson.

Before describing this gifted Welshman any further, I would like to set forth Dumb Dan's theory on the death of good modern heavyweights. This theory, in two sections of ten thousand words each, has been copyrighted under the name of the Morgan Hypothesis and cannot be reproduced without the author's permission (which comes in five thousand words).

Dumb Dan believes that the modern heavyweight, and especially the modern Irish heavyweight, suffers from weak jaws, which in turn are caused by eating too many corned-beef sandwiches and/or porterhouse steaks.

Remember the lines from Lewis Carroll:

And your jaws are too weak
For anything tougher than suet?

Those lines express Dumb Daniel's sentiments perfectly. The remedy? Easy: old-fashioned chuck steaks, which strengthen the masticatory muscles and render the subject impervious to a smack on the chops from Joe Louis or anyone else.

The first time Mr. Morgan explained his theory to me, we were watching Patrick Edward Comiskey, the young Hibernian white hope, as he trained to fight Max Baer.

"He has good chin muscles," mused Mr. Morgan. "His people have nourished him on chuck steak, the salvation of the Irish heavyweight. Mark those mandibles, friend! Strong as steel. Baer won't hurt this boy in a million years."

The next time Mr. Morgan addressed me, we were standing at the ringside at the Baer-Comiskey fight, and the boys were picking young Comiskey out of the ropes, where Mr. Baer had sent him in the first round by means—strangely enough—of a couple of blows on the jaw.

"My worst fears are justified!" whispered Mr. Morgan. "I have just received inside information. This poor young sucker has been feeding on porterhouses. He got hold of a little money before the fight, and it went to his head. First porterhouses, then corned-beef sandwiches, and now his jaws have gone to hell and so has he.

"If they ask me," continued Dumb Dan, warming to his theme, "there is only one thing to do now with Comiskey. Get him back on chuck steaks! Make him chew! Rebuild those flimsy choppers! Get him back on chuck steak, and he will still be a good Irish heavyweight.

"The last good Irish heavyweight," said Mr. Morgan, "was Jim Coffey, the Dublin Giant, who fought Frank Moran back in the old white hope days. When he first come over here, Coffey had jaws like a wolf. Chuck steak did it. He never saw nothing but chuck steak.

"But he got a little prosperous, and he began to go for those corned-beef sandwiches, and his chin went weak. Moran beat him. It taught me a lifelong lesson—keep those big Irishmen on chuck steak. Make 'em strong in the jaws."

A smart sleuth, hearing the Morgan Hypothesis and Mr. Morgan simultaneously, would conclude that Dumb Dan himself has grazed on chuck steak every day of his life, for the Morgan jaws are remarkable for their strength and stamina. Jack Britton fought Ted Kid Lewis thirty-one times (or was it twenty-eight?), and Mr. Morgan tells the story of those fights chronologically, omitting no detail, in three hours flat.

He uses gestures too, to illustrate how Britton got his left into Lewis's ribs. Having played the role of Lewis myself on many of these occasions, I can testify that Mr. Morgan today is a better puncher than Britton ever was.

As for the Morgan Hypothesis, it seems to be sound as a nut. The heavyweight who wants to weather Joe Louis's poison will do himself a favor if he gnaws on chuck steaks morning, noon, and night for a couple of years. The rest should be easy.

"For Louis can be had," says Mr. Morgan ominously. "The champ has gone porterhouse himself."

Bag Hits Baer

from *Newsweek*

Max Baer has been honorably discharged from the Army Air Forces on a characteristic Baer rap—he was hit by a punching bag. Sgt. Joe Louis, home on furlough, said last week he did not expect to be a civilian again for some time to come. Although this state of affairs, Baer on one side of a fence and Louis on the other, is eminently satisfactory to Mr. Baer, who used to display considerable agitation at being in the same country with Louis, it is directly the reverse of the dreams of Uncle Mike Jacobs, the promoter of clean, high-class boxing entertainments.

The discharge of Mr. Baer, especially a Baer incapacitated by a punching bag, is of no great value to Uncle Michael. The release of Louis, on the other hand, would automatically send Mike sprinting to the printer's with an order for 100,000 tickets while his Vice President in Charge of Turning Lights On and Off would screw in the bulbs they have been saving to cut down expenses, and the Vice President in Charge of Changing the Ribbon in the Typewriter of Harry Markson, head of the propaganda department, would blow a note on the staff trombone and dash into action.

How is it, they ask themselves peevishly, at Uncle Michael's Twentieth Century Sporting Club, that Louis cannot get himself hit by a punching bag instead of Baer? The answer, of course, is all too obvious. It is not the kind of thing that Louis does, whereas Max, with no wish in the world to do anything but what is right, slides naturally into these man-bites-dog situations.

It appears that in the case of bag-hits-Baer, the accident occurred before Max joined the Army and its effects were slow and cumulative. While he was minding his own business one day in a gymnasium, a place he may have reached by mistaking the address, a heavy bag slipped down from above him and whaled the old Livermore, California, butcher boy forcefully over his back and shoulders. The record does not indicate whether this was an act of petty vengeance or not, nor does it mention a claim of foul by Mr. Baer, though the blow seems to have come dangerously close to the category of the forbidden kidney punch.

"Give me a rematch," mumbled the loser as they led him away, and while local promoters were negotiating with the owners of the bag, Max entered the Air Forces in what seemed at the time to be a fair enough state of health.

It developed later that the sneak attack by the punching bag had somewhat the same sort of delayed effect that Max's own mighty fists used to have upon Ernie Schaaf, Primo Carnera, and others. Mr. Baer was lamed to a degree which eventually brought his discharge from the service. And Louis, still healthy and worth a million and a half fast dollars at the box office the moment he sheds his uniform, is in the war for quite a spell yet.

The sergeant, mind you, has uttered no complaint on this score. Nor has Uncle Mike Jacobs; not in public, anyway. Gritting his costly new hand-carved teeth, the promoter has gone right on gamely selling second-rate fights at high prices just as though his heart were not breaking within him. It may prove, of course, from a medical examination and a study of the club's books, that Uncle Mike's heart is not breaking within him. Just the same, it must ache a little.

In the New York area, as elsewhere, there are truckloads of money available these days for sports entertainment, and a Louis fight, especially with Billy Conn, might even draw the housewives from the Jamaica or Belmont racetrack, provided it did not conflict in time with the rites of zebra worship out there. It would be the surest over-a-million-dollar gate since Jack Dempsey's heyday.

It would also, no doubt, be a Battle of the Century, and this calls to mind a point raised recently by Uncle Mike Jacobs's Vice President in Charge of Tearing the Leaves off the House Calendar.

"Mike," said the trusted executive recently, "what are we going to do when the twentieth century is over?"

"Why?" said Mr. Jacobs tersely.

"Well, should we change our name to Twenty-First Century Sporting Club?"

"Call my lawyer," said Michael with a roll of the dental castanets. The point is still under debate in the legal department.

The Boy Bandit

from *Newsweek*

James Joy Johnston, a man with, reading from north to south, a derby hat and a lively imagination, will be seventy years old on November 28. I think he is giving his right age. There have been times over the years when Mr. Johnston's statistics on the vintage of his prizefighters were a little misleading, as in the case of one George (Boer) Rodel, who claimed to be a veteran of the Boer War. Mr. Johnston accepted the Boer's tale and passed it along to whom it might concern, though his own keen sense of history told him that to make the story true Mr. Rodel must have been sniping at redcoats at the age of six or eight. However, as I say, James probably is leveling about his personal score of seventy. If he lied on that, it would be downward, not upward, and he certainly does not look or behave like a man who has lived out the Old Testament quote of three score and ten.

He will most likely launch his birthday with a cuppa tea, then go out and sell something or fool somebody, or both, as he has been doing with consistent success and a fine feeling for entertainment values ever since he shipped out of Liverpool, England, for these shores at the dawn of the century.

About ten years ago Mr. Johnston was toppled by Mike Jacobs and associated hustlers from the highest post in the boxing hierarchy, promoter for Madison Square Garden. This should logically have finished a man crowding sixty, especially since Mr. Jacobs had in his hands a surefire box-office weapon in the form of Joe Louis.

Instead, Mr. Johnston rebounded with vigor and put Louis to his own uses more profitably than any other outside manager in the business. Acquiring two mediocre heavyweights, he procured them not one but two fights apiece with Louis for a total of some forty highly remunerative rounds. In one of these fights, the first, he added insult to profit by instructing his puppet, Runnin' Rob Pastor, to flee like a hare for the full ten rounds.

At the time, speaking like a true and loyal manager, James bawled in public places that Pastor had really won that first fight. This was correct under racing rules, for Robin covered the fifty miles he ran in much faster time than Louis; but today, mellowed by a few saucers of tannin, Mr. Johnston will admit Pastor never belonged in Louis's class. He is a shrewd and honest appraiser of fighters when not talking business, and admires Louis warmly. I recall consulting with Mr. Johnston on a printed statement by Gene Tunney some years ago to the effect that he, Tunney, could lick Louis himself if the latter would undertake to smoke two packs of cigarettes a day for six months.

"Did he say what kind of cigarettes?" barked Mr. Johnston. "If he meant marijuana, he might be right."

The Boy Bandit, as he is still respectfully known at seventy, has handled American fighters for the most part, but back in his early years in this country he gave the trade an international flavor with such characters as Gypsy Daniels and the aforesaid Boer Rodel. Rodel once went the full distance with Jess Willard, and the feat was Mr. Johnston's, not the Boer's. A fighter named Bull Young had died just previously, after being knocked out by Willard. Mr. Johnston approached Jess before the Rodel fight and played upon his sensitive mind like a violinist with the information that the Boer had a weak heart and the suggestion that there were plenty of high trees in the neighborhood for the lynching of a man who killed two opponents in a row. Rodel got through that one safely.

Gypsy Daniels was a solid Welshman whom Mr. Johnston painted up to look like a sprig of old Romany: earrings, red headdress, flashing teeth, and dark skin, the latter two departments artificial. He obtained a slight success with the Gypsy, at some cost to Mr. Daniels's peace of mind.

"You've made a bleeding tramp out of me," the fighter complained to his manager one day.

"How so?" asked Mr. Johnston.

"My bleeding father don't like gypsies. He's cut me off without a shilling, won't have me on his place, and now I can never go back to the bleeding Wiles."

Mr. Johnston concedes today that there was merit in the Gypsy's plaint. He even feels a certain amount of remorse, but nothing so strong that a philosophical cuppa tea at four o'clock will not drown it.

Upsy Downsy

from *North American Newspaper Alliance*

The career of Lou Nova, the heavyweight fighter, is divided sharply into two phases, the perpendicular and the horizontal, and there has never been a dull moment in either, to my way of thinking. I enjoyed Lou in the days when nobody could knock him off his feet, and I consider him just as wholesome and educational now, when he saves people the trouble by falling down in several directions at once for reasons which may seem unusual to the lay mind but are always a tribute to his ingenuity.

Lou's latest fall occurred in Detroit the other evening when he swooned in his corner after a fight. It was the decision which caused Mr. Nova to faint, from surprise. At least, so Mr. Nova said, and he is in a better position than anyone else to know how far surprise will drive him.

Deep down underneath, I believe Mr. Nova is in touch with great natural laws and forces. He always has been. His actions depend on which law he happens to be following. Where other athletes comply with man-made laws, like Don't Park By A Fireplug or No Smoking, Mr. Nova is governed by cosmic laws.

In the old days, when he stood up all the time, he obeyed the law of the earth's motion. This was responsible for the cosmic punch and the dynamic stance, two of his greatest inventions. In the dynamic stance, Lou placed his left foot squarely upon his right foot and kept it there. Most other fighters employing this formula would have fallen without being hit. Mr. Nova, however, did not observe the law of gravity. He thought it was unconstitutional; to be more accurate, he suspected it was unconstitutional, and refused to obey it until his lawyers could investigate and advise him on the subject.

Meanwhile, he remained perpendicular. It was most discouraging for his opponents. Max Baer ruined his hands upon Mr. Nova's chin during this period, with never a knockdown to show for it.

A few years ago Lou's legal staff made its report. Newton, it turned out, was right. Gravity was legitimate. It met every test in court.

"How do Brandeis, Frankfurter, and Holmes stand on it?" asked Mr. Nova.

"They love it," replied the attorneys.

"That's good enough for me," said Lou, and began to fall all over the place.

Since his reconciliation with gravity, Mr. Nova has made history in this field. More than any other fighter, he may be said to be in key, in deep, true harmony, with this great doctrine. Newton's apple never did anything that Lou cannot do better.

He is not too proud to pick up tips as he goes along, from gifted fallers. He has studied the methods of Joe Beckett, Bombardier Wells, and Phainting Phil Scott. I remember a fight he had with Tami Mauriello, a young man but a man with a special talent. One of Mr. Mauriello's heels was round. This enabled him to fall on very slight provocation. Nova nudged him gently in the first round, and Mauriello went over on his back.

"Amazing!" said Lou to himself. "In fact, sublime. This fellow has genius. I must remember to file both my heels the first thing in the morning."

Meanwhile, not to be outdone, Mr. Nova went into secret communion with gravity and felt the earth's call as he never had before. Mr. Mauriello was up again by this time, standing earnestly upon his square heel. He tapped Mr. Nova on the mandible, and Lou swayed and fell in one pure line, like a giant redwood. His handlers came in and carried him away, much to the bewilderment of Mr. Mauriello, whose only concern at the moment was to remain upright himself.

Lou's Detroit fight last week may have marked the start of a new aspect of his kinship with gravity. His opponent, Lee Oma, failed to floor him, but as soon as Mr. Oma was declared the winner, Mr. Nova fainted and lay majestically upon his back for several seconds. The physical agent is no longer necessary. The spiritual will suffice. You can now knock him down without a feather.

Death of a Simian and a Scholar

from *Newsweek*

As fine an ape as I knew was Gargantua, the circus star, who passed from this footstool a couple of weeks ago. He is gone but not forgotten. I have postponed my private obituary of this congenial gorilla until I was absolutely sure he was dead. An airplane transporting his remains lost 1,000 feet of altitude when the pilot heard a thumping noise amidships. It turned out to be a loose crate or a gremlin or something, not Gargy come to life.

Although we were acquainted socially, it was my business relationship with the noted entertainer that I valued most highly. In association with Mr. Gene Tunney, a gifted performer in his own right in a lower weight division, I once tried to promote a match of skill and strength between Gargantua and Tony Galento, the spheroid barkeep of Orange, New Jersey. Had Galento not declined the test, we would all have cleaned up.

As it was, the thing fell through, and the four of us went our separate ways. Tunney became a uranium miner. Gargantua has gone to his reward. Galento is a wrestler, and your correspondent changes ribbons on typewriters. It is useless to sit around and speculate on what might have been.

Gargantua was an up-and-coming young ape of about five years, beginning to make his presence felt in show business, when he caught the eye of Mr. Tunney. Tunney was then sports editor of a paper called the *Connecticut Nutmeg*. As an editor he thought he had to take a stand. So he took a stand against Gargantua. "Gorillas are overrated" was the editorial policy of Mr. Tunney.

That, of course, was directly opposed to the policy of another editor, the late Arthur Brisbane, who thought a gorilla could lick any five human beings. Reaching for his Encyclopedia Britannica, Mr. Tunney made some rapid notes and announced that any third-rate heavyweight fighter could lick Gargantua. When your correspondent proposed Galento, a third-rate heavyweight second to none, as a worthy contender, Mr. Tunney leaped at the idea. So I went around to contact the rival camps.

Now it happened that Mr. Tunney had misread his Britannica or got hold of an early edition with incomplete returns. He thought it said that a gorilla had thirteen ribs, as against twenty-four for a human being or an Orange, New Jersey, barkeeper. What a gorilla really has is thirteen pairs of ribs, making twenty-six in all.

"Tunney is being ridiculous," said Gargantua's manager, a Mr. Dick Kroener, whom I found moodily biting his fingernails while Gargantua did roadwork around the inside of his cage. "It never pays to knock gorillas. My principal here can make shredded wheat out of the likes of Galento."

Galento's manager, Mr. Joe (Yussel the Muscle) Jacobs, seemed to share that suspicion, though he put it in another way.

"Let Tunney fight the ape. I will carry the bucket for him," said Mr. Jacobs coldly. "My tiger fights nobody but humans and such. Besides, our engagement book is full up. Ain't it, Anthony?"

"Right to the ears," agreed Mr. Galento. "I would like to belt over this circus bum, but I got no time."

Soon afterward a rumor began to circulate in the prizefight business that Mr. Tunney had deliberately misrepresented the number of Gargantua's ribs in order to lure Galento into the ring with the crowd-pleasing African. Now, since I know that Mr. Tunney was prepared to bet handsomely on Galento, that he is the soul of honor, and that he still thinks gorillas are overrated, I am certain that no such stratagem was in his thoughts. If ever a chap believed in the cause of man over monkey, it is this same Tunney.

However, I am forced to disagree with him. I saw a good deal of Gargantua between that time and the time of his death. We had little to say to each other, both being of a reserved, introspective turn of mind, but whenever I watched him tear an automobile tire in two, I mused on the folly of man and his vaulting ambitions. So, no doubt, did Gargantua. May he walk in green pastures.

The Case of the Chilly Giant

from *Newsweek*

Primo Carnera, the famous toppling tower of Sequals, Italy, once heavyweight boxing champion of the world, is now a wrestler. He gets as much as $2,000 a week at times, which is far better than working. Before he turned respectable, however, Primo treated himself to one final prizefight. A few months after the war ended, he got himself knocked out in Milan by a certain Luigi Musina, seventy-three pounds his junior. It was a most unusual performance, even for Signor Carnera, and will bear further examination.

Primo explained the frightful catastrophe by citing in private testimony one cigarette, one glass of cognac, and one pistol or revolver. When he was taking a preparatory school course to be champion of the world some years ago, Primo studied explanations, both hasty and considered, at the large, shapely feet of Professor Big Bill Duffy, the gifted manager, and his recent statement bears the mark of the master's influence. There is nice color in a cigarette, a stoup of eau de vie, and a roscoe. In this case the three contributing items possess the added advantage of having disappeared, unanimously, into the thin Milanese air.

The points of interest here are the cognac and the gun. Several hundred thousand red-blooded American boys can testify that a glass of Italian cognac of the type now in vogue there might well have got Primo stopped in the seventh round. As for the revolver, one appeared in the same circumstances in Paris in 1914 in the case of the Johnson-Moran fight, which is a tribute to Primo's, or somebody's, wide reading in the classics.

The Carnera-Musina bout was supposed to have some bearing on the European heavyweight championship, but apparently it did not have enough, for all Milan, the flower and the chivalry, stayed away. This caused a vacuum at the box office which in turn sent chills shooting through the dainty torso of Signor Carnera. Wrapping himself in a bathrobe, he made two or three trips into the arena from his dressing room to count the house. What he saw sent him back with his teeth chattering like .50-caliber machine guns, and he soon decided that there was not going to be any fight.

"Against the cold," states the Preem, "I then took a cigarette and a glass of cognac. The cognac hit me in the feet."

Just as this hit, which is nothing very special in the way of marksmanship, was being scored, a party or character entered the dressing room and pulled a gun on Primo. Primo describes him as a "spectator," but a glance at the ticket-sale figures shows this to be doubtful at best. He was more likely a vice president of the firm promoting the fight, since most fight firms do carry a Vice President in Charge of Hardware. The visitor assured Primo that the contest would be held, and to show the big fellow what he meant he proceeded to herd him into the ring at the point of his fowling piece.

The cold, the cognac, the nicotine, the ordnance, and the general absenteeism of the citizens were, in combination, too much for the old Tower of Gorgonzola. He toppled twice in the first round and in the seventh he exercised his inalienable right to sue for peace. Next day, while Milan writhed in torpor at the prospect, Primo challenged Musina to a return match, contending no man could win a fight under such adverse conditions.

Musina declined the offer, reasoning, with what seems to be the stoutest kind of logic, that a return match would draw even fewer people than the first match, which drew nobody. His decision was a blessing to all parties, for it changed Signor Carnera from a boxer into a rich and happy wrestler and drew a curtain over one of the most wretched careers in the history of the art of self-defense.

Mr. Percentage

from *Newsweek*

A fresh-faced and fresh-tongued little Army captain named Joe Gould got into difficulties near the end of the war. The charge on which he was court-martialed and convicted involved the sale of war materials by a firm for which he worked to the Army base at which he worked. The fight managers on Jacobs Beach, where Mr. Gould was once a star and an oracle, took the news philosophically.

"Joe went into the Army in very good faith," they said, "but you can't spend all your life looking for an angle and then suddenly stop looking for an angle because you're in the Army. If there was an angle in the Army, Joe would look for it."

All fight managers pursue angles. They acquire a piece of this and a piece of that. They put situations to work for them. There is a type in society which was known, fifty years ago, as an "easy rider," but fight managers are not necessarily easy riders. Many of them put a great deal of talent, ingenuity, and toil into the exploitation of their angles. Basically, of course, they traffic in the bodies of athletes, but it often takes hard work and mother wit to make a body pay off. Joe Gould had talent and was proud of it. He was one of the few fight managers I know to cast his shadow over two American sports, not including war.

Although some of Joe's activities, being extracurricular, did not get into the newspapers, he was well known before he joined the Army. He managed James J. Braddock, whom he steered with much adroitness and spirit to the heavyweight championship of the world, and he managed Tommy Farr, the Welsh fighter, who never won a fight in this country but made a pot of money while losing five bouts in a row.

Gould rested his fame upon the success (spiritual) of Braddock and the success (commercial) of Farr. Like most managers, he was prouder of his own work than of his fighters'.

"I'm a great manager because I never had a great fighter and I still got places," said Joe one day, in a burst of frankness. "I take off my hat to no manager. Not to none."

"That don't mean anything," interrupted Professor Will Mc-Carney, a fellow nonmanual laborer. "You never take off your hat at all, even when you eat."

This tribute to Mr. Gould's blunt ways was somewhat exaggerated, but it's true that Joe came up a hard road and wasted little time acquiring social polish. He dated back to the days of no-decision fights, when the winning fighter was the one whose manager got to the telegraph office first with a wire to the New York newspapers saying: "Glotz murdered Kluck here tonight in ten rounds," thus forestalling his rival's bulletin: "Kluck pulverized Glotz."

About the tricks of his trade, Mr. Gould was candid—about some of his sidelines, less so. Gould was the good friend of Big Bill Duffy, who was the good friend and lieutenant of the mobster Owney Madden. Sometimes the hand of Madden showed through.

You'll recall that Max Schmeling knocked out Joe Louis while Braddock was champion, in 1936. Mike Jacobs, controlling Louis, wanted Louis to be champion before he fought Schmeling again. So Schmeling was sidetracked, and Gould and Braddock agreed to fight Louis for the championship in Chicago—for a small consideration: 20 percent of the net gate of every future Louis fight.

Faithfully, for some time thereafter, Mr. Gould called around on Promoter Jacobs after each Louis fight and collected his "end." It was nice work, if you could get it. However, Mr. Jacobs notified Mr. Gould and his allies, one day, that he was getting sick and tired of the arrangement. He called it off. Mr. Gould threatened suit. That was the way matters stood until the evening when Mr. Madden and Mr. Big Bill Duffy appeared at a Madison Square Garden fight on what was rumored to be the personal invitation of Mr. Jacobs.

The two distinguished guests were promptly picked up by detectives, who also may have been present on Mr. Jacobs's invitation. Before Duffy and Madden could get free of those detectives and off on their way to Hot Springs, the business quarrel was "adjusted"—certain ious being canceled by one party and the old Louis-Braddock agreement by the other.

There is never a dull moment in Cauliflower Alley.

A little later the great Joe DiMaggio, New York Yankee center fielder, was called before Judge Kenesaw M. Landis to account for the gossip that Joe Gould collected a percentage of DiMaggio's salary as his "manager." DiMaggio denied it strongly, though unable to deny that Gould was a good friend of his who advised him on business matters. Maybe for nothing.

I never took Mr. Gould too seriously in the role of Sinister Influence. But I always knew, when I saw him walking down the street (with his hat on), that I was watching a very busy man.

Life with Eddie

from *Newsweek*

I cherish no spite or bitterness against the members of the society syndicate which invested its doubloons in Beau Jack, a young shoeshine boy and caddy who became lightweight champion of the world. They were lucky with Jack. He turned out fine. I belonged to a fighter syndicate once myself, which did not turn out so good, but I am too sunny and genial a character to begrudge the Jack people their success.

Their success was not financial, strictly speaking. Each of these Stork Club amateurs kicked in with a modest sum toward the outfitting, feeding, and transportation of the Beau in his formative days in the ring, and when he began to pay dividends, they took back their original investment and no more, leaving the profits to Mr. Jack himself, his trainer, and his manager of record, Mr. Charles Hercules Wergeles.

I understand, however, that the syndicate retained a vote in the matter of selecting the Beau's opponents. And it was all too true that whenever Jack fought at Madison Square Garden, the members attended in a body to root him home and bask in his victories and beam fulsomely upon outsiders in the congregation.

It was the vision of this sort of happiness which led the people in my syndicate to invest in a broth of a boy named Eddie, from upstate New York. Eddie was a pleasant fellow and a close student of pinball games, but it developed in the course of the experiment that he couldn't fight much.

He won a couple of bouts in an "amateur" club, and his backers were exhilarated. He then embarked upon a losing streak and spent long periods of time sitting on the floor. This relapse was interrupted briefly by a bout with his manager in which both parties claimed victory, though the bystanders called it a draw. There is no doubt that the punch he hurled at his manager was the best of Eddie's career. He woke up the following morning under new management, namely, mine.

I should mention that the syndicate was not a society syndicate, like Beau Jack's. It included a working girl, a poet-golfer, a drama reviewer, and me, and I believe another piece of the stock was held in shares by a fashion editor, a boulevardier, and an editorial writer. These individuals may have subdivided Eddie even farther, but if so it escaped my attention.

One of the problems with Eddie was weight. He was somewhat too ample. His original manager ordered a diet, and in a week's time Eddie shot down from 219 pounds to 218. The next week he was up to 221, and the syndicate winced visibly.

When his manager trapped him in a restaurant one midnight, browsing over a racing form and a plate of chow mein, Eddie broke down and admitted that he was also getting away with considerable salad dressing on the side. As for his roadwork, he had taken to walking around the reservoir in Central Park, like other people, instead of running, on the ground that running made him feel conspicuous. This struck me as a quibble. At his weight, Eddie was conspicuous any way you looked at him—running, walking, standing, or, in the final stages of his career, lying on the canvas.

Eddie gave the pinball machines of New York a good play. I asked him if he thought this was wise, and he said yes.

"I used to work in a place where they made pinball machines," he told me. "I know how to beat them, don't worry."

Later we discovered that Eddie was getting behind in his rent, and he explained to me that the pinball machines he was playing had turned out to be a different type from the one he had in mind. Thenceforward, he concentrated on horse racing.

For winning a couple of amateur bouts, Eddie collected a couple of watches from the Amateur Athletic Union, and any AAU boxer can tell you that these watches have a hock value of approximately $13; which sum enabled Eddie to eke out his horse studies a little longer than he might have been able to do on syndicate funds.

Eddie was a natural left-hander. His first manager switched him to right-handed style in the ring. When I became manager, figuring he could not bounce on the floor any harder left-handed than right-handed, I let him return to the comfortable southpaw position. And sure enough, I was right. He hit the deck with exactly the same momentum.

The syndicate survived two or three knockouts, but presently we realized that we were weaving and lurching noticeably as we walked down the street, so we bade Eddie a sad good-by. He took the news stoically. Much more regretful was his trainer, a seasoned operative named Battling Norfolk, who got $10 a week as long as the syndicate backed Eddie.

Come to think of it, we still owe the Battler ten bucks.

The Sweet and the Tough

from *Newsweek*

When Billy Conn, the prizefighter, was at the height of his fame, he was invited to go into motion pictures, as many a fighter has done before him with results ranging from the gruesome to the soporific.

Jack Dempsey was in pictures. Gene Tunney made *The Fighting Marine*. The critics likened Mr. Tunney's art to the stately elm tree, on the ground that both were more than somewhat wooden, but I think they did Gene an injustice. He ran the gamut of human emotion from frozen to slightly defrosted, and Duse in her palmiest days never suggested the fundamental sadness of life more surely than Mr. Tunney. Besides, he was the only dignified Marine I ever saw in the cinema.

Joe Louis did a short jolt in films. He performed with great speed, as though anxious to pay his debt to society and get out of there. Jim Jeffries has done bit parts. Maxie Rosenbloom gets good money for his drawing-room comedy.

Perhaps the best fight picture ever made was *The Prizefighter and the Lady*, in which Max Baer scaled the heights of rare old Smithfield. Primo Carnera served as a stooge in this drama, and Mr. Baer attributed his subsequent conquest of Carnera in the ring to the profound psychological treatment he gave Primo, between takes, while they were making the picture.

"I wired his chair and gave him hotfoots all over the lot," explained Maxie. "Preem didn't know if he was coming or going."

About Conn now, I don't know if they were going to cast him for sweet parts or tough parts. Willie has a sweet face and a tough disposition—you might call him a schizophrene, if you smiled when you said it. Willie would rather be tough. He has expressed a desire to muss up the lovely features of Tyrone Power, and if he can't get Power, he will settle for Robert Taylor.

Maybe Mr. Conn would be better off if he didn't have such a pretty face himself. Consider the rise and fall of Kid Broad—an epic of nonpulchritude.

The Kid had a face that only a mother could love, and even his mother managed to control her enthusiasm pretty well. The Kid's face was his fortune.

"They used to put me in pictures like *Beauty and the Beast*," the Kid once told me. "It was a good angle, see, on account of the look of my kisser. I was the beast," added Mr. Broad, to make matters absolutely clear.

The Kid prospered until one day when fate dealt him an ironical blow. He didn't turn pretty overnight. It was worse than that. They found someone uglier.

The late Douglas Fairbanks was casting a picture which called for a particularly sinister thug. The Kid reported for duty with cheerful confidence, but Fairbanks turned him down.

"I need something worse than this," said the actor.

"Worse than me?" faltered Mr. Broad. However, the Kid had a fine, generous nature. Pulling himself together, he said, "All right, I know the guy you want. I'll get him."

The Kid repaired to a nearby gymnasium and returned with a

bush-league wrestler named Luigi Montagna. Montagna had once chopped wood for eight cents a day in Italy. Wrestling was better than that, but wrestling was nothing compared with the green fields that opened to him now, for they hired him on sight. He was—you guessed it—Bull Montana.

Montana soared to fame as the only actor in the world who could make up for the role of chimpanzee by removing his hat. And Kid Broad, the man who gave the Bull his start, was soon forgotten. He languished and pined away. Ironical? You said it. But that's life.

John Arthur Johnson

from *Newsweek*

A lot of people whose judgment I respect think that Jack Johnson, who died in 1946, was the greatest heavyweight fighter of all time—the greatest heavyweight champion, at least. There were a few men, Sam Langford and Joe Jeannette among them, whom Johnson declined to fight after he won his title, and they might have been able to beat him; but it should be remembered that they were colored men, and Johnson had no financial interest in meeting them, nor was he much encouraged to do so by the promoters of those times, whose chief interest was in evolving a "white hope."

The white hope whom Johnson, at the age of thirty-seven, eventually agreed to accommodate was Jess Willard. Willard, when Johnson died, paid high tribute to his talent, saying among other things that he could have handled Joe Louis and Billy Conn simultaneously; but no man likes to knock himself, and speaking of the fight in which he won the title from Johnson in Havana, in 1915, Jess simply said, with a bland look: "I hit him a good uppercut."

Very few people outside of Willard believe this, and maybe Jess doesn't either. A nephew of Johnson's, who lived with the champion while he trained for Willard, bet $5,000 to $8,000 on Willard. That was the kind of fight it was. Johnson had a desperate need to take care of himself economically at the time he surrendered his championship.

So he made his bargain at Havana, and as usual he was double-crossed—this time on motion picture rights. The year before, fighting another white man, Frank Moran, in Paris, he worked for nothing because the promoter, angry at Moran, tied up every sou of the gate receipts. It is hard today—though by no means impossible—to realize how ruthlessly and brazenly Negro fighters were manipulated and cheated in Johnson's time. This fact and Johnson's reaction to it do a great deal to explain the almost chronic suspiciousness and peevishness of his manner, which in turn help to account for his unpopularity with the American public in his heyday.

Johnson, whom I saw quite often in the last fifteen years of his life, was a proud man, as well as a man of intelligence and dignity. Instead of being subdued by cheating and prejudice, or adapting himself meekly to circumstances, as Langford and other great fighters did, he resisted. He insisted on meeting his fellow human beings as an equal—which, in view of his character and preeminence in his field of work, was a fairly modest demand. While he was defeated on nearly every point at issue in this long, contentious career, he never gave up. He died full of the same dignity and self-respect which supported him all his life and which, construed as vanity and cockiness by the press and the public, made him a deep-dyed villain in his native land as long as he was remembered.

There was a good deal of simple vanity in Johnson, too. In his autobiography he told of how a German zeppelin, in the early stages of the First World War, spotted him from above in the London streets and followed him around, twisting and turning to get a direct hit on Johnson. When he announced that he was rewriting *Othello*, or when he sat in a Paris café with a beret on his head, sipping beer through a straw, he was displaying a deep, and I should say harmless, interest in showing the man Johnson to the public in a distinctive way.

Even in Professor Hubert's flea circus on Forty-second Street in New York, where Johnson exhibited himself for a few years in the 1930s in order to make bread and beer money, he was dignified, aloof, and untouched by his surroundings.

"Whenever you write about me," he told me once, "just please remember that I'm a man, and a good one."

As a professional fighter, Johnson was so notable for defensive skill and science that it is sometimes forgotten how tremendously strong he was, and how hard he could hit when he wanted to. Anti-Johnsonites emphasize the time the smaller Stanley Ketchel knocked him down, in Colma, California, in 1909. The fight was an exhibition, and Ketchel was double-crossing Johnson in the fashionable way when he hit him as hard as possible on the chin. Johnson reacted to the double-cross as he always did when he could. He rose and knocked Ketchel unconscious. He was, as he said, a man. He never wanted anyone to forget it.

Fun at the Scales

from *Newsweek*

In the glossary of professional boxing, a "Philadelphia lightweight" is a lightweight who is no lightweight at all. A Philadelphia lightweight cannot make the limit of 135 pounds without cutting off his right leg, and for sentimental and hygienic reasons he hardly ever goes to this extreme.

The Philadelphia lightweight is rare today, because most recent lightweight champions have been able to make the limit handily. Lew Jenkins was a natural lightweight, and so was Henry Armstrong. Lou Ambers lost the championship partly because he sweated his waxing carcass down to taw and was weakened thereby.

If Ambers had fought in the boom times, fifteen and twenty years ago, when a lightweight title fight drew half a million dollars, he probably wouldn't have bothered to make the weight. Nobody else did. I refer you to the roguish maneuvers of the late Benny Leonard and Lew Tendler, two of history's most famous Philadelphia lightweights.

Leonard and Tendler come to mind because of a recent suggestion that Benny and Lew meet again for charity, in an exhibition bout. It would be interesting to watch, if you could hoist either man into the ring without the help of a derrick. Benny, just before his recent death, was pleasingly buxom. Mr. Tendler occupies the space formerly occupied by three Tendlers and a two-car garage.

And yet the boys were just as much lightweights in middle age as they were on the night in 1923 when they fought for the lightweight title to a crowd that paid $452,648 to see them.

Perspiring freely in his training camp before that fight, Mr. Leonard came to a sudden conclusion.

"I can make 138," he told his manager, Billy Gibson, "but you'd have to cut off my head at the neck to get the other three pounds, and I can't spare it."

"Forget it," advised Mr. Gibson. "You don't think Tendler can make the weight, do you?"

"I never thought of that," said Benny, and relaxed.

The weigh-in, a gaudy event, was scheduled for Jack O'Brien's gymnasium on the afternoon of the fight. The press arrived in platoons. Mr. Tendler arrived in a cab. Mr. Leonard failed to show. After waiting a few minutes, Mr. Tendler departed.

"I think I will grab me some fresh air," he explained.

Half an hour later, word sifted through to the watchdogs of the Fourth Estate that the weigh-in ceremonies had been switched to the office of James Joy Johnston, the boy bandit, who was then using the nom de plume of the Cromwell A.C. When the press reached the Cromwell A.C., the two lightweight heroes were buttoning their vests.

"The weigh-in has just transpired," said Mr. Leonard apologetically. "You boys were a little late."

"It was a very interesting ceremony," said Mr. Tendler. "A darb."

"I weighed a hundred and thirty-four pounds," said Benny, thoughtfully stroking his second chin.

"I slipped in there at a hundred thirty-three and three-quarters," said Lew, without blushing. "I guess I will go out and scratch up some filet mignon. The strain has been fearful."

For the sake of the record, I should add that Mr. Leonard won the fight. It was an active and thrilling engagement. Years later Mr. Leonard admitted blandly that the best the boys were able to do on those scales was something in the neighborhood of 138 apiece, huff and puff though they might.

"But what could we do?" he said reasonably. "There was $450,000 in the till, and the crowd wanted to see that title on the line."

Such was life in the golden age of the Philadelphia lightweight. In time Mr. Leonard and Mr. Tendler became a couple of Philadelphia light-heavies. I doubt if either of them could have made 175 pounds after a week's fast. But for sweet charity, and with two strong men behind them in each corner to push, they might still have staged a good stately brawl.

Now Pitching for Bartlett's

from *Newsweek*

Immortality is assured for Shakespeare, Shelley, Pope, and a couple of fellows named Anonymous and Ibid. by inclusion in Barlett's *Familiar Quotations*, and I am glad to learn that Bartlett, in his latest edition, has moved Ibid. over a few inches to make room for Joe Jacobs, better known in his years on this green footstool as Yussel the Muscle. It may well be that Mr. Jacobs is the first fight manager in history to be tapped for *Familiar Quotations*—not that the late shareholder's fame depends on such kudos.

"Joe could get along without Bartlett, but could Bartlett get along without Joe?" was the reaction in the cauliflower market when the boys heard from Uncle Daniel Parker, the *New York Daily Mirror* poet, that Yussel was in. That is a fair summary of the values in this case. No quotation book that calls itself a quotation book can look you in the eye these days unless it includes "I should of stood in bed."

This department notes that the book has been further enlarged to accommodate the second of Joe's great coinages: "We wuz robbed!" The phrase is attributed by some scholars to Anon. and by others to Ibid., but it was the work of Jacobs. It incorporates, as you see, the managerial "We," which is otherwise absent from Bartlett. It was uttered after Max Schmeling and Mr. Jacobs had licked the stuffing out of Jack Sharkey, only to hear the verdict go against them.

According to the poet Parker, who evidently reads Bartlett in his bathtub, the origin of "I should of stood in bed" is wrongly described in the book. It seems there is a nonsensical footnote to the effect that Jacobs gave birth to the words after losing a bet on the World Series of 1934.

As it happens, the great man coined them two feet from your correspondent's ear. It was the only time I ever heard a famous quotation in the making. I used to pal around with Shelley quite a bit, but he always remained mute while we were together. With Joe Jacobs it was quite the contrary, unless he was playing pinochle. On this occasion—1935, it was—he was seeing his first and last ball game. Mr. Jacobs had the seat behind me in the press box at Detroit for the opening game of the World Series, and, though Lonnie Warneke was pitching very nifty ball for the Cubs, Mr. Jacobs did not like it. An icy wind was curdling his blood, along with everyone else's. It was the coldest ball game I can remember.

A neighbor asked Joe what he thought of baseball, and Joe to him these deathless words did speak: "I should of stood in bed." He left the place in the fourth inning. The rest of us had to stay and work. I recall that a flagon of hot tea from the tea fields of the brothers Haig, which I had brought, was all that saved the lives of several fellow convicts and me while we wrote our pieces after the game.

Yussel the Muscle had other claims to celebrity which do not concern Bartlett. He was the only man ever to lose a fight south of the Mason-Dixon Line—that is the managerial "he"—and win it north of same. His man Mike McTigue was the loser to Young Stribling by the vote of the crowd in Columbus, Georgia, but McTigue, Jacobs, and referee Harry Ertle caught the train north and reversed the decision as soon as they reached Pennsylvania. It went down in the books as a draw.

Mr. Jacobs was the only man ever to salute Hitler with a cigar in his mouth—Joe's mouth, I mean to say. He joined a mass "Heil!" to the leader from a prize ring in Hamburg. Since he had to hold his hat in one hand and salute with the other, there was no place for the panatela except between his teeth. "Fuhrer Insulted by Noted Non-Aryan!" the German headlines screamed.

Mr. Jacobs was the only man ever to be hit over the head with a plaster statuette of Schmeling. The statuette was aimed by Joe's business partner, the late Billy McCarney, and the gesture dissolved the partnership. However, McCarney says they remained good friends.

So now Joe, in the heavenly meadows, has a piece of Barlett's *Familiar Quotations*. It is a nice break for both sides.

When in Doubt, Hang the Judge
from *Newsweek*

When Ezzard Charles won the heavyweight championship by licking J. J. Walcott, two years ago, Ezzard's manager, Jake (Madman) Mintz, passed out in the ring. Last July when Walcott won the title, it was Charles who fell, while Jake remained on his feet throughout. That is my idea of a perfect partnership—always one man conscious, to count the house.

Perhaps it was because he foresaw how the evening would end that Mr. Mintz, who is three-quarters brain and one-quarter Westphalian, put on his own show before the fight. It is unethical for anyone, fighter or manager, to enter a coma in advance of the first round, so instead of fainting, Jake howled for ten minutes, breaking the record set by a coyote in a semipro contest near Albuquerque.

As soon as the Walcott-Charles thing went on the air before the largest TV crowd in fight history, Mintz, fully aware of same, took over. His spectacles gleaming with rage, he raced up and down the ring screaming for the elimination of Charlie Daggert, a judge from Philadelphia.

"Nuts to judges from Philly! It's an insult to me!" yelled Jake, as he bounced off the east ropes and dashed for the west ropes. "Gimme judges from Pittsburgh, or I will take my fighter back to the dressing room!"

Six rounds and fifty-five seconds later, Mintz made good his threat. He took his fighter back to the dressing room—feet first, as the trade expression goes. (Of course, the trade expression exaggerates: Charles could walk away from the ring under his own power after the bout; so could Mintz.)

What the millions of watchers wondered was, how about the feelings of Daggert, the judge? Was he hurt by Mintz's screams? Mintz screams very tactlessly. The only indication we have is Daggert's score card—at the time of the knockout, it read 4 rounds for Walcott, 1 for Charles, and 1 even. That doesn't mean much. The referee's score was 5 for Walcott, 1 for Charles, and the referee was a Pittsburgher. My own was 2-2-2 and bam! It's my belief, though, based on past form, that the Philly judge was embarrassed by the shouts of Madman Mintz.

Long ago my father was the official scorer in a ball game in the old Three-Eye League. In those days in some of those ball parks, the scorer sat down on the field exposed to counterjustice. On one ball hit by a tough player, which got past the infield, my father scored an error. Between innings the scorer sat trembling and turning gray, hair by hair, while the victim circled him with a bat, trying to close in. The scorer's life was saved by Dan Howley, later a big-league manager.

When your correspondent, as a reluctant linesman in a tournament, called one against the great Helen Jacobs, she flourished her racket and bared her fangs. Your agent arose and cased the exits, but a ball boy told me to take it easy.

"That's her backhand grip. If she hits you, she's got no power," he said, and maybe he was right.

A truly nervous official was Harry Ertle, a northern referee, who went to the heart of Columbus, Ga., to handle a fight between

Mike McTigue, from Ireland, and Young Stribling, the pride of Georgia.

"A draw," decided Ertle.

"What!" cried many citizens, climbing into the ring to hear better.

"Well, call it yourselves," said Ertle, and hurried off to catch a train for the North. The citizens called it for Young Stribling. The record book calls it a draw.

In the Walcott-Charles square dance, judges from Philly and judges from Tibet could only have called it one way at the end. Charles played with that old Jersey musket once too often. It was loaded.

No Scar, No Memory

from *Newsweek*

CHICAGO—An oddly shocking and confusing thing—neither good nor very bad, neither just nor very cruel—happened to Gene Fullmer, the young Mormon prizefighter, in the boxing hall here the other night. When he went into the ring, his life was at its peak. He was famous, newly rich, powerful, confident, rising. A few minutes later, he fell from power and glory to frustration and relative nothingness. And he cannot tell you of his own knowledge what happened. Not only power and glory are gone—the facts are missing too. Thirty seconds of time, at a climax of his existence, are lost to him.

To know what went on he has to be told. To believe it he has to look at a set of pictures. And this will be true for the rest of his life. It will be a strange, unsettling way to live.

Fullmer missed seeing the punch that jarred his brain off the track of memory. He missed hearing the sudden yell of rapture that filled the hall at the count of ten. He missed the sight—and maybe he can spare it—of Ray Robinson riding five feet in the air on the shoulders of his henchmen.

After he had been levered to his feet, Fullmer walked to his corner with his gray, bumpy face thirsty for information. A baby looks like that sometimes, when he is trying to catch up with the world all at once. "Why did they stop it?" he asked Marv Jensen, his friend and manager. "Well," said Jensen dryly, with a kind of noncommittal tenderness, "mostly because you were counted out."

A minute or two after that, Fullmer stood side by side in the middle of the ring with Robinson, and they talked a little together as they posed for the cameramen. Fullmer spoke earnestly. The same anxious look was on his face. "I don't know anything about it," I heard him say. "I couldn't tell you what happened." Robinson looked down at him, gave a smile, said something, and patted Fullmer gaily on the top of his head. It was the first time in an hour that anything had distracted Ray's attention from the thought of his own work and his own triumph. Perhaps he was struck suddenly by the curious emptiness of the other man's situation—not a scar, but not a memory either, to show for his night's work and his downfall.

Before that, Robinson's mind had been entirely dedicated to the job in hand, as a great artist's should be. They had been telling him in his corner what he'd already figured out: "Hit him coming in, hit him coming in." It's hard to gauge the speed of a strong, lunging man at close quarters, and harder to check him, without a crowbar. But at the start of the fourth round Robinson smacked Fullmer with a quick right lead, as they came together, and slowed him down, and after that he could time his moves. In the fifth he hit Fullmer with a long right to the body. It was a disconcerting blow. Fullmer took a backward step—and when he came on again he was slower, and he was watching the right. It was the last thing that Gene Fullmer saw, or remembered.

Today, every left-hand punch except a jab (and sometimes even that) is called a "hook." It's one of those language trends, a majority rule of speech which I won't try to resist. But a hook, as the word was conceived for boxing, is a short, intimate punch, thrown laterally, inside, with the left side already forward. It was no left hook that stripped Fullmer of his consciousness and turned his life upside down. It was a full left swing, or larrup, if you like, perfectly pivoted, perfectly timed, thrown from two feet outside, moving up and forward straight to the seat of concussion in the point of the jawbone.

"He got the message," Robinson said afterward, abandoning the use of French for his curtain lines and stealing one from Archie Moore.

He then spoke well of God, his wife, his son, Joe Louis, the Bureau of Internal Revenue, and his future in the theater. "I may never fight again," he said at dawn next day. At ten o'clock he began to dicker for 35 percent of the gate with Carmen Basilio. Fullmer will never know how it happened—but he was licked last week by the perfect artist and the perfect dealer in gibberish. In short, the perfect schizophrene.

Cautionary Tales

The Life and Loves of the Real McCoy
from *True*

The hotel manager and the detective stood looking down at the man on the bed, who had killed himself during the night. "Norman Selby, it says on the note, and Selby was how he checked in," the manager said. "Wasn't that his right name?"

"It was his right name," the detective said. "But he was also McCoy. The real McCoy."

Kid McCoy lived by violence, by trickery, and by women. He fought two hundred fights and was beaten in only six of them. He married eight women—one of them three times—and shot another to death. For the murder he paid a light price, lightly. There was vanity in him, and guile, and wit, and cruelty, and some larceny, and a great capacity for enjoying himself. Above all, there was self-satisfaction. At no time in his life—not when he was the world's welterweight champion (with a strong claim to the middleweight title as well), nor when he was a bankrupt, nor a jailbird, nor a Broadway favorite, nor a suspected jewel thief, nor a semiprofessional adulterer, nor a mellow old pensioner, owing his job to a friend—at no time did he do or say anything that displeased himself. No one knows why, on an April night in 1940, he suddenly lost his contentment with Norman Shelby, alias Charles (Kid) McCoy, and wiped it all out with one impatient gesture.

The Kid wasn't sick or broke when he checked in alone at Detroit's Tuller Hotel that night. He had work. He was sixty-six years old, but in good shape, still with a lot of gray but curly hair over his fair-skinned, boyish face, and still nearly as neat, trim, and supple of body as ever. Registering with the night clerk, he had left a call for ten the next morning. It was when he failed to answer the call that the manager came up with a passkey and found him dead. An overdose of sleeping pills had put him out and away. There were two or three notes in his room. In one of them, he asked the paymaster at the Ford Motor Company, where he'd been working, to turn over such wages as were due him to his eighth and final wife. In the longest note, the Kid said, in part:

"To whom it may concern—For the last eight years, I have wanted to help humanity, especially the youngsters who do not know nature's laws. That is, the proper carriage of the body, the right way to eat, etc. . . . To all my dear friends, I wish you all the best of luck. Sorry I could not endure this world's madness. The best to all. (signed) Norman Selby. P.S. In my pocket you will find $17.75."

As to health laws—it was true that McCoy had invented, and tried to sell, a so-called health belt, or health suspender. As to "this world's madness"—most of the madness the Kid had known had been of his own arranging, and he had endured it well and gaily. As to helping humanity—the Kid had always helped himself. An old-timer, seeing the dead man lying there among his last words, would have reflected that never before had McCoy played so sweet, peaceful, and tender a part. The old-timer might have suspected a trick.

Once, in 1895, in Boston, a welterweight named Jack Wilkes was dismayed by McCoy's looks, as they climbed into the ring to fight. The Kid's face was as white as a sheet. There were dark hallows under his eyes. Every few moments, he put his left glove to his mouth and coughed rackingly. When they clinched in the first round, McCoy whispered, "Take it easy, will you, Jack? I think I'm dying, but I need the money." Wilkes took it easy; he mothered McCoy. But in the second round, just after a cough, McCoy's coughing hand suddenly snapped out and pushed Wilkes's guard aside, and his right hand drove against his chin, and knocked him unconscious. For that bout, McCoy had made up his face with talcum powder, and his eyes with indelible pencil. The prop cough was from many dime novels of the time.

In Philadelphia, in 1904, McCoy fought a large, highly touted Hollander named Plaacke. In the second round he began to point frantically at Plaacke's waistband. "Your pants are slipping!" he muttered. "Pull 'em up!" Plaacke reached for his pants with both hands. McCoy hit him on the jaw and knocked him down. "Stay down, or I'll tear your head off!" he snarled. The Dutchman was terrified by the savagery that had suddenly come into the Kid's voice and by the cruelty that transfigured his impish face. He stayed down, and his American manager sent him back to Holland on the next cattle boat.

When McCoy ran a gymnasium in New York, in the early years of this century, he said to a new pupil one day, as the latter came in the door, "Who's that that came in with you?" The pupil turned to look. McCoy knocked him down. "That's your first lesson—never trust anybody," he said. "Five dollars, please."

The Kid got a lifelong pleasure out of teaching this lesson. Once, only a few months before he died, as he was driving along a road in Wayne County, Michigan, his car had a slight collision with a truck. Both vehicles stalled. The drivers got out, and the trucker came at McCoy, braying abuse. "I'm a little hard of hearing, Mack," McCoy said, cupping his hand to his ear. The trucker brought his chin close to the ear to make his point clearly, and McCoy, whipping his hand six inches upward, knocked him cold.

On the morning he was found dead, a true student of the ways of Kid McCoy, seeing the suicide notes, would have looked twice to make sure the Kid was there too. They were not the first suicide notes he had written. In 1924 McCoy was living with a divorcée named Mrs. Theresa Mors in a Los Angeles apartment. When Mrs. Mors was fatally shot by her lover, the police, investigating the crime, discovered near her body a message from Norman Selby which began—as his last one on earth was to do—"To whom it may concern." The message suggested that the Kid meant to end it all—but no dead McCoy went with it. In jail, a few days later, McCoy moved on to still another stratagem, feigning insanity to protect himself from the murder charge. A visitor found him walking around his cell with a blank look on his face, stopping now and then to lick bits of cardboard and stick them to the walls.

"What are those for?" the visitor asked.

"Quiet!" McCoy said. "I'm making a trap for that rat, her husband."

The law, to be on the safe side, called in a team of alienists to examine the sudden madman. "He's at least as sane as the rest of us," the scientists reported. He was. The state, in proving its homicide case against him later, said that the Kid had had no notion of killing himself. He killed the lady, it charged, for a very intelligent reason—she was rich and she wouldn't marry him.

Of all the rich and beautiful women in the life of McCoy, she must have been the only one who wouldn't. It was curious, the way the pattern of the Kid's loves and marriages changed with the changes in his own career. When he was young, tough, and fight-hungry, scrapping first with skin-tight gloves and then by Marquis of Queensberry rules, first on turf and covered bridges and dance-hall floors, later in the ring, outboxing scientists like Tommy Ryan, the welter champion, mauling and knocking down heavyweights like the powerful Tom Sharkey—in those times his love affairs were brief. About his first marriage, at twenty-two to an Ohio girl named Lottie Piehler, McCoy once said: "A few months after I married her, I met a burlesque queen who finished me as a married man." He wasn't finished, he was just starting. But he had to keep on the move. There was less sense of investment, of security, for McCoy, in those early matings. There was even romance in some of them. Certainly, he loved Mrs. Julia Woodruff Crosselmire, whose stage name was Julia Woodruff. Certainly, she loved him. He caught her eye by breaking up a free-for-all fight in a railroad car one day in 1897 on a trip from New York to Philadelphia. In the next few years, they were married three times and divorced three times.

A change set in when the Kid grew older, when he fought only when he had to and felt the pressures and hardships of life as a job-hunter and part-time con man. That was how it was in 1905 when he married Lillian Ellis, the young widow of a millionaire. Julia had recently cut him loose for the last time—as a matter of fact, he had divorced *her*, the only time it happened that way with McCoy.

"She ran away with a man named Thompson," the Kid used to say. "They took a tour around the world, and when they got back, I seceded."

On the morning his engagement to Mrs. Ellis was announced, the Kid was lying in his bed in the Dunlop Hotel, in New York, when the telephone began to ring. "Before I could get my shoes on that day," McCoy said, "the phone had rung a hundred times, and a hundred friends had touched me for a million dollars." Mrs. Ellis told the press that she knew what she was in for. "I know I'm not getting any angel, but I'm satisfied," she said. The Kid himself was so moved that he wrote a wedding poem:

Dogs delight to growl and fight,
But let men be above them,
It's better to have a gal for a pal,
When he really knows she loves him.

In a sense, McCoy said, these lines were his farewell to the fight game. For now, at least, he was through—"Even though Jeff," he said, "is the only man alive who can lick me." He was referring to James J. Jeffries, the retired heavyweight champion of the world.

High-flown though it sounded, the last statement well may have been true. It's possible that for his weight, which ranged from 145 pounds to 170, McCoy was the finest fighter in the world when he was at his best. "A marvel, a genius of scientific fighting," James J. Corbett called him. "Vicious, fast, and almost impossible to beat," said Philadelphia Jack O'Brien. It was a strange fact about McCoy that he did not need his tricks to be great. He cheated because he loved to cheat, just as, in the early days, he married women because he loved them. Fighting on the level, he would still have been the real McCoy.

The phrase which keeps his name famous was born in San Francisco, in 1899. At least, McCoy always said so; and while he was one of the most fertile and tireless liars of his generation, there's a good chance that he was telling the truth. The Kid went to the Coast in March of that year to meet the rough, hard-punching Joe Choynski. A little earlier, in San Francisco, a Joe McAuliffe had easily whipped a man named Peter McCoy. Kid McCoy, following this low-class act with a better one, gave Choynski a savage beating in twenty rounds, knocking him down sixteen times. The press hailed him with gratitude: "Choynski is beaten," a headline said, "by THE REAL MCCOY."

As to how Norman Selby got the name of McCoy to begin with,

there are two stories, both told by McCoy, and both plausible. He was born, probably in October 1873, in Moscow, Indiana, a little farmland crossroads northwest of the town of Rushville. The Selby family moved to Indianapolis when Norman was small. When he was somewhere between fourteen and sixteen, he and two other boys ran away by train to Cincinnati. Cops met them at the Cincinnati station, alerted by their fathers. "Are you Norman Selby?" a cop asked Norman. "I'm Charlie McCoy," he said. The night before, through the train window, he had seen a sign, "McCoy Station." When he made his first prizefight it was under the name of Charlie (Kid) McCoy.

In a story the Kid told another historian, he once saw a burlesque act featuring the exploits of two real-life safe crackers, Kid McCoy and Spike Hennessy. In the theater lobby, for a dime, you could buy a book on the lives of McCoy and Hennessy. The Kid read the book, was taken with the daring, aggressive character of McCoy, and borrowed his name. Either way, there's no doubt that he began fighting early in life as Kid McCoy. Some say his first bout, for $5 or $10, was against Charleston Yalla. Some say it was against Pete Jenkins, in St. Paul, in 1891. In St. Paul, the Kid, who was pausing there to wash dishes, joined the Baptist Church, because you had to be a member to join the YMCA, which had the only sports-training facilities in town. He beat Jenkins in four rounds.

After March 1895, the Kid was a fighter with a reputation; he was "the man who beat Shadow Maber." To Maber, he was "that bloody trickster." Shadow, an Australian fighting in the States and a boxer of note, met McCoy in Memphis. Near the end of one round, Maber heard a strong, clear voice say, "The bell has rung. Go to your corner." He started to turn for his corner, and McCoy, the author of the unofficial announcement, belted him in the jaw. McCoy went on to beat the weakened Australian in ten rounds.

He had marvelous speed and elusiveness, the Kid did, besides his tricks and the cruel, cutting power of his punches. By practicing endlessly, he was able to run sideways, or backward, nearly as fast as the average man can run forward. "In a backward race, in fact," he said once, "I could probably beat any man in the world." He improved the use of his left hand by eating, writing, and throwing a ball left-handed. From every good fighter he fought or watched he learned something. Bob Fitzsimmons, then recognized as world's middleweight champion, was training for a fight in New Orleans while McCoy was down there for a bout of his own. The Kid picked up a few dollars sparring with Ruby Robert.

"You're a cunning bugger," Fitz told him after McCoy, feinting a left, drove his right straight into the pit of Bob's stomach, showing that he had mastered one of Fitzsimmons's favorite moves. "And you can hit almost as hard as I can."

"For the same reason," the Kid said.

"Wot in 'ell do you mean by that?" the Cornishman asked. He did not like to think he was giving away too much.

"You're knock-kneed, Bob," McCoy said. "I figured the reason you hit so hard is because your punch comes up from the knee instead of the waist or the hip."

"————!" said Fitzsimmons unkindly. He considered that the theory was buncombe, and he may well have been right. It was a fact, however, as McCoy then demonstrated, that the Kid had schooled his own knees to come inward by walking around for twenty minutes or a half hour at a time holding a fifty-cent piece between them.

Fitzsimmons (who was to win the heavyweight title from Jim Corbett in 1897) was too big and strong for McCoy, who in those years weighed in at about the welter limit, 145. The welterweight champion of the world was Tommy Ryan, thought by many to be the most skillful boxer extant. Ryan and McCoy were matched to fight for the welter title in Maspeth, Long Island, in March 1896. It was a match Ryan had no worries about. McCoy had sparred with him, too, a couple of years earlier, and McCoy had deliberately made a poor impression—chiefly by a kind of cringing timidity. Once, in a workout, he had asked Tommy not to hit him around the heart. "It makes me sick, Mr. Ryan," he had said. "And it gives me sharp pain that scares me. I wouldn't fight if I didn't have to."

In their fight for the championship, Ryan did his best to hit Mc-Coy around the heart—and every place else where he thought there might be an opening. But there were no openings to speak of. And in the twelfth round, getting impatient and beginning to swing wildly, Ryan exposed his own chin and caught a straight right on the end of it that drained all the strength and science out of him and left him helpless. McCoy then slashed and mauled the champion until the fifteenth, when he knocked him out.

It was in Africa, the Kid used to say, that he developed the "corkscrew punch." The phrase, like others coined by this prince of phrasemakers, became known all over the world. The corkscrew punch, probably, was only a left hook to the head, like other left hooks. Like other hooks, it involved a turning of the wrist, just before impact. But McCoy declared, and the world believed him, that he gave his left wrist an extra, prolonged spin that increased its velocity and its power to cut and maim. "It was the principle of rifling," he said. "I learned it by studying a rifle in South Africa."

It was in South Africa, too, at Bulawayo, that McCoy fought a 250-pound Negro called the King of the Kaffirs. In the first round, McCoy, running backward, lured the giant into McCoy's corner. The King, in sudden pain and confusion, looked down at his bare feet, and the Kid, at the same moment, brought up his right hand and knocked the Kaffir senseless. The floor, as it happened—we have McCoy's complacent word for this—had been sprinkled with tacks by McCoy's seconds just as the fight began.

It was strange, the way the elements of human nature were mixed in this curly head, behind the bland, youthful face and the smooth, bragging tongue. The Kid could not help lying—his picaresque imagination worked day and night to add to his own legend. He could not help swindling—his fight with Corbett, in 1900, after Corbett had lost the heavyweight title, was called by contemporaries one of the most flagrant fixes in ring history. One reporter wrote, "It was the cleverest boxing match ever seen, as it should have been, considering how carefully it had been rehearsed in advance."

But there was far more than greed and deceit in McCoy; there was courage and ferocity. He could fight, against odds, like a tiger. Under such conditions, Maurice Maeterlinck, the playwright, who had seen the Kid fight in Europe, once described him as "the handsomest human on earth." McCoy must have been like that on the night he fought Tom Sharkey—after he had given up the welterweight title, had outgrown a brief claim to the middleweight crown, and was fighting them as big as they came.

Sailor Tom Sharkey was not a giant—he was squat, but massive, and very tough. In forty-five rounds of fighting, the great Jim Jeffries was never to knock him down once. Sharkey and McCoy met on January 10, 1899, at the old Lenox Athletic Club in New York City. It was the biggest gate of McCoy's life; there was $46,000 in the square brick arena that night. The Kid was about Sharkey's height, but he looked like a thin, pale boy beside the Sailor. His legs were slender, his stomach was concave at the narrow waist. Such power as he had was bunched in big arms and low, sloping shoulders. Running like a burglar, he made Sharkey commit himself with rushes and lunging swings. Then the Kid let the gap close. He countered the swings. He hooked Sharkey's head with his left and drove straight rights against Sharkey's teeth and cheekbones. Twice he floored the man whom Jeff could not bring down. By the end of the ninth, it looked like McCoy's fight was for sure, and the patrons were screaming for him to finish it. The truth was, the Kid himself was finished. He had used up all his strength on a head like an oaken bucket; in the tenth, his legs went dead. Sharkey caught him in that round, first with a body punch that seemed to cave in the Kid's ribs, then with a smashing blow on the jaw. Paul Armstrong, the playwright who wrote "Alias Jimmy Valentine," was covering the fight. Of the Kid, at the very last, he wrote:

"He clawed the canvas like some deep-sea crab . . . rattled along on all fours . . . and then bobbled into a meaningless heap."

In 1900, the Kid ran a nightclub in the cellar of the Hotel Normandie, at the corner of Broadway and Fortieth Street. He ran it until a matter of what the police called "larceny from a customer" by McCoy came up—then the customers began to abstain from the Kid's saloon. In 1904, he filed a petition in bankruptcy, having $25,000 worth of debts and no assets. The debts included one of $320 for clothing and another of $569 for repairs to a fast red car. It was natural that the Kid should react to this slump by marrying Lillian Ellis, the rich widow. It was natural that when Mrs. Ellis detached him, after three or four comfortable years, he should marry Mrs. Edna Valentine Hein, the daughter of a silver miner. The Kid impressed Mrs. Hein favorably, before the marriage, by winning a street fight from Mr. Hein.

It was one of the few fights he had in those years. When occasional spells of non-marriage, meaning poverty, overtook him, and McCoy was obliged to fight professionally again, he found the going hard. It was the flesh that was weak—not the two-edged brain. A lad named Young Jim Stewart climbed into the ring in New York one night, during these downhill days, to see what McCoy had left.

He went to the Kid's corner before the bout to pay his respects. McCoy, waving to friends in the crowd, pretended not to see him. Stewart hurt, but not mortally so, returned to his corner. When the referee called them in for instructions, McCoy tramped heavily on the youngster's feet and bumped him accidentally in the eye with his elbow. Next McCoy grabbed Stewart by the nape of the neck with one hand, pulled him down by the head, and cracked him two or three times in the jaw with his other fist. "What I want to know, Mr. Referee," said the Kid, deferentially, "is whether it's all right for him to hit me like this?" "No, it ain't," said the referee. Young Jim Stewart survived these preliminaries, and the fight got under way and went six rounds to no decision.

"Tell me, Mr. McCoy," said Stewart afterward, "did you expect me to soften up with that stuff with the referee?" "God knows, boy," the Kid said. "You can never tell till you try."

In the last fight on his record, McCoy met a British seaman, Petty Officer Curran, in London, in 1914. The bout was scheduled for twenty rounds—a long, weary haul for a man of forty. Three quarters of the way through it, McCoy's feet had gone nearly flat. His nerves were snapping in his body like little twigs. Suddenly, the timekeeper, sitting by the ring in evening clothes, took a tall glass of whisky-and-soda from an attendant and placed it carefully on the apron of the ring. A moment later, the Kid ran into a punch from Curran, fell to the floor near the timekeeper's seat, snatched up the highball, and drank it off. The fight went the full distance. It was close, but McCoy, making his last post a winning one, got the duke.

Though he was still debonair, still a strutter, McCoy was plainly at the end of his rope, financially, when he beat his way home from London at the start of the First World War. The U.S. Army bought his meals for the next few years. Enlisting in 1915—tired, played out, turning to the security of a uniform and steady pay as he had turned to marriage when he was younger—McCoy served on the Mexican border in 1916 and on the home front generally in the wartime years, mostly as a boxing instructor. There was another fling left in him, but in the Army, for a while, he charged his batteries and marked time.

When his enlistment was up, the Kid headed for California. He got a few bit parts in Hollywood, but this career died quickly. In 1922, he became an official bankrupt again—assets: two suits of clothes. One way and another, he took the busy, hot town for a dollar here and a dollar there, and hung on. And in the summer of 1924, he found his way into the life of still another woman with money and a husband she did not like.

Theresa Weinstein Mors was on the point of divorcing Albert E. Mors when she met McCoy. She was in her late thirties and easy to look at. It was not known just how she came to meet the Kid, but on August 4, when their friendship became a matter of record, she described him to the police as her "bodyguard." The police had been called in by Mors, who complained that his wife and McCoy had used him roughly. The visit had been for the purpose of discussing the Mors' property settlement. The Kid, of course, had the habit of discussing things with his knuckles. In this case, however, it was Mrs. Mors who hit Mr. Mors in the mouth, while McCoy protected her.

A divorce followed, and the Kid and Theresa took an apartment together, under the names of Mr. and Mrs. N. Shields. There's good reason to believe that the Kid wanted marriage in more than name. Mrs. Mors, at least for the time being, did not. For this reason, and perhaps for others, it was a quarrelsome partnership. It came as no surprise to the Shields' neighbor, in the next apartment, when, on the sultry night of August 11, at a few minutes after midnight, she heard a woman's voice in the Shields' flat cry out, "Oh, my God, don't do that!" The cry was repeated. Then came a single gunshot. The neighbor investigated, but only to the extent of trying the Shields' door, which was locked. It was not till 10 a.m. on the twelfth that the janitor found Theresa lying dead on the floor of the bedroom she had shared with McCoy. She had been shot once, in the left temple. A .32 pistol lay nearby. A photograph of the Kid had been placed across her breast. Also clearly visible was a suicide note signed Norman Selby leaving his estate to his mother.

At almost the same moment the police discovered the note and the body which did not match it, the Kid himself was running amok a few blocks away, with another gun, in an antique shop owned by his mistress. It was a wild scene he made there. Disheveled, apparently drunk, he burst into the shop with his gun out. He told the men there, mostly employees, to take off their shoes and pants. He put a dance record on the phonograph and, under cover of the noise, went through the pants pockets for money. Then, cursing with all the foulness he could muster from fifty-one years' experience, he went out the door again and, in the street, shot and seriously wounded the first three people he met, two men and a woman. The police caught up with him as he was running blindly through Westlake Park.

Had he been drunk? McCoy, though he'd taken some wine in his time, had never been given to drinking. Had he been faking madness, to set up a defense against a murder rap? Maybe. At any rate, his wildness, real or feigned, subsided after a few days in jail, and at his trial he told the jury in serious, sensible tones that Theresa—"the only woman I ever loved"—had shot herself to death in his presence. It was a story the Kid was to stick to for the rest of his life. The prosecution, in rebuttal, pointed out that Mrs. Mors, a right-handed woman, had been shot in the left side of her head.

The prosecutor told the jury that McCoy had said to his sister, after the crime, "I had to kill that woman." It took the jurymen seventy-eight hours to decide whom to believe. In the end, they disbelieved McCoy. He was sentenced to ten years for manslaughter, and to two terms of seven years each for the larceny and mayhem of his last daffy stand in Theresa's antique shop: a total of twenty-four years.

The rap seemed to mean that the Kid would die of old age in San Quentin. There was one way to escape such a fate—sweetness, light, and good conduct on a scale such as McCoy had never before attempted.

When he came out in 1932, paroled after a little more than seven years, the Kid had established one of the purest records in the history of San Quentin—never a mark against him. With him he brought a canary named Mike, a prison pet as harmless as the new McCoy. His future life was to be mild and pastoral, too. Years before, he had given boxing lessons to a Navy fighter who used the name of Sailor Reese. In 1932, under his real name of Harry Bennett, the sailor had become personnel chief for Ford, in Detroit. Bennett gave the parolee a job as watchman in one of the Ford public gardens. The new line on the payroll read: "Norman Selby. Age, 59. Farmhand." The terms of his parole kept the Kid close to Detroit for five years. When, in 1937, he became totally free—the Kid used to say he'd been "pardoned," but it was really just the formal ending of parole—he went on living in Detroit and working for Ford.

He did make a few trips out of town after the papers came through. One of them was to Rushville, Indiana, near the place of his birth, where he took unto himself an eighth wife, Mrs. Sue Cobb Cowley. Another was to New York, where the Kid and an old fellow-wizard, Philadelphia Jack O'Brien, pottered around town together for a day, cutting up touches and reviewing the past. Wherever he went, the Kid seemed happy. His marriage went well. His job was for life. When he lied, he told contented lies that showed the old vanity, the old satisfaction with Norman Selby, alias Kid McCoy. One day a man asked him if he ever saw his former wives.

"You won't believe it," the Kid said smugly, "but I see them all, regularly. Every year I give a party, and every woman I've ever been married to comes to Detroit to see me again."

He gave a roguish smile. "Why wouldn't they come for me?"

The Kid was not crazy or senile. He simply liked this lie and all the others that celebrated the glory, the beauty, the cunning of Kid McCoy. In everything he did, as his days dwindled down to the last and strangest one, his mind and his body worked smoothly and well.

And then, suddenly, smoothly and well, he killed himself. Perhaps there had been one special sin in his life that was too big for him to live with any longer. If so, nobody knows what it was but Kid McCoy.

Mysterious Montague

from *Golf*

One day in 1937, Inspector John Cosartz of the New York State Police, stationed at Oneida, saw a man's photograph in a newspaper and tied it up with a story that had lived in the corner of his mind for seven years. The name under the picture—Mysterious Montague—was as famous just then as Garbo's or Joe Louis's or Sam Snead's. The face, however, had not been seen by anyone outside Hollywood and its neighborhood for a long time. Its owner had busted the camera of more than one news photographer who tried to sneak a shot of it. Now, finally, another cameraman had gotten away with the goods.

You couldn't blame the cameraman for trying. Mysterious Montague was news, from his natty two-toned golf shoes up the length of his massive, powerful body to his round, dimpled face and curly dark hair. In fact, he'd become a national legend.

He was famous, one, for what he could do with a golf ball, and two, for the company he kept. For a bet, he had once hit a ball three-quarters of a mile in five shots. For a bet of $1,000, using a rake, a shovel, and a baseball bat for clubs, he had won an eighteen-hole match from Bing Crosby. At Palm Springs, he had broken or tied the course record four days running—with 61-61-61-58! Once, in a merry display of muscle, he had stuffed the living, resisting body of he-man film actor George Bancroft into a golf locker.

The movie sports colony had learned to swear by his prowess. Now, in 1937—after a cop with a memory saw a photograph of a legend—the stars had to swear by his character. His real name, it turned out, was La Verne Moore. His home town was Syracuse, New York. Back in the dark old bootlegging days of 1930, he was alleged to have taken part in a roadhouse stickup-and-beating. The police brought him out of Hollywood to Elizabethtown, New York, to stand trial for his supposed share in the crime. And though the evidence against him had grown a bit dim and shaky by then, it was probably the character affidavits of his Hollywood friends—Crosby, Oliver Hardy, Otto Kruger, and others—that helped to win acquittal.

When the news of Montague's double identity broke, his famous cronies and the public understood why he had busted cameras in Hollywood, and why he had never gone in for tournament golf. Watching his power off the tee and his wizardly short game, Crosby and the rest had sometimes urged him to try his luck against pros for money. It has never followed, of course, that a man who dazzles his friends in private golf will also dazzle professionals in open competitions. Montague, with his secret exposed, did try for the United States Open title in 1938, 1939, and 1940. He qualified once in 1940. He shot an 80 in his first round at Cleveland and then dropped out of the tournament.

That showing doesn't cancel the fact of his golfing genius, which has been testified to by the late Grantland Rice, former National Amateur Champion George Von Elm, and other authorities. Some human beings are not geared for the ordeal of public performance; there can be things in a man's temperament that make him prefer the shadows. As time went on, Montague's friends of the movie

world began to drift away from him. What may be more significant, he drifted away from them, too, like a fundamentally wary
spirit who has had his bellyful of fame.

After the trial, he returned to Hollywood, got married, and
dropped into a life of dim conventionality. There have been one
or two public signs of him since then, trying to make a dollar with
a golf course promotion or a real estate deal. Acquaintances say that
the going has sometimes been tough for him, financially. Today,
at fifty-four, he still plays golf around Los Angeles—in obscurity.
And they tell you that he still plays it with the flair that made Rice
speak of him as potentially the finest golfer of his time.

Montague first arrived in Hollywood as mysteriously as he did everything else. He probably got there in 1930. There are no clues as
to how or why he came. There is not much known about his earlier
life, either, except that he was both a wild kid and a strong one.

Police records show that when he was a boy of thirteen or so,
in the country around Syracuse, he was fined $5 for stealing fruit.
A few years later, there was a suspended sentence of six months
for petty larceny. About that time he did a lot of caddying, and he
played football and baseball too. Chick Meehan, then Syracuse's
celebrated football coach, got him into Dean Academy, no doubt
with a football future in mind. But La Verne Moore slipped out
of that life and into professional baseball. In the spring of 1930,
when he was approximately twenty-five, he had a tryout with the
Buffalo club of the International League, as a pitcher. He must
have been a hitting pitcher; in a wallet of his that was found by police in a smashed-up car that same summer, there was a newspaper clipping describing a 500-foot home run hit by "Vern" Moore
in a practice game.

Not long afterward a husky, curly haired, personable young fellow who called himself John Montague rented a room in Los An-

geles and began to hang out at a public golf course in the Holly-wood region, where he bet on himself and consistently won. The jump from there to an intense kind of fame was logical. Hollywood welcomes and lionizes gifted strangers in any line of work. Golfers who knew Montague took him occasionally to courses where movie actors played. To see Montague's golf was to admire it and to want to talk about it; and Monty himself, as they called him, struck the actors as excellent company socially. He was quick-witted and ge-nial. He reached for the check at bars and lunch tables. He drove new Fords or Lincolns. His film-star friends made him a member of the stylish Lakeside Country Club and jockeyed for the privi-lege of playing a round with him.

At his trial, some years later, Monty was reluctant to explain how he managed to live so well at this period. He said, under cross-examination, that he thought he had averaged something like $100 a month from commissions as a car salesman for a firm run by John De Paolo and a Colonel Rogers. When asked how he paid his rent, clothing bills, golf-club fees, and other expenses out of such an in-come, he said, smiling: "Well, I had many things more or less given to me." It seems to be true that he had not only kept famous com-pany, but was, to some extent, kept by it. At one time he was the house guest of the late Oliver "Babe" Hardy, the plump member of the comic team of Laurel and Hardy. It's likely that his friends sometimes shared the profit of their bets with him when they backed him against newcomers. It also seems to be the fact Montague bet strongly on himself in this rich society and seldom lost.

The stars enjoyed being with him at any price. They were used to seeing fine golf, but Monty even outstripped pros in social matches on his own terrain. He was steadily in the 60s at Lakeside. As noted, he shot Palm Springs in 58. His driving was as accurate as it was long. When he bet $500 that he could drive a 1,320-yard stretch of beach, measured by automobile speedometer, in five shots, he not only won the bet but was never off the beach. His irons and his putter were as deadly as a pool shark's cue. It is said that he once knocked a bird off a telephone wire for a side bet with a 6-iron shot. In fact, he admitted it. He took pride in his work in those days.

"I'm modest," he said when asked why he didn't play tournament golf. "But I'll shoot with any man when I'm right," he said at another time. His clubs, which he called "the little fellows," averaged two or three ounces heavier than standard weight. He swung them with 212 pounds of what Gene Tunney described as "fast strength" stacked into five feet nine inches of height.

It was Grantland Rice, who often played in Hollywood with Crosby, Hardy, Guy Kibbee, and other members of the Montague cult, who gave this prodigy the nickname of Mysterious Montague. It was Rice who first described the match in which Montague outscored Crosby with a bat, shovel, and rake—the bat for driving, the shovel for pitching, and the two ends of the rake for the rough and putting. Monty's versatility delighted his companions as much as his straight golf did—the cuteness of his mind as well as the strength of his back. When he deposited the manly George Brancroft in a locker, he put him in upside down, to give the stunt a flourish.

He had a way of shaking hands at first meetings that demonstrated his power and may have helped make him popular in Hollywood, the nation's practical-joke center. I got the treatment once at a party in New York; it took me five minutes to separate my fingers afterward. Montague shook hands with Happy Chandler on the same occasion, and I have never forgotten the look on Chandler's face when it happened. If a politician is not safe shaking hands, whither civilization?

These meetings took place when Montague was brought east for trial, after Inspector Cosartz identified his picture in a newspaper.

The inspector's discovery shocked Hollywood and titillated the East. There were unprecedented crowds at Elizabethtown, New York, where the trail was held. John Brown, the abolitionist, had lain in state in the same courthouse after being hanged for his work at Harper's Ferry. I doubt if Brown's body caused more excitement there than a living man who called himself Mysterious Montague, and who now admitted that he was La Verne Moore.

The trial was a short one, though it depended on long memories. The state charged that Moore, alias Montague, had been one of four masked men who robbed the tavern of a Japanese-American named Kin Hana of $800, beat up Hana's father-in-law with a blackjack, and bound and gagged the entire family. One of the robbers had been killed in an automobile crash after leaving the roadhouse. In the second of two cars used in the crime, state troopers testified they had found golf clubs, clothes, a bag, and a wallet belonging to Moore. They hadn't found Moore. When they finally did find him, seven years later, he had become a celebrity, the pal of the world's most glamorous golfers. The jurors listened to the evidence and the character testimony of these famous men, and set Mysterious Montague free.

Apparently there was something in the Montague story, the story of a handsome adventurer with a secret past, that had a sure-fire Arabian Nights quality. It had made a deeper impression on the public than anyone had realized, including the Mysterious One himself. During the trial, Monty was beset by autograph seekers and got proposals of marriage by mail. After the trial he was given a taste of the limelight that may have helped to scare him back into the shadows forever.

The late Bill Corum, the New York sportswriter, had suggested that Montague play a match for charity somewhere around New York. The match took place at Fresh Meadow near Flushing, Long

Island, on November 14, 1937, a Sunday. It paired Montague and Sylvia Annenberg, a local champion, against Babe Ruth and Babe Didrikson. Your correspondent, who was present, has never witnessed wilder scenes on a golf course. Everyone there was lucky to escape with his life, but it was Montague who had the closest shave.

You couldn't judge anyone's golf by what happened that day. A few weeks earlier, in a private round, Monty had shot the North Hempstead course, which he'd never seen before, in 65. According to Rice, it might easily have been a 61; as it was, Montague beat Alex Morrison by six strokes. At Fresh Meadow, the mob took charge. There were 12,000 people on hand, at $1.10 a head. Most of them were watching golf for the first time. The players began the round facing difficulties. They ended it facing friendly cannibalism.

Thanks to the crowd, the fairways were no wider than bowling alleys and the greens were no bigger than pool tables. People surged over the course, blocking balls and grabbing for souvenirs. When one of Montague's shots knocked a fan's hat off, the man of mystery turned white. At the ninth hole, the crowd completely overran the green. And, then, when Montague broke for his life to the clubhouse, mystery lovers pursued him in full cry, reaching for a tie or shoe to take home.

For the record, the final score for eight holes was Ruth-Didrikson, two up. "Monty was off his game," Ruth rumbled later, as he swigged a beer. "Publicity seems to bother him. What a hell of a thing it would be," the Babe added thoughtfully, "if I was bothered that way."

When Montague went back to Hollywood, there were reports that Everett Crosby, Bing's brother, had signed Montague to a picture deal that would guarantee him $1,000,000. The money soon simmered down to $10,000 for a short golf film. There were further reports that the Will Hays office, then in charge of movie censorship, had quietly barred Montague from the big deal. Just as quietly, Montague took his medicine, though some of it was humiliating: when he tried to have his name changed legally to John Montague, a judge denied the petition on the ground that Monty had falsely denied that there were debts outstanding against him in the name of La Verne Moore.

After that, and after his failure in the Open, Mysterious Montague subsided quickly and maybe gladly into the natural cover of private life. Is there any of the old flamboyance left in him? The chances are that there is, just a little. Once, a couple of years ago, as he and a group of fellow golfers were driving through Los Angeles, someone pointed to a fourteen-story building. Could Montague clear it with a golf shot? Monty allowed that he could. And he got out of the car, teed up, and did.

Battling Siki

from the *New Yorker*

Hell's Kitchen, the region west of Eighth Avenue around the Forties, won its name many years ago and continued to deserve it
until about the time the Eighteenth Amendment was repealed.
Things are different there now. So its residents will tell you, and
so you can see for yourself, if, having known the neighborhood a
little during Prohibition, you visit it even briefly today. Once it was
carpeted, for nearly all its length and breadth, with low, swarthy
brick tenement houses containing a warren of flats, speakeasies, six-
table cellar "cabarets," hole-in-the-wall stores and restaurants, back-
room stills, and "social clubs," where a portion of the manhood
of the district stored guns and ammunition and planned stick-
ups and hijackings. Right along the equator of Hell's Kitchen ran
the Ninth Avenue "L" tracks, throwing a grim, significant shadow
by day and night. Other parts of town had clip joints, or "buck-
ets of blood," scattered through them, but the Kitchen, as a detective friend of mine used to say, was one big bucket of blood. Nowadays the Kitchen is a bit more shiny and much more respectable.
Neon lights and modern shops and garages have pushed their way
into it. The McGraw-Hill Building has gouged out half of what
was considered one of the hottest blocks in Hell's Kitchen in the
1920s—the block bounded by Eighth and Ninth avenues and Forty-

first and Forty-second streets. The Lincoln Tunnel approaches have formed an asphalt plaza west of Ninth Avenue. The sleek New Jersey buses and automobiles bound for and away from the West Side Highway plow across the old badlands in steady procession. The retail liquor traffic thereabouts has become negligible; the city's center of gravity of crime has shifted elsewhere, perhaps to Brooklyn. Broadly speaking, Hell's Kitchen is not a frontier community any more but a sort of vehicular gateway to the heart of Manhattan. However, if you want to conjure up the atmosphere of earlier times, you can still find islands of squat tenement houses here and there to help you, many of them boarded up and condemned, and the empty shells of many basement grogshops. In the unlikely event that you want to visit the scene of the murder, twenty-four years ago, of a man called Battling Siki, which is what I did one day recently for no useful reason, you will come across a few surviving landmarks. You can pace off distances in the same gutter and seamy street—Forty-first—down which Siki crawled forty feet west toward Ninth Avenue, with two bullets in his body, before he collapsed and died. He crawled in the direction of the "L," the cave of shadows that no longer is there. His killer threw away the gun in front of a grimy old house that is now gone; the McGraw-Hill Building is there instead. These changes make the setting less sinister than it used to be, but even now there's plenty to show that it was a drab and lonesome place to die.

Siki, who held the light-heavyweight boxing championship of the world for six months in 1922 and 1923, was born in Senegal, in French West Africa, in 1897, and was killed in Hell's Kitchen twenty-eight years later, in 1925. He was the Kitchen's most turbulent citizen in the short time he lived there. He was thought by neighbors who knew him to have an honest heart and a generous soul, but when he drank the newly cooked liquor of the parish, as he often did, the cab drivers, cops, bartenders, and hoodlums whom he chose, with impeccable lack of judgment, to knock around found it hard to take him philosophically. Rear-line observers, on the other hand, were usually able to be philosophical about Siki. During the three years of his life in which he received international publicity—the last three—he was referred to repeatedly as a "child of nature," a "natural man," and a "jungle child," and at least once as "the black Candide." After his murder, the *New York World* said editorially, "What is all this [Siki's physical strength, his brawling and dissipation] but the sulks and tempers of Achilles, the prank of Siegfried and the boars, the strutting of Beowulf, the armours of Lemminkainen? We have had a walking image of our beginnings among us and did not know it . . . He had, it is true, the mentality of a backward toad . . . But he had the soul of a god."

It strikes me that tributes paid by civilized people to a "natural man," especially one who has walked among us, are apt to sound either patronizing, like the *World*'s, or uneasy, like some delivered by American correspondents when Siki won his boxing championship in Paris in 1922 and was first interviewed. After praising Siki's strength and simplicity, one reporter wrote apprehensively, "He is very black and very ugly." Siki's manager at the time, a M. Hellers, was quoted saying that Siki was a fine lad but "just a little bit crazy." I can discover no support among those who were acquainted with Siki in America later on for the idea that he was crazy, except when he drank, or the idea that he was mentally toadlike. He was illiterate, never having been to school, but he could make himself understood in several languages including English, French, Spanish, Dutch, and German. As far as Candide is concerned, Siki resembled Voltaire's hero in that he had a sheltered boyhood, was thrown suddenly into the thick of the best of all possible worlds, and found society both violent and larcenous. At seventeen, he was involved in a civilized world war. At twenty-five, he was permitted to box a champion on the condition that he lose the match. Having ignored the condition and won the championship, he insured his loss of that title, in all innocence, by fighting an Irishman in Dublin on St. Patrick's Day. He entered American life in the heyday of the Volstead Act. He could not master the strong waters or the social customs of the West Side of New York City. He was killed by gunfire, after surviving a stabbing earlier in the same year. It may seem, offhand, that Hell's Kitchen was a curious place for the curtain to fall on a twenty-eight-year-old Mohammedan born in St. Louis de Senegal on the fringe of the Sahara Desert, but Voltaire has shown that when civilization gets its hands on one of these natural men, it pushes him about at random from curious place to curious place. Candide was lucky to wind up safely cultivating his garden. He came close to meeting his end in an auto-da-fé in Portugal and, another time, on a roasting spit in Paraguay. Siki's story is perhaps more realistic. He failed to last out the course.

The newspaper writers of the 1920s were merely being wishful when they called Siki a jungle child. St. Louis, his African home, is a seaport ten miles above the mouth of the Senegal River, on a bare plain that marks the Sahara's southwesternmost edge. It's doubtful whether anyone in Europe or America today knows what Siki's real name was. Legend has it that when he was ten or twelve years old, a French actress touring the colonies saw him in St. Louis, was impressed by his appearance, and took him into her personal service, giving him, for reasons based on classical Greek, the name of Louis Phal. Whatever its origin, this, Anglicized as Louis Fall, was his legal name when he married, and when he was murdered, in America. He did not become known as Battling Siki until he began to box professionally, in 1913; apparently the word "Siki" was coined or borrowed by French fight promoters, to whom it had vague "native" or colonial connotations. The tale about the actress was told widely in Paris in the days of Siki's first fame, when he knocked out the celebrated Georges Carpentier, but it was never, so far as I know, closely checked up on. It accounts, plausibly enough, for the abrupt shift of Siki from dusty African streets to the perils of Western civilization. The lady is said to have taken him to her villa on the French Riviera and dressed him in a page boy's uniform of bottle green. Subsequently, he worked in one town and another as a bus boy. He was fifteen when he started boxing.

Siki had just time for a handful of fights, most of which he won, before the war of 1914–18 broke out and he was conscripted into the 8th Colonial Infantry Regiment of the French Army. His record was distinguished; in fact, he is reported to have been the bravest soldier in his outfit, which saw action on several fronts and gave a strong performance generally. For heroism under fire, Siki won not only the Croix de Guerre but the Médaille Militaire. After demobilization, he could have had his choice of a variety of ordinary civilian jobs; his record guaranteed him that. However, he went back to the prize ring, where the rewards were intermittent but came in good-sized pieces when they came. He barnstormed in France, North Africa, Spain, Belgium, and Holland. From a tour of Holland in 1921 he returned to Paris, where he lived with a Dutch girl who was thought to be his wife and by whom he later had a child. Siki did not work especially hard at his trade. He fought once or twice a month, which is not often for a "club," or journeyman, fighter, and, while he usually won, he beat nobody of major importance. Between bouts he drank more absinthe than is normal in the profession. American critics were to speak of him three or four years later as a fighter of considerable natural ability who might have been much better than he was. Weighing about 175 pounds, the maximum for light-heavyweights, and standing five feet eleven inches tall, he was a well-muscled young man with a leaping, bounding, lunging style from which he got slapstick effects that amused the galleries, and himself as well. In the early months of 1922, he happened to defeat a couple of men of some slight reputation and thus came to the notice of Francois Descamps, then the most influential and artful character in French boxing. Descamps offered him a bout for the world's light-heavyweight championship with Carpentier, whom Descamps managed.

The prizefight business in Continental Europe in those days was an odd blend of laissez-faire and team play—laissez-faire being understood to mean "Let Descamps do it his way," and "team play" to mean that all hands share in the spoils. Descamps owned a large stable of fighters and also, it was commonly believed in Paris, a large stable of sportswriters. Some of the latter were growing restive in 1922, possibly because of a failure in the team-play system as administered by Descamps. When the Carpentier-Siki match was announced, certain journalists expressed a distrust of it. They suggested that, in Siki, Descamps had laid hold of a small-time, happy-go-lucky trouper with no ambitions beyond getting all the absinthe he could consume, who would be glad to bolster Carpentier's fortunes—Carpentier had not fought for really big money since his knockout by Jack Dempsey in New Jersey, fourteen months before—without making too much trouble for the champion in the ring. Their hints were undoubtedly read by the public. Carpentier was a war hero, the toast of the boulevards, a boxer still regarded, in spite of his defeat by Dempsey, as peerless in Europe, but though the crowd of 55,000 that came to the new Buffalo Velodrome in Paris on the afternoon of September 24, 1922, to see him fight Siki was the largest in European boxing history, it showed before the day was over that it was on the alert for signs of skullduggery. Its suspicions were inflamed during the preliminary bouts by the work of Harry Bernstein, a referee charged by sportswriters with occupying a special compartment in the hip pocket of M. Descamps. In one preliminary, the opponent of a Descamps featherweight named Fritsch was disqualified by Bernstein for hitting too low; in another, the opponent of a Descamps heavyweight named Ledoux was disqualified by Bernstein for not fighting hard enough. Bernstein's rulings brought a volley of *coups de sifflet* from the customers, particularly those in the seven-franc seats, who had mustered their sous at a sacrifice and wished for their money's worth of equality and justice.

The main bout was scheduled for twenty rounds. Carpentier, pale and blond, weighed 173½ pounds, Siki 174. In the first round, Siki fought cautiously and less acrobatically than usual; Carpentier jabbed at him with his left hand. Once, hit lightly, Siki dropped to one knee; Bernstein, who was refereeing this bout, too, did not bother to count. "Get up, Siki, you're not hurt," he said. After the round, ringside spectators saw Carpentier smile broadly and heard him say, "I'll get him whenever I want to." The champion, boxing easily, won the first two rounds. In the third, Carpentier sent a right-hand blow to Siki's jaw, and Siki dropped to one knee again, this time taking a count of seven. When he got up, he rushed at Carpentier and hit him violently in the body with a left and a right. Carpentier, looking startled as well as hurt, went down for four seconds. The rest of the fight was all Siki's. Siki battered Carpentier about the ring in the fourth round while Carpentier hung on to Siki's arms whenever he could and tried to pinion them with his own. In the fifth, Carpentier fell against the ropes. Siki leaned over him ("I whispered him to quit," Siki said later), and Carpentier, pushing himself up, butted angrily at Siki's belly. Carpentier could hardly stand when the sixth round began. Siki hit him at will. A right uppercut followed by a shower of right and left swings sent Carpentier to the floor unconscious one minute and ten seconds after the start of the round. As he fell, one of his feet became tangled between Siki's, assisting the fall.

It was plain that Carpentier was completely knocked out, but at that point Bernstein ruled that Siki had lost the fight by tripping his opponent illegally. The third disqualification of the day was more than the crowd was prepared to stomach. It pushed its way to the ring from all quarters of the stadium and stormed around it, yelling furiously. Police were called up to protect Bernstein. Descamps, meanwhile, for whose blood the demonstrators were also shouting, slipped out of the arena behind a couple of gendarmes. Three judges—Victor Breyer, Jean Pujol, and an Englishman, Tom Bannison—who, before the fight, had been appointed by the French Boxing Federation to make a decision in case there was no knockout, were now appealed to. After conferring briefly with Federation officials, they announced that they would give a final and formal verdict either supporting or overruling Bernstein's. They deliberated for three quarters of an hour while Bernstein stood in one corner of the ring among his police guards and practically no one in the audience went home, or even stopped talking unkindly to the referee. The judges, willingly or not, at last did what the crowd wanted: they declared Siki the winner by a knockout and, in the name of the Federation, awarded him the light-heavyweight championship of the world, plus a subsidiary title of Carpentier's—the heavyweight championship of Europe. Siki said to Hellers, his manager, "Tell America I am ready for Dempsey," and repaired in triumph to his dressing room. The crowd disbanded. The police saw Bernstein safely to the door of his dressing room.

Siki never got a match with Dempsey, but some offers of lesser opportunities did come to him from America. He was lavishly feted in Paris during the first two days of his victory, and after public enthusiasm subsided, his own continued to run high, especially in the Montmartre neighborhood. "No more absinthe. I will train and fight hard as champion," Siki had told a gathering outside the office of the newspaper *Echo des Sports* on the twenty-fifth, the day following the fight. Later that evening, he took a few glasses of champagne, and on touring Montmartre in a rented car with a chauffeur, he reverted to absinthe wholeheartedly at every stop he made. After another week or so he acquired, probably as gifts from fellow colonials, a monkey, which he carried everywhere on his shoulder, and a lion cub, which he led about on a leash. Carpentier was still lying in bed suffering from a sprained ankle, two broken hands, and an unsightly swelling of his nose and lips. Most of the Parisian sporting press was sympathetic toward him but nastily jubilant about Descamps, who, it was implied, had overreached himself and been double-crossed. Rumors to the same effect circulated through Paris for the next several weeks. In early December, the French Boxing Federation precipitated the publication of what was very likely the true story of the fight by suspending Siki—it was charged that while seconding another fighter in the ring, he had struck the manager of his man's opponent. Siki, deprived of a chance to make a living in France, went for help to M. Diagne, the representative for Senegal in the French Chamber of Deputies. Diagne asserted before the Chamber that the Boxing Federation was discriminating against colonials in favor of Parisian city slickers who wanted Siki out of the way, and in support of this theory he gave the deputies the account of the Carpentier bout that Siki had given him. When the Chamber appeared unwilling to take any action, Diagne called a press conference and had Siki repeat his story to reporters. It ran as follows:

A fix had been arranged fifteen days before the bout took place, with Descamps dictating procedure to Siki's manager. As a sign of good faith, Siki was to take a short count in the first round and another count in the third. He was to get himself knocked out early in the fourth. Siki followed the scenario through the third-round knockdown—"I stayed down for seven the first time Carpentier hit me hard enough to give me an excuse," he said—but as he knelt on the floor at that point, he decided not to go through with the frame-up. It was his pride, he said, and his loyalty to the public that made him change his mind. When he got up, he began to fight in earnest. He ignored a sharp reminder from his manager, between the third and fourth rounds, that his end was expected momentarily. (This detail in Siki's narrative gave Hellers a clean bill of health, in a left-handed way; Descamps had been so suspicious of treachery by Hellers that he quarreled with him in public after the bout.) Siki surprised Carpentier with his counterattack and soon demolished him.

When Siki's story was done, M. Diagne explained to the press what it meant: A simple, uneducated man had defended himself and all underprivileged peoples against exploitation by a predatory society. Siki, who was always emotional, wept freely at these words. His tears and his deputy's arguments got him nowhere. Neither did a court of inquiry appointed by the Boxing Federation to investigate Siki's statement. The court, with a flashy display of ingenuity, hired two deaf-mutes to watch the motion pictures of the fight and see if they could lip-read certain remarks delivered excitedly by Descamps to Hellers in Siki's corner during "a critical phase of the battle," after Siki had begun to knock Carpentier around. The experiment (unique, I think, in boxing history) was later described by the court as "successful," but Siki remained suspended. He never fought in France again until after he had lost his championships elsewhere. My own opinion is that being champion constituted Siki's chief sin in the eyes of the Federation. Also, I believe his story of the Carpentier match was substantially correct. A "sign of good faith"—a preliminary fall, or lapse of some other kind, by the loser—is a standard device in the plotting of sports frame-ups. Eddie Cicotte, a Chicago baseball player, hit the first batter he faced with a pitched ball in the crooked World Series of 1919, as a signal to gamblers that the fix was in. Siki's tale confirmed the rumors that were current before and after the fight; it was in keeping with the character of Descamps and of Continental boxing methods in 1922, and it is believed by every European and American I know who was familiar in any degree with the time, the place, and the actors.

As it turned out, the Carpentier bout was the only one of importance in Siki's professional career, except for the next one. The next one was weak and anticlimactic as a show, but it did involve a world's championship, and it demonstrated in a special way how complicated the civilization of the West can be for an unlettered Moslem with no grounding in our rituals and customs. A fairly good light-heavyweight from County Clare in Ireland named Michael Francis McTigue happened to pass through Paris with his staff during Siki's suspension. Finding Siki idle and nearly broke, the visitors proposed a match between him and McTigue for the title. (The world's light-heavyweight championship was one that interested them; the heavyweight championship of Europe had no value in the world market, and has been recognized only sporadically since the day Carpentier lost it.) They spoke of Dublin as a pleasant spot for the Siki-McTigue bout. They mentioned March 17, 1923, as an open date in their engagement book. Siki fell in with these suggestions and met McTigue in the ring in the Irish capital on Saint Patrick's Day. The operation for the removal of his crown was painless. The decision went to McTigue on points. There was nothing particularly wrong with this verdict, I am told by a neutral eyewitness, except that McTigue did not make efforts or take the risks that are commonly expected of a challenger for a world's championship. There was no need to. In the circumstances, nothing less than a knockout could have beaten him, and he avoided that possibility by boxing at long range throughout.

One device by which a civilized man can avoid a predicament like Siki's in Dublin was illustrated by McTigue himself later in the same year. He went to Columbus, Georgia, to fight a Georgian named Young Stribling before a crowd that was strongly and ostentatiously in favor of his opponent. There was almost no way McTigue could avoid losing within the Georgia state limits, so, to protect his planetary interests, he took along a referee from the North. The referee called the bout a draw. Then, yielding to the howls of protest, he announced that he would deputize the local promoter to give the decision. The promoter called Stribling the winner. The referee, on his way back north by train with McTigue and McTigue's manager, signed an affidavit that his own true and considered verdict was for a draw. That is how the result has been listed in the record books ever since.

Siki had only two more European fights, both in Paris, after he lost his title. The last two years of his life he spent in America, disintegrating with headlong speed on bootleg gin and whiskey but nearly always able to make money in the ring when he needed it. When he first arrived in New York, in September 1923, his name had a certain value here, based on curiosity, which it no longer had abroad. He signed on with the stable of a veteran New York manager, Robert (Pa) Levy (Hellers appears to have discarded Siki at the time of his suspension in France), and his first fight in this country was a serious one with a respectable opponent, Kid Norfolk, who beat him in fifteen rounds at Madison Square Garden. From then on, American fight fans were not disposed to think of

Siki as a boxer of top rank, but they liked to watch him. His style was eccentric and funny. He was strong and fast enough to knock out most of the palookas he met, when he felt like it. He was booked as far west as California and as far south as New Orleans, and he earned, according to a fairly reliable estimate I have heard, nearly $100,000 between November 1923 and November 1925. He was one of the best spenders, in proportion to income, that the United States has ever seen. In restaurants and speakeasies he sometimes tipped five or ten times the amount of the check. Once, having made $5,000 from a fight in New York on a Friday, he was turned out of his rooming house the following Monday for nonpayment of rent. Another time he gave away all the money in his pockets to passengers on a Lackawanna Railroad ferryboat on which he was returning from a fight in New Jersey. Scolded for this by his manager, Siki wept. Most of his cash, however, continued to be spent on gifts, liquor, and clothes. In clothes, Siki's taste was unusual but rich. In the first part of his New York residence, when he lived and roamed mainly in the Times Square area, he almost always wore full dress when he went out at night. By day, ordinarily, he appeared in a high hat, a frock coat, red ascot tie, striped trousers, spatted shoes, and a monocle, and he carried a gold-headed cane. From time to time he gave away all the stylish clothes he had on and went home by cab in his underwear. He was particularly open-minded with his high hats. One of these, Siki's gift to the management, hung on a peg in a West Side saloon I used to visit until a few years ago, when the place closed up.

Siki's New York life was divided into two roughly equal periods, the second of which he passed largely in Hell's Kitchen. He had been married in the summer of 1924, at the Municipal Building, to a woman from Memphis named Lillian Werner. The event attracted just enough attention to stimulate newspaper inquiries in

Paris, where neighbors of the Dutch girl with whom he had lived in the suburb of Lanves said she was still there and was still thought to be his wife. She herself was not interviewed or quoted to that effect then or afterward, so far as I know. Siki and his American bride moved into a flat at 361 West Forty-second Street early in 1925. Siki had begun to go downhill physically and professionally by then. His bookings for fights were fewer than they had been, and he did not fulfill all those he made. He got into trouble, almost simultaneously, with the United States Immigration Service and the boxing commissioners of New York State. Siki had come to America on a short-term permit. In July 1925 he was arrested for felonious assault after slashing at a policeman with a knife, at which the government began deportation proceedings. In August the Boxing Commission, annoyed by a facetious exhibition Siki had given at a small New York fight club, summoned him and Levy to its office, suspended Siki, and told Levy to make sure that the fighter was somewhere beyond the three-mile limit within thirty days. The order may seem to have been a usurpation of federal powers, but it coincided with the government's view. At this point, France told the United States that it would refuse to receive Siki if he were deported. Siki, who had wept in the Boxing Commission office when he heard the order to his manager, now took advantage of the stalemate and, in November, filed application for his first citizenship papers. Government decision on his deportation case was still pending when he died.

Siki had the reputation in Hell's Kitchen in 1925 of being dangerous when drunk, mild and affable when sober. As he drank more heavily and fought less in the ring, he fought more in the street, and his opponents were a rough and active group of men. He was known for his favorite joke of hailing a cab, taking a ride, and then challenging the driver to a fight for fare. Occasionally, too, he would invade the Times Square station of the IRT in the early morning in search of amateur boxing engagements. It is characteristic of many boxers that as they lose their ability in the ring they swing their fists more frequently outside it, as a sort of blurred insistence on the claim that they are as good as ever. That, along with the drinks Siki bought or charged up in the bars of the West Side, may account for his pugnacity in his last months. The only instance of Siki's using a knife that I have found was the time he was arrested for drawing one on a policeman. His wife went to night court to plead for him on that occasion. She made a good impression and got him off with a $5 fine. Though he was stabbed in the back himself in August, not long after he had smashed up a speakeasy in the West Forties and spent a few days in the French Hospital on West Thirtieth Street as a consequence, Siki went on using his fists—and now and then a piece of furniture—in nearly all his brawls. He was fined another $5 on December 6 for slapping a patrolman at the corner of Seventh Avenue and Thirty-fourth Street.

At about seven o'clock in the evening on Monday, December 14, Siki's wife met him on the stairs to their flat on West Forty-second Street. The house they lived in still stands, a house of dingy brick with ten walk-up apartments, two on each of its five floors. Siki told Mrs. Siki he was going "out with the boys" and would be back in time to help her pack for a trip they were making next day to Washington, where Siki was to appear in a theater. Shortly after midnight on the morning of the fifteenth, Patrolman John J. Meehan, of the West Thirtieth Street station, walking his beat along Ninth Avenue, had a brief encounter with Siki, whom he knew by sight. Siki, wobbling a little as he turned under the "L" tracks from Forty-first Street, called to Meehan that he was on his way home. The patrolman told him to keep going that way. At 4:15 a.m., Meehan walked past the intersection of Forty-first Street and Ninth

Avenue again and saw a body lying about a hundred feet east of the corner in the gutter in front of 350 West Forty-first. Approaching it, he recognized Siki. The body was taken to Meehan's station house, where a doctor pronounced the fighter recently dead from internal hemorrhage caused by two bullet wounds. Detectives examined the deserted block of Forty-first between Eighth and Ninth avenues. In front of No. 346, some forty feet east of where Siki had died, they found a pool of blood on the sidewalk. It seemed to them that Siki might have been trying to crawl home after he was shot. They could not tell just where the shooting had taken place. The gun, a vest-pocket .32-caliber pistol, was lying in front of No. 333, on the other side of the street. Only two bullets had been fired from it. An autopsy showed that these had entered Siki from behind, one penetrating his left lung and the other his kidneys. The autopsy showed something else which surprised Siki's neighbors a good deal when they heard of it: he had suffered from an anemic condition.

At his wife's request, Siki was given a Christian funeral service at the Harlem funeral parlors of Effie A. Miller. The Reverend Adam Clayton Powell delivered a eulogy. However, seven Mohammedan pallbearers in turbans carried his body to the hearse, chanting prayers as they did so, while a crowd of three thousand people looked on. The body was clothed in evening dress, as Siki would undoubtedly have wished. His estate, estimated at $600, was awarded to his wife in Surrogate's Court after Levy made out an affidavit in her favor. The words of the affidavit, while perhaps not strictly accurate in point of fact, told the broad truth about Siki's place in the world better, I think, than the editorial that spoke of Achilles, Siegfried, and "natural man." To the best of his knowledge, Levy said, Siki left surviving "no child or children, no father, mother, brother, or sister, or child or children of a deceased brother or sister." He lived as man without kin or country, roots or guides, and that, it seems to me, is a hard way to do it.

Siki's murder was never solved. There was an abundance of suspects, but none of them suited the police at all until one day in March 1926 when a young man of eighteen who lived a block or two from Siki's house was arrested and booked on a homicide charge in connection with the killing. Detectives disguised as truck drivers had heard him making incriminating remarks, they said, over a telephone in a bootleggers' hangout at Tenth Avenue and Fortieth Street. On being arrested, he allegedly signed two statements which gave two different accounts of the crime. One said that Siki had staggered into a coffee pot at Eighth Avenue and Fortieth Street in the early morning of December 15 and had thrown a chair at the eight men, including the deponent, who were gathered there. Deponent ran out of the place in alarm and heard shots fired in the restaurant behind him. The other statement, which fitted the physical facts of the killing a little better, said that a short while after the throwing of the chair, he, the young man under arrest, lured Siki to Eighth Avenue and Forty-first Street on the promise of buying him a drink. At the corner they were joined by two other men, one of whom, as the party walked west on Forty-first, shot Siki in the back. The young man was held in the Tombs for eight months, until the fall of 1926, and then was released by the court without trial, presumably because the state was not satisfied with its case. I might add that in May 1927 this same young man got five to ten years for second-degree robbery, committed in April in the vicinity of Ninth Avenue and Forty-second Street against a tourist from another state. That was clearly the wrong part of town for a tourist to go to.

Other Precincts

The Roller Derby
from *Sport*

It develops that there are certain parts of this country in which the thing called the Roller Derby is still unknown. The people in such places live in the same state of uneasy innocence as the Indians did before the white man came along, bringing them civilization, un-cut whiskey, glass beads for all hands, and two or three variations of hoof-and-mouth disease.

It's a matter of record that the Indians could not get this kind of civilization fast enough, once they had a look at it, and the same thing is true of the Roller Derby. Those in America who have not yet seen the Derby are sending out loud, clear calls to know what it is all about. The more advanced tribes who have tasted the Derby by television or been exposed to it in person are clamoring and stam-peding for more—or so we are told by Mr. Leo A. Seltzer, who sells the stuff to the natives.

Of course, Mr. Seltzer's definition of a stampede is flexible. Back in 1935 B.T. (Before Television), when he tried his first Roller Derby on the public for size, Mr. Seltzer was satisfied with a stampede of three hundred or four hundred people, at any wide place in the road. He did not care how many of them wore shoes. Today, in the age of so-called video, he measures his clients by the million. The incidence of shoes among them is getting higher. Some even wear neckties. In short, Mr. Seltzer feels he has finally got hold of the bon ton, and got them where it hurts.

The Roller Derby, mark you, is a sport. Its backers will stand up and raise their right hands and swear it is. And they are right. Defenestration is also a sport, for those who like it (defenestration is pushing people out of windows). So is extravasation (extravasation is blood-letting, with a license). So is lapidation (lapidation is stoning people to death, or near there). So is the grand old game of suttee, which consists of barbecuing live widows over a charcoal fire.

So, for that matter, is wrestling—and here we are getting close to the meat of the matter. For wrestling is the thing that the Roller Derby threatens to replace, in certain ways. When the television business started to warm up, after the war, it was found that many set owners took a morbid interest in the actions of wrestlers like Primo Carnera and Gorgeous George. The more grotesque, the better. Then televised wrestling began to seem a little cold and stately. That was the spot into which the Roller Derby stepped.

Mr. Seltzer and his staff of calculators estimate that of the more than a million new addicts who paid to see his skaters in the last year, 91 percent were won and brought over by the telecasts of noted television broadcasters like Joe Hasel of WJZ-TV, in New York City, where the Roller Derby broke into Madison Square Garden this year and took its place in Garden history with the Democratic Convention of 1924 (also a sport). That is a pretty solid estimate, that 91 percent, for Mr. Seltzer did not just pull it out of the air, like a butterfly. He went around to the customers in person, feeling their pulses, and asked them, "What in the world brings you to my place, friend?" Most of them said television, which is good enough for Mr. Seltzer. He now feels that, after thirteen lean years or so, the tide has turned, that the nation is his oyster, that America is about to break out with Roller Derby teams and leagues at every pore.

Your correspondent set out the other day to learn the details of the sport, on behalf of those tribes which have not yet put their wampum on the line to see it. It was a most interesting visit. As I knocked at the door, they were just pulling six inches of light, seasoned timber out of the flank of Miss Marjorie Clair Brashun, daughter of a plumber from St. Paul, Minnesota. Miss Brashun, known to the trade for what seem to be satisfactory reasons as Toughie, is one of the leading female skaters of the Roller Derby troupe. Since she likes to wear wood next to her skin, she had gone on skating for some time before the house doctors learned that she had bumped into the guard rail of the track and acquired a piece of it internally.

The sight of Miss Brashun being defrosted caused a slight argument among the Roller Derby people as to whether she is four feet eleven or four feet ten in height. Personally, I think it might be one or the other. I have never gone close enough to a live rattlesnake to put a tape measure on it, and in the same way I am willing to be an inch or two wrong about Miss Brashun.

"The girls in this sport are tougher than the boys," said Mr. Seltzer.

"That's right," snarled Miss Brashun.

"If the girls have a fight on the track," said Mr. Seltzer, "they go right on fighting after the match, maybe for two or three years. In their spare time they spit in each other's teacups. But the girls have a weakness. They are tender in the coccyx."

The coccyx, it should be said, is a vestigal bone at the southern end of the spine. Women skaters wear a special strip of sponge over this area, since they are always falling upon it and making it ring like a bell. In fact, their uniforms are padded all over, and so are the men's—with hip pads, shoulder pads, and thigh pads, topped off by a helmet borrowed partly from football and partly from Marshal Rommel's Afrika Korps. There is lots of padding, but not enough.

A Mr. Billy Reynolds went to the hospital recently with six breaks in one leg. A Miss Margie Anderson (out of Miami) had twenty-four stitches taken in her shapely Gothic torso. A Miss Virginia Rushing broke her pelvic bone in a warm debate, but went on skating for several weeks before she noticed it. Your correspondent would estimate that the number of stitches embroidered in Mr. Seltzer's troupe each week is about the same as Betsy Ross took in making the first flag.

Before establishing the fact that the Roller Derby is, like cutting throats, a sport, let us glance at its history for a moment. Mr. Seltzer, who operates out of Chicago, is an old dance-marathon man. You can tell by the way he stands erect and looks at the world through a clear eye that he got out of that business long ago. At the peak of the Depression he rounded up a few roller skaters and went on the road with the first Derby. For a while, like Virginia Rushing with her pelvic bone, nobody noticed. Things were tough and slow. Once, among the southern hills, twenty-two of the skaters were killed in a bus accident. It may be, in view of the way they made their living, this was an easy and merciful death, but probably not, for the skaters seem to enjoy the work.

Today, old-timers come up to the Derby's doors in each town it plays and introduce themselves as former members of the troupe. Recently a deaf-mute pants presser approached the Seltzer staff and opened conversation with the following written message: "I'm an old Roller Derby ace." He was, at that, and the sight of him reminded Mr. Seltzer that the man was probably responsible for the fact that the Derby today enjoys a strong deaf-mute following wherever it plays.

Now that the show—beg pardon, sport—has struck gold, it plays mostly the big towns in the television belt. It carries a squad of any-where from thirty skaters up (there were sixty-five at Madison Square Garden), half of them men, half women, and a portable Masonite track which is eighteen laps, or two quarts of blood, to the mile. It also packs a stack of referees, medical men, and penalty boxes. The referees put the skaters into the penalty boxes if the medical men have not previously put them into local hospitals.

There are certain laws of God and man the violation of which, I am told, will get a skater thrown out of the match for the night, but I hesitate to imagine what those could be. The penalty boxes take care of the rest, as in hockey. As in football, blocking is en-couraged. As in six-day bike racing, you can jam and sprint at will. As in osteopathy, you can probe for new bones in your fellow man. As in wrestling—well, I was especially interested in the work of a Mr. Silver Rich, who has developed a two-handed kidney punch from behind which puts me strongly in mind of the technique of the five wrestling Duseks from Omaha. It is extremely legal by Roller Derby rules.

The squad is divided into separate teams of boys and girls, the boys playing the boys for fifteen minutes, then the girls playing the girls for fifteen minutes, and so on alternately, while Mr. Selt-zer counts the house. In a wholesome, high-spirited way, Mr. Selt-zer calls the teams by the names of towns, such as Brooklyn, New York, Philadelphia, and Cleveland. A player like Miss Toughie Bras-hun (but there are, I am glad to say, no other players like Miss Bras-hun) will represent Brooklyn in the same way that Mr. Luis Olmo, the Dodger from South America, represents Brooklyn—that is, she wears a Brooklyn shirt.

There is a further similarity, and Happy Chandler can sue me if he likes, between baseball and the skating dodge. The skaters do not like new equipment. They hone, grind, cut, gouge, and chew on their skates and shoes as ballplayers hone their bats, break in their gloves, and cut their shirtsleeves. They sometimes get friends to break in their shoes, or they file down their wooden skate wheels so close that Mr. Seltzer has to supply them with three or four new sets of wheels apiece per evening. The wheels are wooden because metal wheels set up such a vibration that Miss Brashun, for instance, could not hear herself thinking up a plan to murder Miss Gerry Murray, her deadliest rival, in cold blood, if she wore them.

As in bike racing, the fastest skaters on each team sprint for points—one point for passing one rival within two minutes, two points for three, and five points for passing the whole enemy team of five. The other skaters form packs to deter hostile sprinters from passing. At the end of the match, the winning and losing teams split a percentage of the gate on a 60-40 basis and walk, or are carried, home to supper. In their spare time, roller skaters are often married to each other. Miss Brashun is the bride of a skater named Ken Monte, while Miss Murray is Mrs. Gene Gammon in private life. Like other people, skaters have children, and these, Mr. Seltzer hopes, will grow up to be skaters too. The supply is short, and he cannot afford to miss a bet.

That raises the question of where Roller Derby skaters come from. Some of them used to be bike riders, some of them used to be ice skaters, some of them used to be ballplayers, and some of them used to be homegirls. A Miss Peggy Smalley was a homegirl on a high hill in Tennessee when the Roller Derby suddenly surrounded her. The skate shoes they gave her were the first shoes she had ever seen. If it weren't for the skates, she would throw them away. It is claimed that one of the boys in the troupe deserted the St. Louis Cardinal chain for the Derby because he could make more money that way. That may be a gratuitous sneer at baseball, but on the other hand, thinking about the Cardinals, it may be true. Mr. Billy

Bogash, recognized as the Ty Cobb of roller skates, makes consistently better than $10,000 a year, and when a good girl skater and a good boy skater have the presence of mind to marry each other, the pair can knock down from $15,000 to $20,000 per annum, as well as everything that gets in their way.

Pending the arrival of the next generation, Mr. Seltzer has got to dig up and train new skaters to keep the market supplied. Toward this end he runs a skating school in Chicago, where prospects are polished at the house's expense. It takes about a year of training to get a skater ready for the "pack," and three years to make a top point-sprinting performer. Like piano teachers who dislike to take on pupils who have learned to play "Yankee Doodle" with one finger, Mr. Seltzer prefers absolutely fresh recruits with no fixed skating tricks and no bad habits. A bad habit in roller skating, for instance, would be kindness. Those things have got to be pruned out of the subject while he is young.

The new Roller Derby helmets, which were put on view for the first time at Madison Square Garden, are not entirely popular with skaters, especially the ladies (I use the word in a general sense) among them. Neither are all the pads. There is a certain vanity among girl skaters, when they are not too busy tattooing their initials on the shins of the next girl, and they point out that Mr. Seltzer's scheme of padding, while technically useful on the track, does not coincide with nature's scheme. They prefer nature's. As for the helmets, there are two things against them. The ladies like to have their hair float behind them in the breeze when they skate. It looks better. Also, the helmet protects the hair of their victims. A lady skater who cannot sink her hands wrist-deep into the coiffure of an enemy, take a good hold, and pull the scalp at the roots feels frustrated. She feels that her individual liberties have been violated. She wonders what to do with herself.

"Have a heart," said Miss Toughie Brashun to Mr. Seltzer the other day. "I have my eye on a hair-do that I want to rip open from here to Texas."

"Nothing doing," said the chief sternly. "Helmets will be worn. Safety first. Players desiring concussions must obtain them on their own time. Security and dignity are the rule of the sport."

"That's what you think," muttered Miss Brashun, baring her fangs. The final issue remains in doubt. As we go to press, history awaits the outcome.

Sleeper for '44

from *North American Newspaper Alliance*

It warms the cockles of your correspondent's old heart to be able to go down in history, along with other aspects of last Saturday's Army–Notre Dame game, as the fellow who picked Notre Dame to win.

I advertised this hunch as my "sleeper" for 1944. As we proceed to press it is still sleeping soundly, so much so that neighbors have petitioned the city to bury it before later and more indelicate symptoms set in. A rival prophet who bet on Dewey to carry Texas is suing me for infringement of copyright, while my heirs have started proceedings to have the great Lardner industrial holdings, including an uncashed mutuel ticket for the Aqueduct racetrack, taken out of my custody. All in all, this daring and memorable prediction may cost me more trouble than it was worth.

However, I had to make it. A tradition born in 1904 demanded it. In that year my ancestor, the noted Indian soothsayer, Chief Illegal Use of Hands, picked Notre Dame to beat Wisconsin. Wisconsin won by 58 to 0. Up till last Saturday this was the most overpowering defeat Notre Dame had ever suffered.

Naturally, the Chief's guess attracted wide attention at the time. The Republican national committee offered him a handsome fee to pick William Jennings Bryan the next time he ran for president (which, incidentally, the Chief did). A poll of sophomores at Bryn Mawr College named him as the man they would most like to be cast away with on a desert island with a pair of dice and $100,000. A party of his fellow members of the Potawatamie Tribe called upon the Chief on the Monday following the football game and questioned him closely.

"How did you arrive at your conclusion, Chief?" they asked him.

"I refuse to answer," replied Illegal Use of Hands, "on the ground that a medicine man is bound to protect his sources."

"Don't worry about that," said the spokesman. "You are no longer medicine man for this tribe. Your license has been revoked as of noon yesterday. You may speak freely."

"The secret is my own," said Chief Illegal Use of Hands, folding his hands (illegally) across his chest and taking a defiant attitude. "The formula will never pass out of my family. It was used by my ancestor who picked the North at the Battle of Bull Run, and his ancestor before him who predicted that July would follow August in 1672. They passed the recipe on to me, and I will pass it on to my descendants, and on some far distant date when Notre Dame is beaten even worse than this time, it will be one of my family, nobody else, who picks Notre Dame to win."

As the Chief said, so it came to pass. If you notice a slight discrepancy in the sequence, it's because the family changed its name from Illegal Use of Hands to Lardner for reasons of convenience following an oil stock swindle a few years after the Chief's death. Practically nobody I know remembers the time Wisconsin beat Notre Dame, 58–0, in 1904 except Mr. Joe Fogg, well-known Cleveland barrister who played on the Wisconsin team in 1903 and is in no position to deny that Chief Illegal Use of Hands picked Notre Dame the following year.

It was by use of the Chief's formula that I forecast victory for Notre Dame over Army last week. When Army won by 59 to 0, my obligations to the memory of the grand old sachem were fulfilled, and no further prognostications along this line will be forthcoming until Notre Dame loses by 60 to 0, which will probably be in the time of my great-grandchildren.

The Old Postgraduate Try

from *Newsweek*

The thing called school spirit is notably hard to prolong over a period of years. So I admire the gameness of Slinging Sam Baugh, the oldest virtuoso in professional football, in calling a dressing-room meeting of the Washington Redskins recently and urging them to go out and win one for the fans, for themselves, and—I think Sam invoked this for whatever sentimental weight it might have with the team—for him.

It is easier, of course, to say "Fight for the Redskins!" than "Fight for your $8,500!" but I believe that many people feel that it amounts to the same thing, so that they are cynical about the possibilities of stimulating a pro ball club on a purely spiritual basis.

They could just as well be cynical anywhere along the line. The average football player undergoes a long series of calls on his spirit. It can begin in grade school. I remember being exhorted by coaches to go in there and fight when I was ten, playing a pretty static, though well-meaning, center. On the sidelines my schoolmates added their solicitations to the tunes of school songs borrowed from Amherst, or Yale, or Wisconsin.

Then may come junior high school. The song "Jones Junior High (it's the best junior high in To-le-do)," which swept the Pacific war theater like pellagra in 1945, must have been meant to needle many a brave young man into dying for Jones when it was sung in earnest back on the campus. Then may come high school, or prep school, entirely new sets of stimuli, but with the same old trimmings.

Then the subject gets to college, where they give him what used to be considered the final opportunity to strew his chitlings over the field for alma mater. Alumni, to be sure, are also full of fight, but there is not so much quid pro quo about it with them, since the chief danger they face is choking on an ice cube.

Professional football puts the newest, the heaviest, and what is generally agreed to be the fatal strain on a player's capacity for martyrdom. He plays for cash, and the public does not expect him to play for higher values as well—I mean, these members of the public who recognize values higher than cash, and they tell me there is such a fellow somewhere in New Jersey, and another in northern Nebraska.

Just the same, Sam Baugh gave the Redskins a fight talk week before last in which money was hardly mentioned. As assistant talkers he had two of the next-oldest men on the club, Al Demao and Joe Tereshinski. Among them they represent a record for longevity of school spirit that will probably never be surpassed.

The Redskins, favorites in their division of the National League that year, had been losing games consistently. Slinging Sam sent the coaches out of the room, as was his privilege after bleeding and dying for the George Preston Marshall wet-wash service for fourteen years. Then he gave the boys twenty minutes' worth of inspiration. It was nineteen and a half minutes longer than Sam had ever talked at one time. Among other things, he said that he would like to play on one more championship team before retiring his ancient bones, including the most spectacular right ulna in the game's history.

Mr. Demao and Mr. Tereshinski recalled glorious incidents from the Redskins' past—like the time 10,000 Washington fans marched up Broadway behind a brass band to the strains of "Hail to the Redskins" by Mrs. Corinne Griffith Marshall, the team's most beautiful rooter.

The surprising thing was that the team broke out at once with signs of stimulus. Its jaws tightened, its knuckles whitened, and it walked from the meeting in deadly, ominous silence. It almost won its game the following Sunday with the N.Y. Giants. Perhaps it was too much to expect it to win right then. Even Notre Dame teams do not "win one for the Gipper," or Centre College teams pray their way to victory, unless someone has had the prudence to load them with football players in advance. I suspect the Redskins are not as good as Slinging Sam nearly kidded them into thinking they were. But they are something above the ordinary, anyway, as long as they have Sam.

Rooney's Ride

from *Newsweek*

This is an age of machines in the horse-racing world, of overnight pari-mutuel laws, of jerry-built tracks and daily doubles and dusty stretches and one quick coat of paint—which makes it easy to understand why the old-fashioned gambler points his nose toward the green hills of Saratoga every year, when August comes around.

They take your money just as fast in those mellow surroundings as anywhere else—perhaps faster. Your agent, known up there in the north country as Ace-Deuce Lardner, has paid out money, rather than vice versa, for the privilege of advertising the place where Gates and Arnold stopped Burgoyne. Nevertheless, you keep going back to shuffle the warm bricks of Broadway at noon, to ride to the track after lunch in the hack of an affable bandit, to watch and play the horses, to touch at the lake in the evening for steak and frogs' legs and roulette, to wind up at dawn throwing dice with the frankly predatory mob at the old Chicago Club, hard by the railroad station, which used to be your next stop, if you still had the fare home.

Saratoga, Dick Canfield's town, is the stronghold of the old-fashioned gambler. The old-fashioned gambler is not a guy with a frock coat or a waxed mustache. He is any private citizen who comes along with his private roll to buck the house at the house's game and to stay with it till he makes his killing or takes his licking.

The poolroom and syndicate systems being what they are, few gamblers are known by name any more. The last lone wolf to "make a score" in a free, wide, and purely innocent way was a deadpanned little Irishman from Pittsburgh named Art Rooney, owner of the Pittsburgh professional football club. He made his score at Saratoga, which is only right.

Some people have heard of "Rooney's Ride," but because the Irishman speaks only six words a month in a good year, the blow-by-blow details of his killing were not known until recently, when Mr. Joseph Madden, a literary saloonkeeper, published his third straight undefeated and untied book of memoirs, *Set 'Em Up*.

Some seasons ago, Mr. Rooney arrived in New York City accompanied by $300 and the old Pittsburgh light-heavyweight fighter, Buck Crouse. Their object was to spend a quiet weekend and get back to Pittsburgh alive. However, on Saturday, at the Empire City track, Mr. Rooney ran his $300 up to $21,000. This seemed to call for a couple of steaks at Mr. Madden's place.

"What's your next move, Artie?" inquired Mr. Madden.

"Back to Pittsburgh," said Mr. Rooney tersely. "First train."

The upshot of this conversation was that Rooney, Madden, and Crouse set out for Saratoga two hours later in Mr. Madden's $150 car, which had four bad coughing spells en route. Mr. Rooney and Mr. Crouse got out and pushed it over the hills, Mr. Madden retaining the helm.

On Monday—opening day at Saratoga—Mr. Rooney sent $2,000 on the back of a horse named Quel Jeu, at 8 to 1. The race came to a photo finish in the rain. Mr. Madden had $2 on this animal and swallowed his cigar when the picture showed him the winner.

"Ain't you happy?" he yelled at Mr. Rooney.

"We were lucky, Joe," said Mr. Rooney solemnly.

There were four photo finishes that afternoon. Rooney's biggest race was the fifth, when he tried to bet $15,000 on another 8 to 1 shot, but could only place $10,000.

"In that race," recalls Mr. Madden, "the four houses came out of the fog and hit the finish line in a heap—it looked like a dead heat for all four nags.

"As I had a few clams on this event, I nearly died waiting for the picture to come down. But Artie lit a cigar, got out of the crowd, and went to the men's room, and when I brought him the good news there, he was telling the colored groom the difference between the single wingback and Warner's double-wing.

"'I will finish explaining later,' he said. 'I gotta hot tip in the next race.'"

Rooney won $256,000 that day. He, Mr. Crouse, and Mr. Madden celebrated in the evening with a banana split apiece at a soda fountain.

Has Mr. Rooney still got the dough? Please do not change the subject while I am looking up trains to Saratoga.

An Angel on Horseback

from *Newsweek*

Between races at the Hialeah racetrack in Florida not so long ago, a customer yelled an epithet at Edward Arcaro, the country's best jockey, and Eddie almost jumped the fence to horsewhip the heckler. His touchiness was surprising, at first glance. Jockeys as a rule are immune to the remarks of postrace quarterbacks—especially Mr. Arcaro, the best of the jocks and therefore the most accustomed to second-guessing—and the epithet in this case, Banana Nose, was pretty mild. The fact was that Mr. Arcaro felt misanthropic because he had just found a method of self-torture previously unknown to jockeys. He had backed a play. I don't know how much he went for; the grapevine said $30,000.

The play was a thing called *Crescendo.* In the language of the track, it was the sort of entry that would have paid $96.20 to win, $34.80 to place, and $11.70 to show. However, it did not win, place, or, to the best of my knowledge, even show. Some of the boys around the barn were puzzled by Eddie's bet, for he has been in circulation quite a while and is generally thought to be two degrees sharper than mustard.

"Who touted you, Eddie?" inquired a friend.

"Nobody touted me," said Mr. Arcaro morosely. "I didn't even have a clocking, although they tell me it took three hours to cover the route, ridden out. You know how it is. Some of them go all the way. Some stop."

Crescendo stopped in Philadelphia, I am told, which is a good furlong short of Broadway. During the short and erratic gallop which brought it that far, Mr. Arcaro was riding his four-legged friends down in Florida and doubtless lashing at the flanks of *Crescendo* in his mind while ostensibly bringing his bat down on Class C handicap horses and $4,000 platers. An angel on horseback is a rare sight, and I expect some of the other jocks were tempted at times to slip Eddie a notice from Wilkes-Barre or a clipping from Scranton as they pulled alongside him in the stretch, in the hope that the out-of-town notices would stop him cold, like *Crescendo*. It is a tribute to Mr. Arcaro that he went on riding winners. He is a talented man aboard a zebra.

This very talent, however, has contributed to Eddie's recent touchiness. It is not only a matter of backing plays that stop south of Newark. It is also the way the horseplayers back Mr. Arcaro. If you have followed the charts, you know that Edward's mounts seldom leave the gate at longer odds than 2 to 1. His skill is widely recognized, and for at least a couple of years the players have been betting on Arcaro horses simply because they were ridden by Arcaro. If there is one sort of horseplayer more unscientific than another, it is the kind that bets on jockeys. In the words of Mr. Arcaro himself:

"Any jock looks good on a good horse."

If everything in the horse department of a race is even, then the best jockey will prevail. A good ride may be worth two, three, or four lengths to a horse in certain circumstances. But it will not make the five to fifty lengths' difference that some of those abject platers or outright stiffs require, and Mr. Arcaro rides his share of abject platers and outright stiffs. The trouble is, the bettors usually force them down to favorite, or thereabouts. Mr. Arcaro will go off on an 8 to 5 horse that ought to be a 10 to 1. The horse will come in just about where he deserves to come in, and as Mr. Arcaro strolls back to the jockey room, with a mud-stained shirt and the woes of the theatrical world on his shoulders, the railbirds will yell: "You bum, Arcaro!"

Or, if they are more the fruit-minded type, "Banana Nose!"

If a jockey had to get mixed up with plays, you would guess it would be a steeplechase jockey. There is the spirit of the footlights in steeplechasing, the fragrant odor of greasepaint—to the extent, in fact, that the boys sometimes rehearse their races, with or without costume. A steeplechase rider expelled from racing for life in Maryland—which is allergic to theatricals—remarked of the formal performance that followed the rehearsal: "A blind man could have seen I was pulling the horse." This is known as mugging, or overplaying. There may have been a certain amount of it in *Crescendo*, which hung in Philadelphia. Or it may have been just a natural stiff, an 80 to 1 shot. With Arcaro up, the wonder is that the critics did not back it down to 6 to 5 and then scream for their money back.

Little Bill

from *Newsweek*

William M. Johnston, a freckled, sandy-haired salesman who once played tennis on the side, and was twice national champion, died one day in California at the age of fifty-one. Usually the death of an athlete, whether two- or four-legged, wins several linear feet of sentimental prose in the newspapers. Jim Jeffries got yards of it at the same time without even dying, just by being sick. Little Bill Johnston was passed over lightly with a few paragraphs. This is an apportionment which seems all wrong to me. America has seldom had among its great athletes a more gallant, honest, and attractive fellow than Johnston.

I grant you that he may have looked like a better guy than he was just because he played tennis. It is a strange phenomenon, which I will try not to probe here, that the majority of tennis stars are so designed by nature in the character department that any nice person, male or female, stands out among them like a lighthouse. That is one of the reasons why crowds used to pack the Forest Hills stadium at the national championships in the hope of seeing Johnston beat Bill Tilden. They knew he had very little chance to do it. So did Johnston. But he always tried his hardest, and that was good enough for the crowds.

However, there was something more positive than that in the

popularity and attraction of Johnston. Almost alone he resisted the temptation to become a tennis bum, at a time when nearly every other great or even pretty good player without a private income was a pro and a lackey masquerading as an amateur. In the thirty years that tennis has been an important spectator sport, no great player has ever played in so few tournaments as Johnston. He played in the nationals. He played for the country in the Davis Cup. Then he went back home to sell some insurance, because he had to live and he did not want to live as a tennis bum.

Things are a little healthier today. A good tennis player can turn professional openly without losing his prestige and his public. Twenty years ago only Vincent Richards among the leaders was bold enough to take this step, and Richards was a number of years younger than Johnston, who dated from the time of McLoughlin and Brookes and ended his career in 1927.

Little Bill, playing when he could afford it, which was seldom, was by all odds the greatest player in the world except for Tilden. It was his misfortune to be contemporaneous with Large Bill, probably the foremost genius in the game's history. This caused his fans more anguish than it did Johnston. He plugged along. And he had his compensations. He could always beat the other players, against whom Tilden sometimes flagged.

The English, the Australians, the Japanese, and the French—and they had virtuosos in those days—all looked alike to Johnston. He played sixteen Davis Cup challenge matches in his time—fourteen at singles, two at doubles. He lost only three, and two of those came in 1927, just before he decided to hang up his shoes and go home to stay. He murdered Shimizu and Brookes and Patterson and Anderson and Borotra and Lacoste. More often than not he took them in straight sets.

His height, to the best of my recollection, was about five feet six, and he never weighed more than 125 pounds. In fact, it seemed to me that the difference between him and Tilden as players lay chiefly in Tilden's height. Little Bill was a steadier competitor, a harder fighter, and there was no weakness in his strokes. Of all the players I have seen, only big Jim Anderson and Ellsworth Vines hit the ball harder off the forehand. And they did not have Johnston's consistency, nor could they compare with him in the other shots.

In spite of his conquering international record, I guess the clearest memories of those who watched Johnston will always be of his foredoomed struggles with Tilden. A tiny fellow, half-bald, with his shirt clinging drenched to his thin chest, he stood back there and slammed the ball as hard and as long as he could at the big man who had his number, year after year. Then the end would come, and there would be a second's pause, as Johnston's shoulders drooped a little and his jaw muscles tightened. He did not like to lose those matches. Then, with a grin, he would trot up and shake the tall man's hand. Then, since his year's short holiday was over, he would climb on a train and go home and go to work.

Strong Cigars and Lovely Women

from *Newsweek*

This department is disposed to agree that Mrs. Fanny Blankers-Koen, the Netherlands jumper and loper, is the greatest woman track athlete in the world. She has the rest of the field whipsawed.

I will also concede that she is a mother. The latter fact, which is mentioned in every story about Mrs. Blankers-Koen, seems to have inspired an admiration bordering on ecstasy, merely because mothers are scarcer in the track world than they are in, say, the Republican Party or the songs of Al Jolson. While I revere Mrs. Koen's motherhood, it does not startle me. I have known many mothers who could run like a thief—beg pardon, like the wind—when there was something in it for them.

It's when the boys in the jury box go on to say casually, as they have been doing in the last few weeks, that the lady from Holland is the world's greatest woman athlete (no qualifications, mind you) that I demur. The greatest at track, yes. But has she ever pitched an inning for the St. Louis Cardinals? Has she ever beaten par by judging the wind's effect on the smoke from a ten-cent cigar? A woman athlete must be many things before I give her my vote across the board.

For that matter, has Mrs. Koen ever run a boxing show? You will have deduced by now that I am speaking in loyal defense of my friend, Mrs. Mildred (Babe) Didrikson Zaharias. The Babe, with her husband, the reformed wrestler George Zaharias, was recently licensed to promote boxing in their home town of Denver. It does not follow automatically that Mrs. Zaharias will turn boxer herself, under her own auspices. But in the present degraded state of pugilism, she may be tempted to, to make ends meet.

It is nice to hear news of Mr. and Mrs. Zaharias, a couple who have, to my mind, achieved the pinnacle in married harmony. For evidence I refer you to the Women's Western Open golf championship a few years ago on a day when a high wind was whipping the course. Mr. Zaharias, observing that the gale had affected his consort's work off the tee, went to the clubhouse and bought a supply of his favorite stogies. He then returned to the golf match, puffing smoke like the steamboat Robert E. Lee. "Over here, Babe," he called.

Watching her husband the Babe was able to gauge the wind's direction to a nicety. It goes without saying that she won the match. She also lost her audience. The smoke from Mr. Zaharias's heater, while true as the pole star, had too keen a fragrance for the rest of the gallery to manage before lunch.

Mrs. Blankers-Koen married her trainer. That is high romance indeed, but it seems to me that the Zaharias wooing was even more beautiful. Mr. Zaharias won his wife because he was practically the only man she had ever seen who could outdrive her—for distance, that is.

Sharing radio air with the Babe on a program not long ago, your correspondent hesitated before pronouncing the historic name of Zaharias.

"Does the accent come on the antepenult, Babe?" I asked with deference.

"Never mind the antepenult, boy," said the Babe calmly. "Just put the accent on the 'har—' and everything will be fine."

With that question settled, I cautiously brought up the subject of the longest fly ball I ever saw hit—by Jimmy Foxx, off Babe Didrikson, who was pitching an inning for the Cardinals in an exhibition game in Florida. I pointed out that it was quite a belt.

"Yes," said the Babe with womanly nonchalance. "I would have been in a spot if Terry Moore hadn't run and caught it in his Wilson glove."

By a coincidence which we will not analyze now, the Babe happened to be working for some people named Wilson, who made gloves. Whether Mr. Moore wore that kind of glove, I don't know. My recollection is that the ball did not land in a Wilson glove or any other kind, but in the next county. Mrs. Blankers-Koen might have caught it. Nobody else.

What Was That Again?

from *Newsweek*

Dizzy Dean, in his day one of the greatest of baseball pitchers and rhetoricians, still flourishes in the latter field, as a broadcaster of ball games in St. Louis. His medium is known loosely in the trade as Dean English. When a group of local schoolteachers attacked this rich patois in Diz's second year on the radio, alleging that Mr. Dean was poisoning the wells of culture in and around St. Louis, the public came to his support with such a tall majority that Dizzy routed the pedagogues and went right on doing what came naturally.

In some of its aspects—like "slud" for "slid" and "throwed" for "threw"—Dean English is sound stuff and may supersede the original models as time goes on. Another phase of it—what you might call the "confusion" or "what-was-that-again" style of speech—is so widespread anyway that I am surprised it should have been noticed at all in the radio talks of Mr. Dean.

"Don't fail," chanted Diz one day, in a burst of advertising zeal, "to miss tomorrow's double-header here at Sportsman's Park!"

No doubt the great man meant to say something else; he is not paid to promote absenteeism at the ball game. But think back a few years to a song which began "I got spurs that jingle, jangle, jingle." It was widely popular. Millions of people, high school and college students included, sang its words in good faith. Among those words was the following passage:

> *I got spurs that jingle, jangle, jingle,*
> *As I go riding merrily along,*
> *And they say, "Oh, ain't you glad you're single?"*
> *And that song ain't so very far from wrong.*

This is a fair specimen of "what-was-that-again" English. I am not referring to the "ain'ts." "Ain't" was high-toned English two centuries ago and may be high-toned again someday. But the fourth line of the chorus says the opposite of what I think the author means—he means the song of the spurs "ain't so very far from right."

If millions of educated bathtub singers could repeat those words for weeks on end without realizing that there was a gimmick in them, it strikes me that the officials were calling the plays pretty close on Diz Dean when they tried to penalize him for offside syntax.

Let us glance for a moment at the football prose of the stately Associated Press, which does not tolerate a sportswriter unless he can get at least one metaphor in his lead paragraph. He merely has to get it in. He does not have to get it out again. In fact, an AP football man who ends a metaphor the same way he began it is obviously cooking at very low heat. What is the point of moving in one direction if you can move in two simultaneously?

Having thrown in a couple of metaphors myself, for the regular price of admission, I now cite the AP lead on the first football story that comes to hand:

"A whirlwind finish . . . today gave twice-beaten Michigan State a 19-to-16 football victory over Penn State and wrecked what 20,000 Nittany Lion partisans hoped would be just another hurdle on the road to an unbeaten season."

"Nittany Lion" is sportswriter's code for Penn State, and no football story is genuine without it. But what about this hurdle-wrecking? Not only is hurdle-wrecking an odd sport, probably out of season at this time of year, but how and why do you wreck a hurdle and who got wrecked in this case?

As I understand the thought here, Michigan State was the hurdle, since it stood on Penn State's road to an unbeaten season. That is suicide in a diabolic form, for no sign of it appears in the score, which came out in favor of Michigan State. Ed.'s note: also known as the Spartans. Having wrecked itself, as a hurdle, Michigan State would seem to have left the road clearer than ever for an unbeaten season for Penn State. Yet the sight of the wrecked hurdle left the twenty thousand Penn State partisans weeping and desolate, if I read their emotions correctly.

We will not at this time go into the question of why the partisans hoped the other team would be a hurdle, and why they hoped for a hurdle at all. I am turning the entire body of evidence over to Dr. Dean to be checked for fingerprints.

Mr. Jacoby and the National Folly
from *Newsweek*

In Dallas a gentleman named Al Hill has published a book, a privately printed edition of one (1) copy, called *How I Beat Oswald Jacoby at Canasta*. This leaves your correspondent the only man over seventeen in this country who has not yet written a canasta book. I plan to rectify the oversight by next St. Swithin's Day.

Mr. Jacoby himself has written two canasta books, both of which are selling like hotcakes (better than hotcakes; as they say in Wall Street, hotcakes just ain't moving). The Jacoby score of two books may, of course, be out of date by the time you read this. I have not seen the maestro for several days. He may have let fly with another canasta book in the meantime.

While calling on him last week, I asked Mr. Jacoby how many canasta books he thought there were in circulation already, as of that moment.

"Oh, somewhere between sixty and sixty-five," he replied. "Call it sixty-two point five."

"That's funny," said Mr. Jerry Nagler, who is hired to keep Mr. Jacoby's light from getting under a bushel (in card-playing circles they tell you that the bushel has not been made which is big enough for that). "When I counted up this morning there were only thirty-two."

"It is now past noon," said Mr. Jacoby calmly. "I feel sure that thirty more canasta books have been published today. Get a newspaper this evening and look at the late scores."

Regardless of the scores there is no doubt that canasta, which is said to be Uruguay's answer to civilization, has had a deep, bruising effect on the body politic in the U.S.A. It is, as you know, chiefly a partnership game, like bank robbing. Mr. Jacoby says it is currently the hottest of all partnership games. He estimates that in the last year it has cut down bridge playing by 90 percent.

It has also cut down my old friend, Mr. Ely Culbertson, by $240. That was the sum Mr. Culbertson bet against Mr. Jacoby and his partner, John R. Crawford, in their recent charity match with Theodore Lightner and Samuel Fry, Jr. In order to give Mr. Culbertson something more than a mere spectator's interest in the match, Mr. Jacoby covered the bet himself, giving odds of 7 to 1 on his side. He and Crawford won in a gallop.

Mr. Crawford was part of the reason for the 7 to 1 odds. He is an ex-G.I. of thirty-three with a growing reputation as a card player. Newspaper reports have suggested that he does not care too much for publicity, because it makes it hard for him to get a good game. Mr. Jacoby describes this Crawford theory as pure Roquefort.

"When a card player gets a national reputation," he says, "everybody wants to play with him. The more money they have, the more they want to play."

Under questioning, Mr. Jacoby said that he rates Crawford as the best all-around card player now in action. This rating followed a short soliloquy in which Mr. Jacoby listed the card games at which he is Crawford's master. It was a fair-sized list. You can see at a glance where that leaves Mr. Jacoby in the national ratings.

It may be asked, what about Mr. Al Hill, the Dallas citizen who wrote the privately printed book *How I Beat Oswald Jacoby at Ca-*

nasta? The answer is that the spirit of good, clean fun runs high in Dallas. Mr. Hill is a social player, an amateur. Mr. Jacoby is strictly a pro. He has been a pro since the age of ten, when he used to play cards with one of his aunts, and gave her the business without compunction.

Canasta, Mr. Jacoby was saying the other day, is a game of pleasure and low stakes. Poker remains the most skillful of card games. Your correspondent, a poker player, agreed with this, and Mr. Jacoby shot him a stern look.

"I have noticed," said Mr. Jacoby, "that whereas the most cautious card players in the world are actuaries, the most reckless and unsound are reporters. I have also noticed," continued Mr. Jacoby, "that no drinker of alcohol can be a good card player."

With these words, the maestro buried his nose firmly in a stein of homogenized milk and the meeting broke up.

The Best of the Browsers

from *Newsweek*

Last year toward the time of the Harvard-Yale football game, a couple of Harvard students challenged Herman Hickman, the prominent (280-pound) coach of the Yales, to an eating contest. Stung by Hickman's fame as a freestyle grazer, they offered to meet him at a neutral trough, before or after the game, and eat right down the line with him for a purse and side bets.

Naturally the coach ignored this callow proposition. Recognized in several states, especially Connecticut, Tennessee, and Virginia, as the world's champion trencherman, he felt it beneath his dignity to eat against children. Known far and wide as the Scourge of the Smokies, celebrated in two continents for his work in the fields of ham and fried chicken, Hickman deserves an opponent worthy of his mettle. And I think the opponent—and the occasion—are at hand.

From time to time Coach Hickman leads a team of college all-stars in a football game with New York's professional Giants, coached by Steve (Carbarn) Owen, the well-known one-man group. Mr. Owen is said by connoisseurs to be the strongest hand with a knife and fork ever produced west of the Mississippi.

I do not propose anything so trifling as an intercoach eating contest between the halves of the game. It takes Coach Owen and

Coach Hickman twenty minutes to roll up their sleeves, summon their caddies, and select their cutlery for the opening course. Before they had killed their first barrel of oysters, the teams would be back on the field, punting and passing and spilling the horseradish and generally fouling things up. What we need here is a species of twi-night doubleheader—Owen vs. Hickman, table stakes, from 4 p.m. to 8:30, football thereafter.

Eating contests have always appealed to the truest sporting instincts in your correspondent. Stories of the old-time, bare-knuckle eaters—Irvin S. Cobb (great on corn), Babe Ruth (outstanding with spare ribs and pig's feet), Enrico Caruso (peerless with pasta), and Jim Thorpe (had no weakness)—have thrilled me since boyhood. An eater with skill and stamina, who can go to his right or to his left, is a spectacle as brilliant as Citation pounding down the stretch.

As it happens Mike Jacobs and the late Damon Runyon, some fourteen years ago, thought they had hold of the best eater in the country for his weight. Their boy was Walter Stewart, the noted Tennessee locust, now sports editor of the *Memphis Commercial-Appeal*. They were going to put him into the ring against all comers. But just as I was challenged in behalf of my own man, Stewart sprained a wrist lifting an order of side meat, and had to retire. He was a good man but brittle.

My own man, Harry George, then deputy executive stage carpenter of the Metropolitan Opera, was the best eater of his time, recognized as such by both Caruso and Scotti. He held the world's record for lamb chops at a sitting (twenty-seven). Once resting backstage in a rocking chair, he consumed a case of beer and a case of sandwiches during one performance of *Madame Butterfly* (his favorite), finishing the last beer and the last sandwich on the last note of the opera.

There are no Georges today, but Coach Hickman and Coach

Owen are true virtuosos all the same. Incidentally, coaches dominate the art of browsing today. One authority, Joe Madden, the bartender who has written six books, contends that professional crapshooters eat slightly more than coaches, because they exercise harder and stay indoors. But he rates coaches high.

The only thing that might upset present ratings would be the arrival of a foreign challenger—like, say, Ronnie James, the British prize fighter. Mr. James went to Australia a few years ago to fight for the Empire welterweight title but had to default, because in Australia he suddenly encountered meat and became a middleweight overnight. There is no telling what an eater can do unless he has something to eat.

Maybe in Memoriam
from *Newsweek*

Every five years or so, to keep my stake in the wrestling game from moldering, I lay claim to the world's championship in behalf of my Italo-Saxon lion, Hereward "Muscles" Quattrociocchi, through whose veins (on the left side) courses the blood of the Caesars and (to starboard) the purple hemoglobin of Hengest and Horsa.

There is no question that Muscles is the highest-born wrestler in existence—that is, if he still exists. When last heard from he was in Kurdistan, wrestling exclusively with leopards between the Greater and the Lesser Zab rivers. That was some time ago. A rumor leaked out that one of the Kurdish leopards forgot whose turn it was one night and confused Muscles with a Wiener schnitzel. This report, if sound (it could be a Kurdish canard), may be said to weaken my claim.

However, alive or dead, Quattrociocchi is the only wrestler I own, and in the present anarchic state of wrestling, I have no hesitation in asserting his rights. Dead or alive he can beat any of the contemporary world's champions. That is natural for a man who blends in one container the genes of Caligula and the heritage of Alfred the Great and Hardicanute.

Today if you call for a world's wrestling champion, one of the following will raise his hand: Gorgeous George, Antonino Rocca,

Gene Stanlee (Mr. America), Yukon Eric, Frank Sexton, Primo Carnera, or Don Eagle. It depends on which way you are looking. If you are prudent you will keep your eyes shut.

Eagle, an aboriginal, wears a scalplock and not much else. He knows the secret of the Indian Death Trap, which was handed down to him (with kid gloves) by Chief Little Wolf. I know the secret myself but will not divulge it, except to say that it would surprise you. That accounts for the look of amazement, not to say consternation, on Eagle's pan.

Gorgeous George is the fellow who wears or drinks perfume. I forget which. They tell me the difference is insignificant. Stanlee got the name Mr. America because he is descended from a family named America on his mother's side. Rocca, a South American, bounces around, but so do checks. Carnera you know. If you don't I can introduce you. Eric and Sexton are a couple of fellows named Yukon and Frank.

The threadbare quality of this kind of talent leaps to the eye. The fact is, there has not been a true test of championship standing since the heyday of Henri Deglane, who later turned square and became a war hero. While he wrestled Deglane was a yardstick. The champion was the man who had bitten the largest piece out of Henri's leg. Some truly important nibbles were taken, but for my money, no one in this special field of anthropophagy excelled Hereward "Muscles" Quattrociocchi.

Muscles, if alive, is a fine specimen of wrestler in the further sense that he is cultured. Most wrestlers are. Not long ago a spelling bee was conducted on the radio between a team of wrestlers and a team of boxers. The boxers, after a little early difficulty with the word *cat*, always a tricky one, went down on (if memory serves me) *apple*. Long after the last pugilist had gone off limping to his stall, the wrestlers were still cutting through words like *canaliferous* and *pterodactyl* like a knife through margarine.

Culture, however, is all the present crop has got, except for George's scent, Eagle's scalplock, Stanlee's press clippings, and Carnera's appetite. Muscles Quattrociocchi has drawing power. Once, wrestling a Bedouin chieftain for the championship of one of the better-known oases in the Sahara desert, he broke the attendance record for water holes. It is said that forty Arabs and thirty-eight camels came by during the six days the match lasted. True, they didn't stay long, but that can be set down to the restless, nomadic nature of those desert tribes.

It is sad to think of a bundle of energy, charm, and erudition like Muscles being eaten by a leopard. I'll say this, though, to console his fans: if it happened, somebody had a mighty sick leopard on his hands for the next couple of days.

The Life of T-ts Sh-r

from *Newsweek*

I hear that the editors of newspapers from Boston became disturbed
one day when a hasty survey confirmed their suspicion that nine
out of ten "Broadway" columns and similar boilerplate pieces syndicated out of New York contain the name of—well, just a moment,
I have the name here somewhere. I will glance through my notes.

Let's see. It says here that I owe the Old French Hand Laundry
$18.30. That would be for three weeks' work. Forget it. Here is a
notation of a bet I made that Williams would hit fifty home runs.
Irrelevant. Mrs. Lincoln . . . no, I guess that's Mrs. Lardner . . .
the handwriting is a little obscure around this point . . . wants me
to stop at the taxidermist's and get that shark stuffed on the way to
the office. Why doesn't she run her own errands? Ah, here we are:
The name that the Boston editors are getting tired of because it
appeared in twenty-six columns in one week is Toots Shor.

Toots Shor is a former prizefighter or Indian guide or congress-
man or something who runs a refectory in New York where you
can eat lunch, if that's your idea of fun. His sideline is being mentioned in columns, and he also runs a small subsidiary business of
getting his picture taken advising people how to do things.

When times were better, Shor went down to Washington and was
photographed advising President Roosevelt. He has also advised

Horace Stoneham, Melvin Ott, Larry MacPhail, and several generals and admirals. It is safe to say that none of these made any serious detour from the strategy outlined by Shor, whether they finished in last place or first. More lately he has run into a slump and was last seen advising Billy Conn how to fight Louis. A true friend would have advised Conn not to fight Louis, but Shor is a "how" man rather than a "not" man. He told him how.

In spite of the photographic slump, things are booming with Shor in the print business, as you can see from the reaction of those editors in Boston who decided to form a Society for the Prevention of Mention of Toots Shor. I am afraid there is not much chance of success for this movement. The man Shor is diabolically cunning. Witness the way he has streamlined his name. Shor is obviously short for something, like Shore. Or maybe it is short for Short. At any rate, the name is so terse that it will fit into any kind of column, and sometimes—mark the devilish ingenuity at work here—when a columnist gets down near the end of his column and wonders if he has room to mention Shor again in the same piece, he finds he has room.

The editors in Boston will have their troubles deleting the name of Shor and trying to fill the blank spaces with the name of Senator Vandenberg, for instance, or Leopold Stokowski. In the end they will have to go back to Shor, like a tired swimmer. (That last jest is offered to columnists free of charge as part of our shopping service.)

The way the thing works, a columnist thinks of a line that may be funny—at least, he thinks he thought of it himself, although actually he heard Bennett Cerf use it, which means it was originated by Marcus Tullius Cicero in 48 B.C. He tries it on his secretary for effect.

"Is that comical?" he asks.

"Nyah, it smells," replies the amanuensis tactfully.

"Then I'll credit it to Shor," says the columnist, and does so. Or perhaps the writer has been over at the Waldorf-Astoria shooting grouse at a time when he was supposed to be working. To cover his movements, he writes as follows:

"The other Wed. evening I dropped into Toots Shor's and asked the host what time it was. 'Eleven thirty-three,' said Toots, quick as a flash. He is never at a loss for an answer."

I got my information about the anti-Shor revolt in Boston from Mr. Jimmy Powers, the motorboat editor of the *New York Daily News*. Mr. Powers is not a Shor-mentioner himself. He is a Dinty Moore–mentioner. Whenever Mr. Powers finds himself desperate in the middle of his column, as is not infrequently the case, he changes the subject and says that he ran into Chester A. Arthur or Henry Clay or some other Broadway figure, gnawing a marrow bone at Dinty Moore's, where he asked him if he would rate Ty Cobb over Cary Grant. The fellow usually says yes.

What Price Olympic Peace?
from *Sport*

Unofficial statistics show that good will prevails over bad will in the Olympic Games by a ratio of about nine to one, which is why the Games are still in business—and a fine thing, too. Nonetheless, in memory and in history, it is the bad will that sticks out, like Sandy Saddler's thumb. The mind of man (a trouble-loving organ, at best) turns back with relish to such dates as these:

A.D. 400—Somebody stole the statue of Zeus from the Olympic Stadium in Greece.

1948—Somebody stole the Olympic flag from the stadium at St. Moritz.

1904—The first man home in the marathon turned out to have traveled twelve miles of the distance by automobile. He was excused from marathon running for life.

1908—The American tug-of-war team resigned because the English team's shoes were too big. The British tuggers were, of course, cops.

1928—The French Olympic team was barred at the gate by a Dutch gatekeeper.

1932—On returning home to Argentina from the Games, the Olympic heavyweight boxing champion was put in jail for fighting.

1936—Avery Brundage threw a lady off the American Olympic team for drinking champagne with sportswriters.

1948—A young male member of the American team heard that Avery Brundage was planning to make a test run down the bobsled course. "I hope he breaks his leg," said the young man, for publication.

1952—A maiden in a white nightgown floated around the arena, promoting peace. She was run off the premises.

1956—A man in a white flannel nightshirt floated around the arena, promoting peace. He was run off the premises.

Apart from the man in the nightshirt, alleged to be a Communist, the Olympics of 1956 have been mild, to date. American girl figure skaters were reprimanded, though not fined, for intramural cattiness. A male skater from Minnesota told the press that America should stop giving its money away, and save it to spend on amateur skaters, as the Russians do. This is pretty quiet stuff; the indications are that major rhubarbs will not break out this year until November, in Melbourne, Australia, which can take a hint. The government is said to be insuring everything in the country that is not nailed down, and to be putting a double guard over the museum which houses the nation's proudest possession, the heart of the racehorse Phar Lap. It is every Australian's belief that Phar Lap was poisoned in the U.S.A. What is to keep some foreign hop-step-and-jumper from stealing what is left of the big fellow?

At its best, however, the 1956 Olympics does not figure to produce a ruction to match the one in 1904, when Fred Lorz tried to revolutionize marathon running. With most connoisseurs, this is the favorite Olympic rhubarb. Boiled down, it appears that Lorz, representing the Mohawk A.C. and America in the Games and St. Louis, developed cramps while he was still seventeen miles from the finish. The motorcar had just been invented. A motorcar was going Lorz's way. He climbed aboard, and soon outdistanced the field, to which he waved as he passed it. Five miles from home, the car took a tip from Lorz and broke down. Fred did the last five miles on foot, breezing. He breezed into the stadium and was about to accept his prize from the president's daughter, Alice Roosevelt, when word got out that he owed his long lead to the internal-combustion engine.

Lorz was not lynched by the crowd. However, he was barred for life by the AAU, and became as popular in amateur sports as Benedict Arnold is with history students. There seems to be no doubt that Lorz was joking. There seems to be no doubt, either, that he had the narrowest escape from death of any Olympic counterfeiter since Pisidorus's mother.

Pisidorus was a runner in the ancient Greek games at Olympia. His mother was also his trainer. Women were barred from the stands in those days. The mother of Pisidorus disguised herself as a man, took a seat, saw her boy win, and expressed her satisfaction with tribal yells. It was this that tipped off the law. "That fellow is getting quite a bang out of the race," said one badger to another. (Badgers, or badge-wearers, or officials, are as old as Olympic history.) "True," said the other badger, looking closely at the noisy fan, "and the reason is that she is a dame." The boys studied the rules and found that the penalty was death. Eventually, however, this was commuted to a handshake and a season's pass to the Games, for the public was on the lady's side, and the heat was removed from Pisidorus's mother by another rhubarb, when a boxer named Eupolus was convicted of bribing three of his Olympic opponents to take it easy. They fined the stuffing out of him.

Centuries passed, the old Olympics died, the modern Olympics were born, and we find the badgers still at work. Prince George of Greece, who stood six feet five inches tall, was officiating in the

1,500-meter walk at Athens. Wilkinson, of England, was a great walker, as walkers go—but few walkers go very far without cheating. Like trotting horses, they tend to "break" into a run. The Prince noticed that Wilkinson had begun to run like a cheap silk stocking. He stepped out onto the track and waved the Englishman off. "You are all through," he said, except that he said it in Greek. Wilkinson went right on going, but, as he came around on the next lap, Prince George struck a blow for badgers everywhere by throwing a block on him and tossing him off the track.

"Why didn't you stop the first time?" Wilkinson was asked later.

"I don't speak Greek. I thought he wanted my autograph," said Wilkinson, as cool a walker as ever broke into a gallop.

At London, in 1908, British and American athletes declared war on each other, and Italy challenged the winner. Trouble began with the tug-of-war—a gentle event on the face of it. The American team came out full of confidence, but stopped dead at the sight of the British team's shoes. Each boot was a city block long, and covered with cleats. "I didn't know the fleet was in town," the American captain said. "You have to use shoes, not gunboats." The shoes were normal, however, for cops' shoes—the British team being made up of Liverpool policemen, whose feet are bigger than Pinkertons' feet. So the tug began. The Americans surrendered just in time to avoid being pulled into the English Channel. They refused to try any further tugs.

A second U.S. rebellion occurred in the 800-meter run. As the leaders hit the stretch, Carpenter and Robbins of America were ahead of Halswelle, the famous English half-miler. Suddenly, someone off the track shouted "Foul!" A British badger, roused from a sound sleep, reached out and cut the tape, which was then passed by Carpenter, Robbins, and Halswelle in that order. The race was ordered re-run. Halswelle re-ran it alone, in a walkover, and was called the winner. The U.S. runners sat out the event in their hotel rooms, refighting the American Revolution. They might never have come out again, except for meals, which are indispensable to amateur athletes, if the marathon race, run on the last day of the Games, had not made everybody forget every battle but the last one.

This was the marathon in which Dorando Pietri of Italy, the favorite, reeled into the stadium ahead of the rest of the field, looked wistfully around him, and fell on his face, through for the day. He was hauled the rest of the way to the finish line by loving arms—in British sleeves, to hear the American press tell it. With Dorando still unconscious, or thereabouts, there came into view a New York ribbon clerk named Johnny Hayes, just running out his race. Hayes crossed the line and became the startled winner of the 1908 Olympic marathon. Dorando was disqualified for starting the race alone but finishing as a group. "Robbery!" yelled the headlines in Italy. The howling continued until Thanksgiving night of the same year, when someone thought to sell tickets to a Hayes-Dorando rematch in Madison Square Garden.

Every Irish-American and Italian-American in New York bought a seat in the Garden, or tried to break down the doors. Bands played, and the customers beat time to the music on one another's jaws. Dorando—and his fans—went home early. Not even all the Irishmen in the house waited for Johnny Hayes to finish that night, since they had breakfast to eat. But Johnny, a loser by the distance from Marathon to Pittsburgh, had the consolation of his Olympic medal, which was more than Jim Thorpe was to have four years later.

Thorpe's case was *the* rhubarb, and the only rhubarb, of the 1912 Games in Stockholm. The big Indian won the decathlon and the pentathlon, and got his medals all the way home before Francis Albertanti, a New York sports editor, revealed that Jim had once or

twice played baseball for money, under the cunning alias of Jim
Thorpe. The King of Sweden got the medals back, the world went
to war with guns, and it was eight years before the war in short pants
was resumed. En route to Antwerp, in 1920, the American Olympic team mutinied against its keepers because—the boys said—the
beds aboard the transport *Princess Matoika* were for horses, and
the meals were for dogs. "All right, so go home," said the Olympic
committee. The boys looked around at the Atlantic Ocean, and
saw that this was not the place for it. The mutiny was adjourned to
Antwerp, where the team lived in barracks. The committee fired
a hop-step-and-jumper named Dan Ahearn for decamping to a
hotel, an unheard-of move for a hop-step-and-jumper. The whole
team struck. Ahearn was reinstated, and finished sixth in the hop-
step-and-jump.

By 1928, the Winter Olympics had begun to prove that snow
is just as hard on the nerves as sunshine. Irving Jaffee of the U.S.
got through his clocking in the 10,000-meter skating event at St.
Moritz in what seemed to be unbeatable time. But the home committee noticed that the ice was defrosting fast, and called off proceedings with four finalists still waiting to skate their turns. The
race was ruled no contest. The International Olympic Committee protested; Jaffee protested; the Swiss team, coming to see Irving off on the train for home, carried banners reading "JAFFEE,
WINNER OF THE 10,000-METER RACE! LONG LIVE AMERICA!" But the
records still say it was no race, and Jaffee had to wait for 1932 and
Lake Placid to show he was the world's best. Meanwhile, the summer Games of 1928 set a new high in defensive play, at Amsterdam.
The French team marched up to the gate on opening day, but a gatekeeper stopped them. France protested. Holland apologized. Next
day, the French came up to the gate again, and again the keeper
turned them back. France protested. Holland apologized. It was one

of the greatest one-man stands since Horatius at the bridge—but the Dutch finally removed their star gatekeeper and France got into the Games in time to win the marathon on closing day.

To lure competitors to the summer Games of 1932, the town of Los Angeles invented a new event by suppressing a weather report. Some Europeans feared that Los Angeles was too hot. To prove it wasn't, the Chamber of Commerce took thermometer readings in 1931 for the dates corresponding to the Olympic dates. The worst heat wave in the city's history ensued. The chamber studied the readings and threw them in the ashcan. As a result of this shrewd move, everyone came to Los Angeles the next year—including, against great odds, the Brazilians and the Argentinians.

The Brazilian team had no money, so its government put the boys on a ship with fifty thousand sacks of coffee and told them to beat their way north by selling the stuff en route. Coffee sales were so poor that when the athletes docked in California, forty-five of them couldn't afford the $1 landing charge. The rest went ashore, and the ragged forty-five sailed up and down the West Coast peddling coffee until the Games were over. Argentina was racked by civil dissension in 1932. At Los Angeles, the Argentine team got its coach fired by cable, and the new ruling faction then produced the heavyweight boxing winner in Alberto Lovell, later a good pro. On the voyage home, civil dissension was resumed, with fist and gun. The ship's captain radioed ahead to Buenos Aires, and the police met the boat and put Señor Lovell and his medal in jail.

All the world knows how, in 1936, on the ocean voyage to Berlin, Eleanor Holm, the backstroke swimmer, wet her lovely whistle with a champagne cocktail or two and was detached from the team by Mr. Avery Brundage, the noblest badger of them all. "The athletes rode in the steerage, dry," reports Miss Holm. "The sportswriters rode first class, which was wet. The sportswriters invited me up, and I went." Miss Holm adds that, dry or fueled, she could have won her event with one hand.

The world also knows how, in Berlin, when U.S. Negroes began knocking over medals like bowling pins, the late Adolf Hitler was accused of congratulating no winners except white winners, and it became an international hassle. A more obscure, but actually livelier, issue developed that year on the soccer field, when Peru was penalized for flaws in etiquette and was instructed to replay a game it had won from Austria. The Peruvian delegation withdrew from the Games in a body.

It's a matter of Olympic record that soccer and hockey, in which mayhem is committed by hand and by club, respectively, are the leading sports in the production of international ill will. In the 1948 winter Games, hockey came close to wrecking the entire Olympic system before a stick was drawn. America sent two teams to St. Moritz, on opposite sides of the ship—one backed by the American Hockey Association and the Ligue Internationale de Hockey sur Glace, the other by the AAU and the IOC. The first team was thought to be more professional—as amateur hockey teams go—than the second. Yet the Swiss host committee loved the "outlaw" AHA team on sight, and the outlaws went right to work playing the schedule on behalf of America, while the AAU-Olympic team watched and booed.

Every day for a week, Brundage and the Swiss committee wrestled two falls out of three in a hotel room. Daily, the fate of the Games hung in the balance. Hockey was wiped off the books, then reinstated (when the outlaw team finished fourth). In the end, the Ligue Internationale was suspended by the IOC.

In the heat of the battle, it was not much noticed that the Canadian hockey team was thrown off the ice one day for roughness. Or that fiends in human form got to the U.S. bobsleds by night and loosened the steering screws. Or that America's badgers—covering the team's retreat from Switzerland, when the Games had ended—lost the international combined bookkeeping-and-room-service event to the Swiss hotelkeepers. Usually, the public does not hear of it, but in 1948 the blood of the U.S. management boiled over on two counts:

1. By adding special charges for milk and hot baths, the hotelkeepers billed the U.S. finance committee bowlegged and broke its budget in two places.

2. The U.S. complained that there would have been more money to pay the tabs with if the Swiss gatekeepers at the Games had not passed in so many relatives and other freeloaders.

The following summer, in London, British-American war broke out again, on a small scale. The U.S. 400-meter relay team of Barney Ewell, Lorenzo Wright, Harrison Dillard, and Mel Patton won clearly from the British team in the final. But the judges ruled that England had won, because the Americans had committed a foul in passing the baton outside the legal zone. The winning medals went to the British runners. Then someone thought of consulting J. Arthur Rank's motion pictures of the race. The films showed that America's baton-passing had been as clean as a baby's mind—and the medals were pried loose from the British just in time to save the English-speaking Union.

There is a moral in this: Films can prevent rhubarbs and restore peace to the Olympic Games. That leaves the question, who gets the film rights? As 1956 began, they were having a rhubarb about it.

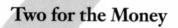

Two for the Money

Titanic Thompson

from *True*

One day not long ago, a St. Louis hotel detective tipped off a cop friend of his that there was a fellow in a room on the eighth floor who packed a gun. They decided to do a little further research. They went into the room without knocking, and it didn't take long to find the gun. It was pointing at them. The man who held it was tall, dark, thin, well dressed, and fiftyish.

"Take it easy," he said. Then, observing the cop's uniform, he set down the gun, a small Army model, on a table, and smiled pleasantly. "I thought it might be a stickup," he said. "I have to be careful."

Down at the station house, where the man was taken to explain why he was armed and why he drew his hardware so quickly, they got a polite and possibly a truthful answer. He happened to have $3,930 on him. He was expecting to claim a racehorse with it. When he carried cash, he liked to feel protected. He had a license for the gun. His name was Alvin C. Thomas. At this point, the police lost interest in the details of the story and merely sat looking at the speaker with the frank curiosity of zoo-goers looking at a duck-billed platypus—for Alvin C. Thomas, as they knew and as he readily confirmed, is also Titanic Thompson. All the cops in the house took a good, long stare. Then they released him, and he went on his way.

On a small scale, Titanic Thompson is an American legend. I say on a small scale, because an overpowering majority of the public has never heard of him. That is the way Titanic likes it. He is a professional gambler. He has sometimes been called the gamblers' gambler. He does not resent his fame among fellow hustlers as a "man with a million propositions," as a master of percentage, but he likes to have it kept within the lodge. In the years of his early manhood, no one knew of him except gamblers, a few rich suckers, a few golf pros, and, by rumor, the police of New York City, the Middle West, and California, his favorite bases of operation. The cops had heard that he clipped people at everything, from golf to throwing quarters at a crack in the floor. But the people he clipped were mostly members of his own profession. Those outside it, honest suckers, did not complain. Suckers seldom do. Besides, they believed—and often they were right—that they had been beaten by pure skill.

One night in 1928, the most celebrated card game in American criminal history took place. As a result of it, Arnold Rothstein, a so-called underworld king, was murdered. And then it turned out that someone named Titanic Thompson had sat in on the game and might know something about the killing.

That was the end, for a while, of Titanic's obscurity. Members of the Grassy Sprain Country Club, near New York City, blurted out a story that had been on their minds for a month. One day, sometime between the Rothstein killing and Titanic's arrest as a material witness, Leo P. Flynn, a big-time fight manager and matchmaker who once handled Jack Dempsey, had brought a stranger out to the club. Leo was known there as a sport and a pretty fair golfer. This time, though, he didn't want to play golf himself. He wanted to match the stranger, whom he called Titanic, against the club professional, George McLean.

A side bet of $2,500 was arranged, with Flynn backing Thompson and several members pooling their funds in support of the local pride. That day, McLean won. He won with ease—the stranger, though he hit some good shots, did not seem to be in George's class. Besides, he was left-handed, and top-notch left-handed golfers are almost as rare as left-handed catchers. The McLean faction listened to Flynn's talk of a return match. McLean listened to the stranger's mild appeal for a ten-stroke handicap.

"I'm not in your league," said the unknown, running his hand through his floppy dark hair, "but I think I can do better than I did today. Give me a real edge in strokes, and we'll bet real dough."

The handicap, after some needling back and forth, was fixed at eight strokes. The real dough, supplied mostly by Mr. Flynn and another golfing sport, a Mr. Duffy, was $13,000, and the members covered every dime of it in behalf of their pro. Mr. Duffy, it happened, was Big Bill Duffy, a jolly henchman of Owney Madden, the racketeer. The members did not know this, but it would probably have made no difference if they had. They did not see how you could fix a golf match, and they did not see how an amateur could beat a good pro. It may not have occurred to them that for $13,000 Titanic was not, strictly speaking, an amateur.

The stranger shot much better, or luckier, golf this time than he had in the first match, but at the end of sixteen holes he had used up his eight-stroke advantage. The match was dead even, and McLean prepared to close in. On the short seventeenth, his tee shot stopped six feet from the pin. Titanic studied the distance and dropped one four feet closer. Perhaps that shot unnerved McLean. At any rate, he missed his putt. The stranger sank his. Titanic stood up. He halved the last hole in par, and Mr. Flynn and Mr. Duffy picked up the $13,000—of which they gaily gave Mr. Thompson his share—and called for drinks for the house. The members went home to brood on the fact that a golf match can indeed be fixed—"fixed upward," as gamblers say—if the fixer is a talented athlete who knows how to hide the symptoms until the price is right.

On the day the news broke of Titanic's arrest in the Rothstein case, Grassy Sprain started the legend rolling. It has been gathering strength ever since. Generally speaking, New York newspaper readers forgot Thompson soon after the trial of George A. McManus for Rothstein's murder (Titanic was a state witness who gave the state no help at all). To most of the rest of the world, he was then, and still is, unknown. But in the small circle in which his name is famous, Titanic Thompson stories have been collected, pooled, and warmed over slow fires for nearly a quarter of a century, till now they amount to a kind of saga—the sharpshooter's *Adventures of Robin Hood.*

Rothstein's death reminded Broadway story-swappers of what might on other levels be called the Adventure of the White Horses. The horse-playing set to which Titanic and Rothstein belonged had formed the habit of spotting white horses from the train that took them to the Belmont or Jamaica track. One morning, some twenty of these smoking-car handicappers made up a pool, of $50 each, on the number of white horses that would be counted on the trip that day. Rothstein's estimate was surprisingly high; Titanic studied the tycoon thoughtfully before he made his own guess, just one horse above Rothstein's. There was an outburst of white horsemeat along the Long Island Rail Road tracks that day—a batch of fifteen animals at one crossing, a batch of twelve at another. The first batch had been planted by Titanic, the second by Rothstein.

"That will teach you not to be close with your money," said Titanic to Rothstein, as he pocketed the pool. "For thirty bucks, you could have had a whole livery stable."

Bear in mind that if Titanic had taken from the rich to give to the poor, as Robin Hood and Jesse James are said to have done, the legend-makers of the gambling world would want no part of him. He would be the wrong kind of hero. But Mr. Thompson has always taken very frankly to give to himself, or to split with the people who stake him. He has seldom made a bet he wasn't sure of winning. He always carries a gimmick—sometimes his hidden athletic skill, sometimes his trained knowledge of percentage, and occasionally a little something extra.

Here are some of the tales they tell:

1. Titanic once bet a peanut vendor $10 he could throw a peanut across Times Square in New York. He took a peanut from a vendor's stack, palmed a loaded one in its place, and pitched the phony goober up against the marquee of the Hotel Astor, across the street.

2. Billy Duffy once backed Titanic in a bet against a powerful amateur golfer noted for his long drives. Titanic offered to let his opponent make three drives on each hole and play the best drive of three. It sounded like a big margin to spot a strong hitter, and the party of the second part snapped the bet up. Playing his best drive, he piled up a big lead on the first nine holes. By that time, his arms were so tired from three full swings at a hole that he could hardly knock the ball off the tee. Titanic breezed home in the last nine.

3. Titanic once bet $10,000 that Nick (the Greek) Dandaolos, another high operator, would not sink a twenty-five-foot putt. Kissed by the goddess Athena, the Greek holed the ball. Thompson, however, was not one to let $10,000 of his money rest long in someone else's jeans. He bet Nick double or nothing that he could hit a silver dollar with a gun eight times out of eight, from ten feet away. After the ceremony, the Greek gave back the ten grand and kept what was left of the dollar for a souvenir.

4. Titanic's mathematics were as sound as Pascal's. In fact, they

were based on the reasoning of the great seventeenth-century Frenchman. He once bet a fellow gambler that two of the first thirty persons they met and spoke to would prove to have the same birthday. Strong in the thought that he had 365 days running for him, the second hustler was pleased to accept. Suspecting, not unnaturally, a frame-up, he was careful to approach total strangers and chance passers-by, who could not be known to Titanic. He lost the bet on the twenty-eighth question, when a duplicated birthday turned up.

"To tell you the truth," said Titanic afterward, "on each of the last five guys we spoke to, the odds were better than even money in my favor. I'll explain the mathematics to you some time."

Your correspondent will also be glad to explain the mathematics some time, to any reader. He does not quite understand them, but he knows what they are. Titanic's reasoning on the birthday proposition was founded on the fact that the chance against him at first was 364/365th, which, when multiplied by the succeeding chances—363/365th, 362/365th, and so forth—came fairly soon to represent 1/2, one chance in two, or even money.

5. Tony Penna, the golf professional, tells of a bet by Titanic that he could throw a pumpkin over a three-story house. The pumpkin, when he produced it, was the size of an orange—but still a pumpkin. Going perhaps into the realm of pure myth, Penna adds that Titanic once bet he could throw a baseball over the Empire State Building. He won it (says Penna) by taking an elevator to the top platform and throwing it from there.

6. Titanic once bet a dice impresario named Nutts Nitti that he could find a hairpin in each block of a stretch of twenty consecutive New York blocks. He won. The hairpins had been planted in advance.

7. Titanic once bet he could throw a quarter at a potato, from

fifteen feet away, and make it stick to the potato at least once in ten tries. Encountering resistance from his opponent, he agreed to settle for seven tries, and scored on the fourth one.

8. Titanic was motoring into Omaha, his temporary base, with a friend one day. As they passed a signpost on the road, Titanic, without looking at it, offered to bet that they would reach the city limits within ten minutes. The signpost made it ten miles to town. The friend, a noticing sort of man, took the bet. He lost. Titanic had moved the signpost five miles closer that morning.

9. There is a standard prop in Titanic's repertory—a two-headed quarter, which he uses with more than standard speed, skill, and acting talent. His opening line, after dinner, is "Let's toss for the check." His next line, while the coin is in the air, is "You cry." If his opponent cries tails, Titanic lets the quarter fall—heads. If the other fellow cries heads, Titanic swings his hands nonchalantly, catches the coin, puts it back in his pocket, and speaks to this effect: "Oh, to hell with gambling for ham and eggs. Let's go Dutch."

10. Titanic is credited with being the man who introduced Rothstein to the art of betting on automobile license plates, at Rothstein's expense. He bet Rothstein, as they stood on a Broadway corner, that the first New Jersey plate to come along would make a better poker hand than the first New York plate. Thirty seconds later, from his parking spot around the corner (there were parking spots in those days), a colleague of Titanic's drove into view in a New Jersey car. His plate number carried three threes.

11. In a Hot Springs, Arkansas, stud poker game, a player named Burke became justly incensed one evening because he could not win.

"That deck is ice cold, and so is the other one," he bawled. "I ain't had a pair in an hour."

"You ought to know," said Titanic soothingly, "that the odds are against getting a pair in any five-card hand. Now if you dealt yourself six cards—"

"With these cards," yelled Burke, "I couldn't pair myself if I dealt all night!"—and the way was paved for a Thompson proposition. Titanic offered to let Burke deal himself ten cold hands of six cards each. Before each hand, he offered to bet that there would be a pair in it. They say that the agony of Burke, as he paired himself in eight of the ten hands and thus lost $300 by the sweat of his own fingers, was something to see. Titanic had known that the addition of a sixth card changes the odds on catching a pair from 13 to 10 against to nearly 2 to 1 in favor. And to bet even money on a 2 to 1 favorite, he would walk quite a distance and stay quite a while.

12. In his early days, Titanic, going through a storeroom in the basement of a sporting club in Ohio on his way to the men's room, spotted a rat and nimbly tipped a barrel over the animal. Later, in the course of the dice game upstairs, he raised the subject of the prevalence of rats in Ohio sporting clubs and made a bet that he could find and shoot one any time. The bet was taken, Titanic returned to the cellar, shot the dead rat, and brought it back to the table with him.

13. Titanic, shooting right-handed, lost a close golf match to an amateur who played in the 90s. Next day, he bet the winner double their first bet that he could beat him playing left-handed. Left-handed, his natural style, Titanic shot an 80. The victim continued to shoot in the 90s.

14. Titanic once bet he could drive a golf ball 500 yards. The bet was popular on all sides, and the interested parties followed Titanic out to the golf course of his choice, on Long Island. He picked a tee on a hill overlooking a lake. It was wintertime. His drive hit the ice and, it seemed to his opponents, never did stop rolling. It went half a mile if it went a yard.

Titanic, as the district attorney found out in the Rothstein case, does not talk much. All that anyone knows about his origins and early life comes from stray remarks, spaced far apart, that he has let fall to other gamblers on the golf course or at the card table. This writer has seen him only once. It was in the "private" or "upstairs" crap game at the old Chicago Club in Saratoga. Joe Madden, the literary barkeep, pointed him out to me from the sidelines. I saw a slender fellow about six feet tall, his dark hair cut long, wearing a neat gabardine suit and two fair sized diamond rings. When Titanic left the game a little later, Madden said, "He's going down to the drugstore to get a load of ice cream. That's his dish."

"That's his dish for breakfast," corrected one of the gamblers at the table. "But he don't eat breakfast till he gets up for the races, maybe two o'clock in the afternoon."

A discussion of Titanic's habits ensued. It reminded me of a session of fight men on Jacobs Beach or in the press room at the Garden, discussing some figure of legend like Stanley Ketchel. I asked where the name Titanic had come from. The answer was one I'd heard before, the only one I've ever heard. It may or may not be true.

In a poker game in New York on Thompson's first tour of the East, one player said to another, "What's that guy's name?"

"It ought to be Titanic," said the second player. "He sinks everybody."

The logic here was a little unsound—if I remember the ss *Titanic* story, "Iceberg" would have been the right name. But gamblers are seldom good on names. Thompson, for instance, is an easy garbling of Titanic's real name, Thomas. There seems to be no doubt, judging by police files, that he was born Alvin Clarence Thomas, in the state of Arkansas, about 1893. He still talks with a slight southwestern accent. As a boy, he once said, he acquired the throwing skill that served him handsomely later by killing quail with rocks. He was a good horseshoe pitcher and an expert shot.

Athletic talent is a rare thing in a professional gambler, but what surprised the golf pros of the Pacific Coast and the Southwest, who knew him in his early days and accepted him as an athlete to begin with, was his lightning speed of mind at gambling. He would make twelve to fifteen bets in a single hole, keeping track of them in his head while others took time to make notes. He would lose one bet and make another on the next shot that would bring his stake back doubled. Penna and others noticed that his bets during the match often were bigger than his bet on the match as a whole.

"Yeah, that's right," said Titanic, when someone spoke of this. "I like to bet 'em when they're out there on the course with me. Especially on the greens. Why? Figure it out for yourself."

It was hard not to figure. When a golfer is out there on the course, any new bet he makes is probably made with his own money, without the help of a backer. When he bets with his own money, he gets nervous. Especially on the greens.

In Titanic's youth, they say, he was impatient with mental slowness of any kind, but it could not have been long before he came to recognize that quality, in the people around him, as so much bread and jam for him. Among the money golfers that knew him at one time and another were Penna, Dick Metz, Len Dodson, and Ben Hogan. He always told them, as he often told the cops when they picked him up on the curious charge of shooting golf too well, that he was a "former pro." It may have been so, but the chances are that he was a former caddy who, on discovering his own skill at the game, almost immediately became a professional gambler rather than a professional golfer. It was a nice economic choice. The best professional golfers in the country, even in these days of rich prizes, do well to earn $30,000 a year from tournaments. Titanic has sometimes made $50,000 in a few weeks of well-timed chipping and putting at golf resorts.

"I've been broke," he told a Coast newspaperman once, "but never for more than six hours at a time. When I tap out, somebody I once helped loans me a stake, and I'm back in action again."

Titanic Thompson broke into the Rothstein game as a young man because he was good company and a good player—though the state of New York tried to prove, a little later, that trained fingers had something to do with it. The fateful game that led to Rothstein's death and to Titanic's first appearance in print took place on the night of September 7–8, 1928. It was held at the apartment of Jimmy Meehan, a regular member of the circle, on the West Side of New York. Rothstein, because he was rumored to have a finger in every branch of organized crime in the city, was the best-known player in the game, but all the others were noted figures in the gambling, bookmaking, and horse-playing worlds. They included Martin "Red" Bowe, Nigger Nate Raymond, Sam and Meyer Boston, Abe Silverman, George A. McManus, and Titanic Thompson. The game was stud poker, but as it went along it took on a pattern familiar in that group—it became a "high-card" game, with the biggest money being bet on the size of the first-up card in the stud hand.

There were rumors along Broadway in the following week that Rothstein had lost a packet. There were also rumors that the winners had not been paid in full. It took a gunshot, however, to make the story public property. On November 4, 1928, someone put a revolver slug into Rothstein's body in Room 349 of the Park Central Hotel. Rothstein staggered from the room and died just outside it. The killer pushed aside a screen and threw the gun into the street below. The New York newspapers went to town. It became the biggest crime story since the murder of Herman Rosenthal by Whitey Lewis, Dago Frank, Lefty Louie, and Gyp the Blood.

The overcoat of George McManus, a smiling gambler, brother of a police lieutenant, had been found in Room 349. Soon afterward McManus was indicted for murder, along with three gunmen who never did show up for trial. On November 26, the D.A., Joab H. Banton, arrested Jimmy Meehan, Red Bowe, Sidney Stajer (Rothstein's secretary), Nigger Nate Raymond, and Titanic as material witnesses. All of them but Bowe were held in $100,000 bail. For some reason it was Titanic, then and later, who caught the public's fancy—maybe because he was said to be a westerner, a lone wolf, a romantic and single-duke gambler of the old school.

It turned out that Titanic had a wife, Mrs. Alice Thomas, who had been living with him at the Mayflower Hotel. A few days after his arrest, she paid him a tearful visit at the West Side prison on Fifty-fourth Street. Titanic then sent for the D.A.'s men, made "important disclosures" (the papers said), and was released on $10,000 bail. What kind of minstrel show he gave to win his freedom is not known. Unofficially it was reported that he had admitted to being in Room 349 just before the murder, leaving when he saw that there might be trouble. Whatever he said, it was plain that the D.A. thought he had laid hold of a fine, friendly witness. The D.A. was very wrong.

When the McManus murder case came to trial, in November 1929, Titanic was running a nightclub and gambling spot in Milwaukee. He was also running a fever in a Milwaukee hospital. So important was his evidence considered by the prosecution that the trial was delayed for a week. Titanic, in Milwaukee, showed for the first time that he was in no mood to blow whistles.

"I don't know what they want me as a witness for," he told reporters, whom he received in scarlet pajamas in the hospital. "I wasn't with Rothstein on the night of the murder and hadn't seen him or McManus for two months previously. We played cards at that time, and McManus lost a lot of money. That's all I know about the case."

When he did get to New York to testify, the courtroom was packed. Titanic sat in the rear of the room, twisting his fingers nervously, till he was called. The crowd buzzed as he took the stand. McManus, in the dock, sat up and smiled at Titanic. Titanic nodded to McManus. Ferdinand Pecora, later a famous judge, then assistant D.A. and a strong trial lawyer, moved in on Titanic confidently. It had been established that McManus had lost $51,000 to Rothstein in the celebrated high-card game while Rothstein was losing about $219,000 to some of the others. Pecora's pitch was obvious. He implied that Rothstein, possibly with Titanic's help, had fleeced McManus of the fifty-one grand. Titanic would have no part of this hypothesis. After identifying himself by saying that he gambled on everything from golf to horse races, and referring to McManus as "a square and honest guy," he began to spar Pecora to a standstill.

"Was the game on the level?" asked the prosecutor.

"It couldn't be any other way on high cards," said Titanic with a deeply scornful gesture. "A man who never dealt in his life was peddling the papers. We had to show him how to shuffle."

To "peddle the papers" is to deal. The crowd was delighted with this local color.

"Now, think," said Pecora angrily, after a while. "Wasn't this game crooked?"

"Anyone ought to know," said Titanic, still scornful, "that that's impossible."

"Couldn't a clever dealer give the high card to any man he chose?"

"Certainly not," said Titanic. "It ain't being done."

On other questions, his memories failed.

"You see," he told Pecora patiently, "I just don't remember things. If I bet on a horse today and won ten grand, I probably would not be able to recall the horse's name tomorrow."

While the public gasped at this spacious statement, the defense took over for cross-examination. At once, Titanic's memory improved, and his attitude got friendlier. He said that McManus had shown no ill will after the game.

"He's a swell loser," said Titanic tenderly. "Win or lose, he always smiles."

In short, he probably gave the state less change for its money than any state's witness in recent memory. And it's a matter of record that George A. McManus was acquitted in the murder of Arnold Rothstein.

It's a matter of record, too, that Titanic was annoyed by his notoriety during the trial. For several months afterward, he complained that he could no longer get a "good" game of golf, by which he meant a game with gravy on the side. He may have misstated the case a little. Recently I asked Oswald Jacoby, the card wizard, about a story in the newspapers that said that John R. Crawford, an ex-G.I. and a spectacular newcomer to card-playing circles, resented the publicity he got in a big canasta game for charity because no one wanted to play cards with him anymore.

"Don't you believe it," said Mr. Jacoby. "People always want to play with a man with a big reputation. The more money they have, the more they like it."

Be that as it may, Titanic, in Tulsa soon after the trial, was bothered by the galleries that followed him—but he did find one man who wanted to play golf with him just to be able to say he'd done it. Titanic fixed up "a little proposition" for him and won $2,000. There must have been other men with the same ambition, or else

Ti's celebrity began to fade, for we cross his trail again in Little Rock, Arkansas, soon afterward, playing golf for $2,000 and $3,000 a round.

True, even a roving gambler likes to stop and run a new "store" now and then, but since the time of his first fame, Titanic has found it more comfortable to keep on the move. He and a large restaurant operator and racketeer, whom we will call Tony Rizzo, were moving by train not long ago from California to Tony's base at Hot Springs.

"Tony," said Titanic, "do you ever regret being illiterate?"

"Whaddya mean?" said Tony, hurt. "I ain't so dumb."

"I'm going to teach you to spell two ten-letter words," said Titanic. "The words are 'rhinoceros' and 'anthropoid.' If you can still spell them when we get off the train, I'll pick up the checks for this trip. But take a tip from me—keep spelling them or you'll forget them."

For the rest of the trip, Rizzo kept spelling out, in order, the letters r-h-i-n-o-c-e-r-o-s and a-n-t-h-r-o-p-o-i-d. He still knew them at the Hot Springs station. Titanic paid off.

The gambler set the second stage of the proposition for Tony's restaurant. He first brought an unknown partner, a respectable-looking fellow as shills go, into the act. He rehearsed the shill in the spelling of the ten-letter words, including "rhinoceros" and "anthropoid." The next night he sat down in Rizzo's restaurant, as usual, with Owen Madden and other lovable tourists. Rizzo himself, as usual, was sitting at a table by himself, wolfing his pizza in solitary grandeur.

"Do you know," said Titanic confidentially, "that that Rizzo just pretends to be ignorant? He puts on a dumb front for business. The guy has got diplomas from two colleges."

This speech aroused great skepticism at Titanic's table, which in turn aroused bets. Titanic covered a thousand dollars' worth, his argument being that Tony could spell any ten-letter word, any one at all, that Mr. Madden and the boys chose to mention. As Titanic expected, a pause followed, while the boys tried to think of a ten-letter word to give to Tony. They were somewhat embarrassed. At this point, Titanic's partner hove into view, and Titanic hailed him.

"Excuse me, sir," he said, "but you look as though you might be able to help us. May I ask your business? A lawyer? Fine. Would you mind writing down ten-letter words on a piece of paper here, for these gentlemen to choose from?"

The stranger obliged. Looking around, he wrote down the word "restaurant," which appeared on Tony's window. He wrote down several others he found on the bill of fare, such as "cacciatore." In and among the rest he inserted the words "rhinoceros" and "anthropoid." He turned the paper over to the boys, who immediately set to work making scratches in the morning line, to protect their bets. They scratched "restaurant"—Tony saw it on the window all day, he might know it. They scratched "cacciatore." "He's Eyetalian," said Mr. Madden, "and he might know all that kind of stuff." This left them, in the end, with "rhinoceros" and "anthropoid." At random, they scratched "rhinoceros." They summoned Mr. Rizzo and desired him to spell the word "anthropoid."

"Sure," said Tony, taking a deep breath. "R-h-i-n-o-c-e-r-o-s."

Titanic paid off the $1,000. The bet belongs to his legend partly because he lost it and partly because he won the money back, with galloping dominoes, the same night. As I said before, he is prosperous just now. A fellow gambler who ran across him in Evansville, Indiana—you might find him anywhere—says that Titanic's pajamas and dressing gowns, always brilliant, are more brilliant than ever. His supply of jewels, rings, and stickpins is at high tide.

A man like Ti, my informant explains, buys jewels whenever he is in the money, to sell or hock when times are hard.

The Titanic legend would not be so solidly honored in the gambling world, it would not be complete, if the quiet Mr. Thompson had never used the gun he always carries, in defense of the money he takes from the rich to give to himself. The police of Little Rock, years ago, found a letter in Titanic's room which demanded "2 thousand cash or you will be sorry." The police of St. Louis more recently found him ready to draw at the sound of a door being opened.

And in Tyler, Texas, a few years back, it was proved clearly that in matters involving Titanic Thompson and his money there is very little kidding. Titanic had had a good day on the golf course. His caddy noticed it. The caddy was sixteen years old, but he had grown-up ideas. At a late hour the same evening, a shot was fired in Tyler, and the police arrived to find the caddy with a bullet in him, while Titanic stood in attendance.

"I shot him," said the gambler. "It was self-defense. He tried to stick me up for my roll."

The young man died the next day. A mask and an unfired gun were found on his person, and the plea of self-defense was allowed. Titanic moved along, with a stronger toehold on history than ever.

The Sack of Shelby

from the *New Yorker*

Jack Kearns became almost legendary in the prizefight business between the two world wars because of his ability to make money in large, bold scoops without recourse to day labor. After the second war, to show that his hand—green thumb, prehensile fingers, and all—was still in, he repeated an old trick by steering still another fighter to a championship. The fighter, Joey Maxim, who became world's light-heavyweight champion under Kearns, will not shine brightly in history books. He is just a footnote sort of fighter—cute but pedestrian, the critics agree, and practically punchless. I remember that there was something like boredom in Kearns's voice, one day in the late nineteen-forties, as he sat on a desk in Madison Square Garden, shortly before Maxim's bout with the Swedish heavyweight champion, Olle Tandberg, and delivered a routine hallelujah to his latest means of support.

"This kid is better than Dempsey," said Kearns. His soft blue eyes stared vacantly at the floor. "He don't hit quite as hard as Dempsey, but otherwise he's better."

Since Kearns managed Jack Dempsey when the latter was heavyweight champion, it may be that he thought he held a lifetime of dispensation from some celestial chamber of commerce to misuse Dempsey's name for advertising purposes. It may be that he was right; at any rate, no thunderbolt split the ceiling to strike him down for his blasphemous words. His audience, composed of managers, trainers, reporters, and press agents, shifted its feet and withheld comment. There was nothing to be said—nothing polite. Then one of the managers, an old-time boxing man, began to warm to the recollection of the team of Dempsey and Kearns. He turned the talk to happier times.

"Remember Shelby, Doc?" he asked. "You and Dempsey broke three banks in Montana."

Kearns's eyes came to life. "We broke four banks," he said. With rising enthusiasm, he went on to describe his withdrawal after the sack of Shelby, Montana, in 1923, with two bags of silver in a railroad caboose. His listeners drew closer. The career and prospects of Joey Maxim were, for the time being and without regrets, tabled.

To boxing people who have heard of the place, the memory of Shelby is precious for many reasons, one of them being that it brought a man of their own profession—namely, Kearns—into singlehanded combat with a state 147,138 square miles in area, producing copper, gold, silver, zinc, lead, manganese, oil, corn, grain, and livestock. No one who was involved in the Shelby affair, including Kearns and Dempsey, is any longer a perfectly reliable authority on the facts of the story, owing to the blurring influence of the autobiographical instinct on boxing memoirs. However, investigation shows that Kearns's performance compared favorably—for tenacity, at least—with those of the predatory railroad barons Jay Gould, Daniel Drew, Commodore Vanderbilt, and James J. Hill. As it happened, it was on Hill's Great Northern Railway, which opened up the north of Montana in the 1880s, that Kearns rode into the state with a fiery purpose, and out of it again with great haste, in 1923. The scope of Kearns's raid had been exaggerated somewhat by his admirers, himself among them, but there is no doubt that it had a profound effect on no fewer than two Montana counties, Toole and Cascade. Furthermore, the name, spirit, and wealth of the whole state were invoked by those Montanans who struggled with Kearns firsthand. They stated more than once at the time that "the honor of all Montana" was at stake. Montana today is perhaps in a sounder financial condition than Kearns, but that only goes to show the extent of its natural resources. It took an oil strike to draw Kearns to Shelby, in Toole County, in the first place, and it took another oil strike, years later, to complete Toole County's recovery from Kearns.

The raider, who was born John L. McKernan, had his sixty-seventh birthday in 1950. He was still a dapper figure then, when dressed for pleasure, but his hair had grown thin and a paunch showed at the conjunction of his pants and sweater when he climbed into the ring on business, as he did at the meeting of his man Maxim with Tandberg, in which Maxim won a close decision. That bout netted Kearns and his fighter approximately $1,500. The loser, by terms of an arrangement based on his drawing power, got $15,000. Later, finding good soil in London, Kearns and Maxim did better. But the spark will never burn as high in this team as it did in Dempsey and Kearns. The bout between Dempsey and Tom Gibbons in Shelby, on July 4, 1923, brought Kearns and Dempsey nearly $300,000. The loser got nothing whatever. In those days, Kearns was forty years old and at the height of his genius.

A good many people in 1923, including writers of newspaper editorials, likened Shelby after the fight to a Belgian village ravaged by the Huns. They ignored or overlooked the fact that Shelby, like no Belgian village on record, had opened the relationship by begging to be taken. Kearns and Dempsey had never heard of Shelby before its citizens went to the trouble of raising $100,000 to entice them there. In the popular view, Dempsey was the archfiend of the episode. His reputation as a draft dodger in the First World War, carefully cultivated by managers of rival fighters like Fighting Bob Martin, the AEF heavyweight champion, made a strong impression on the public; during the Shelby crisis, people were quite willing to consider him a profiteer as well as a slacker. They lost sight of Kearns in Dempsey's shadow. It was only the men directly concerned with financing the Dempsey-Gibbons match who realized that Kearns was the brains and backbone of the visiting party. In language that will not bear repeating, these men marveled at Kearns's almost religions attachment to the principle of collecting all the cash in Montana that was not nailed down.

It was the booster spirit that got Shelby into trouble—the frontier booster spirit, which seems to have been a particularly red-blooded and chuckleheaded variety. Up to 1922, Shelby had been a village populated by four or five hundred cowhands, sheepherders, and dry-dirt farmers. In 1922, oil was struck in the Kevin-Sunburst field, just north of town. The population rose to over a thousand. It was not much of a jump superficially; the significant difference was that all the new citizens had money. Some of them were oil speculators, some of them were real estate men from the West Coast buying up land to sell to oil speculators. A few were merchants selling standard boomtown merchandise, much of it liquid, to the oilmen and real estate men. Kearns had not yet seen Shelby with his own eyes when he first tried to describe it to skeptics in the East a year later, but his description was not far wrong.

"It's one of those wide-open towns," he said spaciously. "Red Dog saloon, gambling halls—you know, like you see in the movies."

It was old Blackfoot country. South of Shelby, the Marias River wound toward the site of a vanished fur-trading post on the Missouri. Not far north was the Canadian border. The Great Northern Railway ran west from Shelby to Glacier Park and the Pacific, east to Duluth and the Twin Cities, south a hundred miles to the nearest real town, Great Falls. In Shelby proper, there were the railroad depot, a few stores, a few houses, a couple of new banks, the Silver Grill Hotel, where fifty extra beds filled the lobby at the height of the boom, and half a dozen saloons.

In one of the saloons, on an evening in January 1923, a bunch of the boys were whooping it up in a civic-minded way. The party was headed by Mayor James A. Johnson, a large man of fifty-eight who had made a comfortable fortune ranching and had added to it in the boom through oil leases and the ownership of the First State Bank of Shelby. Sitting around him were men named Zimmerman, Sampson, Dwyer, and Schwartz. It was Sam Sampson, a storekeeper and landowner, who first suggested that the best way to make the nation and the world Shelby-conscious—that being the object of everyone in town who owned property—would be to stage a fight there for the heavyweight championship of the world. Dempsey was champion. The two most talked-of contenders for his title at the time were Harry Wills, a Negro, and Tom Gibbons, a white man from St. Paul. The barroom committee skipped lightly over Wills. Gibbons was its choice on two counts: the color of his pelt and the fact that he was a Northwestern man, from a state with which Montana had close commercial connections. The committee toasted Gibbons, Shelby, and itself. Then Sampson began to send telegrams in all directions. He wired Dempsey and Gibbons and their managers, and received no replies, which was not surprising, in view of Shelby's overwhelming anonymity. He also sent a telegram to Mike Collins, a journalist and boxing matchmaker in Minneapolis. Collins, a friend of Gibbons, agreed to come to Shelby at the committee's expense and study the possibilities.

His reaction on stepping off the train at the Shelby depot was recorded himself at a later date. "I was startled," he said. Shelby was small and raw beyond the power of a city man's imagination. Mayor Johnson and Sampson led Collins across a few rods of the Great Plains to a saloon, where the mayor gave Collins the impression that Mose Zimmerman, another committeeman who owned land, was ready to finance the championship fight out of his own pocket. To substantiate this, the mayor rounded up Zimmerman, who denied indignantly that he was ready to contribute anything but a small, decent, proportionate piece of the total. The mayor looked sad. Collins walked back to the depot to catch the 8 p.m. train for Minneapolis. As things turned out, he was the first of a series of people who started to wash their hands of Shelby by catching a train. They were all called back at the last minute. A Fate straight out of Sophocles had matters in her grip.

Before the eight o'clock train arrived, Mayor Johnson arranged a mass meeting of citizens in a saloon. Collins was persuaded to address it. He said starkly that Shelby had no boxing arena, no population, and as far as he could see, no money.

"You would need a hundred thousand dollars before you even talk to Dempsey and Gibbons," he added.

At this point, Shelby startled him for the second time. The mayor and his friends raised $26,000 on the spot, the contributors receiving vouchers for ringside tickets to the fight in exchange. Collins noted that the vouchers were marked July Fourth. The phantom battle already had a date and ticket sale. This show of sang-froid won him over. A short time afterward, he set out, in the company of a gentleman named Loy J. Molumby, state commander of the American Legion, to stump Montana for the balance of the money. Traveling from town to town in Molumby's private airplane, they brought the total of cash on hand to $110,000 in little more than a week's time. The moment had come, Collins freely admitted, to let Dempsey and Gibbons in on the secret. It was now, he said, just a matter of convincing them that there was such a place as Shelby and showing them the money.

The two things were achieved in reverse order. It was after seeing the money that Dempsey and Gibbons—or, rather, their managers, Kearns and Eddie Kane—brought themselves to believe in Shelby. The rest of the country, having seen no money, did not believe in Shelby for some time to come. At the beginning of May, the boxing critic of the *New York Tribune*, Jack Lawrence, spoke of a meeting that would take place soon at Madison Square Garden between the Dempsey and Gibbons parties.

"There," he wrote scornfully, "they will probably hear a counter-proposition from the lips of Tex Rickard that will waft Shelby, Montana, back to the pastoral obscurity from which it emerged so suddenly."

Lawrence was wrong. Kearns and Kane bypassed New York and Rickard went to Chicago to inspect the cash and negotiate the Shelby deal with Molumby and Collins, who were now the accredited agents of Mayor Johnson's town. It is apparent that both managers were remarkable for the grandeur of their vision. Kane showed it by agreeing to let Dempsey and Kearns have everything the bout drew, up to $300,000, at the box office in Shelby, if there was a Shelby, before taking a percentage for Gibbons. The Gibbons share was to be 50 percent of the receipts from $300,000 to $600,000, and 25 percent of everything above that. Three hundred thousand dollars was exactly what Kearns and Dempsey had made from the spectacular million-dollar-gate fight with Georges Carpentier, which Rickard had promoted two years before on the threshold of New York City. Kearns was now counting on gouging the same sum from an infinitesimal cow town that had no boxing ring, no professional promoter, and no large city within five hundred miles. At least, he said he was counting on that. Almost no one in New York believed there would be a fight. Kearns's friends suspected, with characteristic misanthropy, that Doc was up to some sort of practice ruse to keep his hand in and his brain lean and sharp for coming campaigns. Rickard, who did not think much of either Gibbons or Wills as an opponent for Dempsey, having sped Kearns west with a tolerant wink, went on with plans for his own notion of a Dempsey match, with the Argentine Luis Firpo, for autumn delivery.

Kearns, however, was in earnest. It pleased his fancy to undertake this western adventure on his own. He wanted for once to be free from eastern entanglements, free from his professional peers. Gibbons and Kane, the parties of the second part, would be amateurs at Shelby in everything but name. At Shelby, every power, privilege, and bargaining weapon would belong to Kearns. If he could carry $300,000 out of a town of one thousand population, he would become immortal in his profession. If he couldn't he had dictated terms that said firmly that all money paid to him and Dempsey in advance was theirs to keep. If they got $300,000, there would be a fight; if they didn't, there would be no fight, and no rebate. Molumby agreed, on behalf of Mayor Johnson, to deliver a second installment of $100,000 to Kearns on June 15, and a third, and last, on July 2, two days before the fight. This was Molumby's last major gesture in connection with the Dempsey-Gibbons match. Like half a dozen other Montanans who tried to learn the boxing business in the next few weeks, he flunked the course.

A slight difficulty occurred in the secondary negations between Kearns and Kane. The difficulty was that they had not spoken to each other for four years and had no wish to start speaking now. Kearns said much later that he could not remember the reason for the breach, which may or may not be true; boxing men usually are shy about revealing the causes of their Grade A feuds—the ones that last anywhere from a year to life. Quartered two floors apart in the Morrison Hotel in Chicago, Kane and Kearns conferred by messenger. The messenger was Collins. One question was who was to referee the fight. It was purely nominal, for Kearns had already decided on his good friend Jim Dougherty, sometimes known as the Baron of Leiperville, Pennsylvania. After four trips by Collins up and down the hotel's emergency stairway, Kane accepted Dougherty. He had no choice. Kearns, as the champion's manager, was in command. Kane, managing the challenger—and a poorly recommended challenger, at that, in the opinion of most critics—could consider himself lucky to have gained a chance at the title for Gibbons. That chance was something, although Gibbons was older and smaller than Dempsey. Beyond it, there was a possibility of making some money if the fight was successful, which was the dream that Mayor Johnson had sold to Collins and Collins to Kane. Kane and Gibbons were gambling, like the men of Shelby and the men of the rest of Montana who backed them. That explains, in part, the deep affection Montana came to feel for Gibbons as the time of the fight drew near.

A few days after the terms were signed, Collins, as "matchmaker," or supervisor of arrangements, announced the ticket price scale: from $50 ringside to $20 for the rear seats. There were no seats at the moment, but Mayor Johnson had persuaded Major J. E. Lane, a local lumber merchant, to build an arena at the edge of town to accommodate forty thousand people. There was no money for Major Lane, but the mayor got him to take a $70,000 chattel mortgage on the arena. Training camps were staked out for both fighters. On May 16, Kearns entrained for Montana with a staff of sparring partners for Dempsey, who made his own way there from his home in Salt Lake City. Kearns was glad to leave the decadent cities of the East, where the newspapers, when they mentioned Shelby at all, still questioned the reality of the fight and half questioned the reality of Shelby. He found Shelby in a holiday mood. The mayor and his friends had recovered from the strain of getting up the first $100,000, and had not yet begun to worry about finding the remaining two hundred thousand. The ticket sale would take care of that.

Kearns beamed upon these unsophisticated burghers with boots on their feet and guns in their belts. He addressed them at a Chamber of Commerce luncheon at the Silver Grill. With all the sincerity he could muster on short notice, he told them that Gibbons was a great fighter, "the best boxer in the world."

"I would not be surprised," Kearns told the meeting lovingly, "if the winner of this contest fought Harry Wills right here in Shelby on Labor Day. You will be the fight capital of the nation. We have come here," he added, "at something of a sacrifice, since we were offered half a million dollars for the same fight in New York. However, Shelby spoke first, and Shelby wins out."

Then Kearns took a rapid look at Shelby, whose facilities could all be seen at a glance with the naked eye, and caught the six o'clock train to Great Falls. All Montana, and Shelby in particular, was well pleased with itself at this point. It is hard to say at just what hour between then and June 15, the first day of open crisis, misgivings began to set in. They must have come soonest to Johnson and Molumby, who were in charge of the ticket sales and cashbox. Kearns ostensibly had no notion of how things were going. When he was told, Montana was stunned by the change in the manner of the free-and-easy stranger.

Kearns had made his base in Great Falls, partly because it was a town of thirty thousand that offered some freedom of movement, and partly because Dempsey was training there, at Great Falls

Park, a mile or so outside the city limits. Before June 15, Dempsey trained well and seemed happy. The park, in a hollow in the hills of Cascade County, just east of the Missouri River and in sight of the Little and Big Belt mountains and the Birdtail Divide, was a pleasant place, surrounded by cottonwood trees, that had formerly been a scene of revelry. Dempsey lived and sparred in a roadhouse that Prohibition and repeated government raids had closed down. Sometimes the champion fished in the Missouri. He had a pet cow, a Hereford bull, a wolf cub, and a bulldog in camp, as well as two of his brothers, Johnny and Bernie; his trainer, Jerry (the Greek) Luvadis; and his stooge, Joe Benjamin, with whom he played pinochle. His sparring partners ranged from giants like Big Ben Wray, seven feet two inches tall, to small, clever middleweights who could simulate Gibbons's style. Gibbons trained in Shelby. He lived with his wife and children in a house on the great, treeless plain, not far from the arena. If anything more was needed to make Gibbons a favorite and Dempsey unpopular in Shelby after June 15, Gibbons's choice of training quarters did it. The town saw him and his family every day. Gibbons at that time was thirty-four, six years older than Dempsey. He had a long and fairly successful career among middleweights and light-heavyweights, though the gifted little Harry Greb had beaten him just the year before. He was a polite and colorless man, with a slim waist, big chest, and a high shock of pompadoured hair.

On June 15, the day appointed for the payment of the second $100,000 to Kearns and Dempsey, Kearns went to the Great Falls station to take a train to Shelby. He said later that he was going in all innocence to ask Mayor Johnson for the money, that he did not know that the mayor and Molumby were at the moment wretchedly chewing cigars in a room in the Park Hotel in Great Falls, having just confessed to George H. Stanton, the leading banker of Great

Falls, that the day of reckoning had found them approximately 98 percent short. They asked him what to do. Stanton, like all Montanans, had followed the Shelby adventure closely. As the principal capitalist of that part of the state, he had followed it more closely than most, and he probably had a fair notion of the truth before he heard it from the unhappy promoters. However, he told them it was a hell of a note, and he sent someone to get Kearns off the train. Kearns came to the hotel room looking hopeful. It was his first business contact with Stanton; it would have been better for Stanton if it had been his last. The promoters explained the situation, or what they could understand of it. They admitted frankly that it confused them. It seemed that a great many tickets that had been mailed out, unbonded, to various parts of the state and country were not yet paid for. It seemed that expenses were unexpectedly large. It appeared that there was $1,600 in cash for Kearns and Dempsey. Whatever suspicions Kearns may have had before this, the cold facts undoubtedly shocked him. He flew into a rage.

"Why don't *you* take over the promotion and the sale?" suggested Stanton. "From all I can see, you own the fight right now."

"I won't promote!" screamed Kearns. "These guys are the promoters. I'm trying to train a fighter. Let them get our money or there won't be any fight."

Kearns left the room in a black mood. He went back to the hotel that evening, at Stanton's invitation, and found that most of the money in Great Falls was represented there: Stanton, president of the Stanton Trust & Savings Bank; Dan Tracey, hotel owner; Russell and Arthur Strain, department-store owners; J. W. Speer, lawyer and former judge; and Shirley Ford, vice-president of the Great Falls National Bank. From there on, Kearns was told, the honor of Montana was at stake. The fight would have new promoters. The money would be raised. It *was* raised, within twenty-four hours. At 5:15 p.m. the next day, June 16, the press was summoned to see Stanton present Kearns with a check for $100,000, seventeen hours and a quarter after the deadline of midnight, June 15. Kearns put the check in his pocket and congratulated Montana. "A dead-game state," he said. Stanton accepted his kind words modestly, though it must be said that he gave newspapermen present the impression that he himself had put up $73,000 of the money, which was not strictly true. He had supplied cash in that amount, but it was underwritten almost entirely by Mayor Jim Johnson, of Shelby, with land and oil leases from his own estate. The Strain brothers and the O'Neill brothers, Lou and John, who were oilmen, made up the balance.

While Molumby and Mayor Johnson sat humbly by—the latter quite silent about his contribution to the salvation of Montana's honor—Dan Tracey delivered a tough speech. The Great Falls committee had appointed Tracey head man of the fight. The old promoters, he said, were through as head men. He would protect the interest of his Great Falls friends. He would see that they got every nickel back. He would countersign all checks from now on. He paused, and Kearns advanced to shake him by the hand.

"This reassures me," said Kearns. "I will stick to Shelby and ignore the countless offers I have got from other states for this fight. I am sure," he added thoughtfully, "that we won't have any trouble about the last hundred thousand dollars—due midnight, July second."

Mayor Johnson mopped his brow with a handkerchief.

"This is a great relief," he told the press. "I wasn't cut out to be a boxing promoter."

Molumby had nothing to say. Earlier that day, he had been denounced by an American Legion post in St. Louis for involving the Legion in Dempsey's affairs.

The reign of Tracey as head man lasted eleven days. It was a time of stress and brooding. The backers of the fight knew that since raising the second $100,000 had been like pulling teeth, the collection of the third hundred thousand would be on the order of a major amputation. The advance sale of tickets brought in no money to speak of. People could not be expected to buy tickets unless they were sure the fight would take place, and the promoters could not persuade the strong-minded Kearns to guarantee the fight before he was sure of the money. The Great Northern canceled a plan to run special trains from the East and the Pacific Coast. The promoters and their friends snarled at Kearns whenever they saw him and nervously fondled the butts of their guns. Frank Walker, of Butte, Montana, a lawyer and later postmaster general under Franklin Roosevelt, came to Great Falls to add weight to the heckling of Kearns. Kearns, however, rode his choppy course serenely and nonchalantly, true to his lofty principle of $300,000 or no contest.

The strain was much harder on Dempsey than on Dempsey's manager. If Kearns was Public Enemy No. 1 to the financiers of Montana, Dempsey was the people's choice for the part. He was sharply aware of it and of the artillery on the hip of nearly everyone he saw. He said later that he pleaded with Kearns, to no avail, at this time to waive the final payment, to promise a fight, and to take over the box office management. The champion's state of mind showed in his work. He looked slow and easy to hit in training, and his sparring partners complained of his viciousness when he hit them. On his twenty-eighth birthday, June 24, seemingly angry at his failure to catch Jack Burke, a middleweight, he knocked down another sparring partner seven times in five rounds and broke the jaw of the giant Wray, who subsequently took his meals through a tube.

The crises came fast now. On June 26, Stanton, conferring in Shelby with Tracey and Mayor Johnson, who had been reduced to assistant promoter, was told that the lumber merchant and the contractors were about to foreclose on their mortgage on the arena. Stanton stalked angrily to the railroad station, but he was called back into conference, inevitably, at the last minute. Half an hour later, he announced that the creditors had agreed to accept payment on a pro-rata basis from the gate receipts. He said that all was well. Tracey, the tough talker of June 16, could not bring himself to share this view. The mortgage crisis had broken his spirit. On June 27, he resigned his job.

"The money that my people put up is nowhere in sight that I can see," he said. "I can't be sure they'll get it back, and I'm through."

Shelby was excited the next day by a telegram received by Mayor Johnson from Minneapolis signed "Louis W. Till," which it assumed to be from Louis Hill, board chairman of the Great Northern, assuring the mayor that he was "on way with cash and securities so Tom can have chance to put profiteering Dempsey in hospital." The wire turned out to be a hoax. On June 29, Stanton made a final, desperate move. After consulting with Great Falls leaders on a list of names and sending telegrams to all parts of the state, he proclaimed "twenty lifelong friends" had pledged $5,000 each to meet the final payment to Kearns and "save the honor of Montana." The announcement was given out now, Stanton said, to dispel doubts that the fight would be held. But the payment to Kearns would not be made until the agreed date of July 2, because, he went on sulkily, some of the new sponsors "are disposed to follow the lead taken by the champion's manager and adhere rigidly to the conditions of the contract." It was their opinion, he said, that Kearns "would get out of the fight if he could." Enlarging on the patriotism of his twenty lifelong friends, Stanton said that cancellation of the bout "would have cast reflections on the state that would have been far-reaching in effect." The Northwest, he added, would now save the fight; the Dakotas, Wyoming, Idaho, Washington, Oregon, and western Canada would send at least fifteen thousand people. The members of the committee would take a loss but "are game enough to see this thing through."

Kearns, ignoring the slurs on his good faith in this manifesto, expressed satisfaction. Dempsey forced a smile and acknowledged the gameness of all Montanans. But on July 2, facing the press, with Kearns present, in Great Falls, Stanton revealed that he had been unable to cash the pledges of his lifelong friends. Eight of them had come through as advertised, he said, but in the circumstances he did not feel like keeping their money. He looked defiantly at Kearns. Kearns shrugged. He retired to discuss things with his lieutenant from New York, Dan McKetrick. Then he told Stanton that he would make the "gamble" that had been forced on him. He would take over the fight, and the gate receipts with it. From that moment, concern about paying Kearns was outweighed by a vivid fear that Kearns and Dempsey would slip across the border before July Fourth with the money they had already collected, leaving Shelby to whistle for its world championship fight. There is no evidence that either man contemplated doing this, but practically everyone in Montana was convinced that both of them did contemplate it. Kearns later recalled that Frank Walker, in a state of deep emotion, shook his fist beneath Kearns's nose on July 3 and warned him not to try to escape.

Shelby had built up to the fight, within its limits. There were concession booths and stands all the way from Main Street to the arena. Entertainers had come from every corner of the state. A tent show called the Hyland-Welty Comedians was playing the town; it starred a certain Patricia Salmon, the toast of the out-of-town reporters, who for $50 a week did three song spots a day, yodeled in front of the curtain, and played the lead in *Which One Shall I*

Marry?, *Thorns and Orange Blossoms*, *The Tie That Binds*, and *The Sweetest Girl in Dixie*. An acquaintance of mine from Billings, Montana, drove to Shelby for the fight with his father, an early patriotic ticket buyer. The sign he remembers best on Main Street was "Aunt Kate's Cathouse." All tourists slept in their automobiles the night of July 3. The great northwestern migration to Shelby had not materialized, but there were enough cars parked on the plain by the arena to show that there was an interest in the fight. Part of the interest was speculative; many people had not bought tickets but counted on getting in anyway.

Dempsey came from Great Falls in a private railroad car on July Fourth, arriving in the early afternoon. A switch engine pulled his car to a siding near the arena, where a crowd of men instantly surrounded it. "There were no cheers," according to Dempsey. His party, which included a Chicago detective named Mike Trent and a celebrated hanger-on of the time, "Senator" Wild Bill Lyons, both strongly and ostentatiously armed, took counsel. Some of the crowd were trying to climb aboard. Lyons told the engineer to keep the engine hooked on and to run the car up and down the siding till it was time for Dempsey to get off. When that time came, the crowd pressed close around the champion, but there were no gunshots or blows. "Trying to run out, were you?" called some of the men. A messenger from the ringside reported that it was still too early for Dempsey's entrance, since the program had been delayed. The crowd, however, got solidly behind Dempsey in a physical sense and pushed him firmly to the arena doors, where he waited with half a dozen retainers by a soft-drink stand, listening to comments on his character and lineage.

The reason for the delay was the public's reluctance to pay official prices for the tickets. Kearns had opened the gates in the morning, after surrendering $500 from the advance sale for the privi-

lege to a crew of federal revenue men who were on hand looking
hungrily after their country's interests. At noon, however, there
were only fifteen hundred people in the grandstand to watch the
first preliminary bout. Thousands milled around outside the gates,
many of them shouting, "We'll come in for ten dollars!" These
were the aristocrats of the mob. Kearns began to accommodate
them at 2:30, while people inside pushed down from high seats to
empty ringside seats, the working press sweltered over typewriters almost too hot to touch, and two bands—the Montana State
Elks band on one side of the ring and the Scottish Highlanders of
Calgary on the other—alternately administered soothing music.
A blind war veteran was singing a ballad in the ring when Kearns
was finally overrun by the rest of the crowd outside, which came in
for free. Dempsey entered at 3:36, thirty-six minutes late. "It was
the most hostile crowd a heavyweight champion ever faced," he
said a few years later, through a ghost writer, and he was probably
right. There was some hissing, he recalled, but mostly "sullen silence." Gibbons made it harder for him by delaying his arrival till
3:45 and taking ten minutes to have his hands taped in the ring.
A few empty bottles came down near Dempsey's corner, tossed
by spectators who blamed the champion for the delay. Dodging
glassware in the corner with Dempsey were Kearns and Bill Lyons, who wore chaps and a sombrero as well as his arsenal. A number of what Kearns called "my Chicago hard guys" sat watchfully
at the ringside just below.

It was a very bad fight. Dempsey, outweighing Gibbons 188
pounds to 174, but stale and nervous, could not land his punches
squarely. It was widely said later than he would not, out of fear for
his safety, but that theory conflicts with the testimony of Dempsey
and the opinion of expert eyewitnesses. Gibbons won a few of the
early rounds. He opened a cut over Dempsey's eye in the second.

Dempsey complained afterward that Kearns, never the most sure-handed of seconds, poured cut medicine inside the eye between rounds, making him half blind until the seventh. From the sixth round, it was Dempsey's fight, easily. The crowd stopped crying, "Kill him, Tommy!" and cried "Hang on!" That was all Gibbons tried to do—he had every reason to know he was working for nothing, and Dempsey's strength soon made him sure he couldn't win. Gibbons scored one moral triumph when he survived the twelfth round, a new record against Dempsey, and another when he survived the fifteenth and last, and forced the bout to a decision. The last round was one long clinch; Gibbons wrapped his arms around Dempsey, and the onlookers shouted derisively at the champion and threw cushions. Gibbons made no objection to referee Dougherty's decision for Dempsey. Neither did the crowd. Dempsey got out with the utmost dispatch when the verdict had been given. The Chicago hard guys, led by Detective Trent, hustled him aboard the private car on the siding. At the Shelby station, his car was hooked to a train for Great Falls. He spent the night at the Park Hotel in Great Falls and caught a regular train the next day for Salt Lake City. Both of Dempsey's eyes were discolored when he boarded the Salt Lake train and exchanged a few last words with the residents of Great Falls who had come to see him off.

"Don't hurry back!" called his well-wishers.

"I won't, boys," said Dempsey sincerely.

Kearns's departure from Montana was a little more complicated. To this day, he holds the colorful view that he narrowly escaped injury or death from the guns of the West in getting out with the money. The money, the proceeds of the last day's ticket sale, amounted to about $80,000 in silver and bills. Kearns and McKetrick counted it in the presence of the federal tax men and stuffed it into a couple of canvas sacks. It is altogether possible that if Kearns

had then honored an earlier promise to meet with certain fight fans
and Shelby citizens in a saloon to talk things over before saying
good-by, he and the cash would not have left the state intact. The
temper of Shelby needed only a sprinkling of ninety-proof rye to
boil over. But Kearns, holding to his higher purpose, which was
to keep all the money, less tax, broke the date. He and McKetrick
made straight from the box office for a caboose attached to a locomotive that stood waiting in the twilight at the station. The getaway transportation had been chartered with the help of the federal
men. As Kearns and McKetrick boarded the caboose, they observed
in the street nearby the shadowy figure of a small man with a uku-
lele. This was the late Hype Igoe, a New York sportswriter with
a turn for minstrelsy, who, having written his fight piece and lin-
gered in Shelby to take on fuel, was delicately strumming chords
for his own entertainment. "This is the New York special, Hype,"
called Kearns. Igoe accepted the invitation and got aboard, and the
special rolled out of Shelby.

Still playing a cautious game, the Kearns party spent the rest of
the night in the cellar of a barbershop in Great Falls. Kearns passed
up the Salt Lake City express next day, and for $500, out of one
of the canvas bags, hired a locomotive and coach from the Great
Northern's Great Falls agent. He and his friends joined Dempsey
the next day.

On July 9 began a series of events that canonized Kearns in the
boxing business. The Stanton Trust & Savings Bank of Great Falls
closed its doors that day. Stanton insisted that the closing had no
connection with the Dempsey-Gibbons fight; he blamed it on post-
war conditions in general. However, all other reports from Montana
then and later agreed that the public knowledge of Stanton's association with the fight caused a run on the bank, which the banker

could not meet because of the temporary withdrawal of $73,000 in cash from his own account to pay Kearns on June 16. The state bank examiner, L. Q. Skelton, came to Great Falls to take over the bank. He saved himself an extra trip to the neighborhood by taking over Mayor Johnson's First State Bank of Shelby as well, Johnson having stopped payment to depositors on the morning of July 10.

It was now revealed for the first time that much of the cash paid by Stanton to Kearns had been secured by Johnson with his personal property, which he began making over to Stanton soon after the fight. On July 11, the First State Bank of Joplin, Montana, an affiliate of Stanton's bank, closed down. Newspaper reports from Joplin stated that all closings to date were "generally accredited" to the championship bout in Shelby. Boxing people never doubted this for a moment. Kearns and Dempsey have been pointed out ever since as winners over three Montana banks. The better-informed students of the situation, like Kearns, feel that the score should be four, for on August 16 of the same year, almost unnoticed by the press, the First National Bank of Shelby was closed by order of its board of directors, following withdrawals of something like $100,000 in the first month after the fight. This left Shelby with, for the time being, no banks at all and practically no assets. The oil boom subsided not long afterward. The arena was torn down and the lumber salvaged by the mortgage holders.

Kearns has related that Mayor Johnson wrote to Dempsey and himself that summer asking for a loan of $25,000, and that it was granted, and repaid within a year. It is certain that the mayor was comfortably well-off when he died in 1938, thanks mainly to another strike in the Kevin-Sunburst oil field, a few years after the first one, which reanimated the town. The career of Patricia Salmon, the tent-show actress, took an opposite course. Her New York press reviews from Shelby in 1923 won her a contract with Florenz Ziegfeld and a season in the *Follies*. It was thought for a time that she, Dempsey, and Kearns (and the U.S. government) were the beneficiaries of the Shelby fight. But Miss Salmon was a one-year wonder. Her star declined as Johnson's rose, and in 1928 she was towed off the floor of Madison Square Garden with a set of swollen feet after performing consecutively for a hundred and thirty-five hours and forty minutes in a dance marathon that she hoped would bring her publicity and another job in the theater.

A word should be said about the early unpopularity of Dempsey, for it contributed much to his discomfort at Shelby and to the public's reaction in Montana and elsewhere. Like other entertainers in both world wars, Dempsey, in 1918, did a certain amount of morale-building among war workers. There is evidence he was popular with sports followers, including Army and Navy men, in 1919, when he won the championship (Willard, the champion, who had also failed to see service, was much less so). The change in Dempsey's case did not set in until after the managers of heavyweights with war records, all of them outclassed as prizefighters by Dempsey, began to play up their wartime service in interviews and advertisements. Dempsey did not speak to Jimmy Bronson, who managed Fighting Bob Martin, for more than twenty years after this campaign, though Bronson actually had nothing to do with the wide circulation of a 1918 photograph of Dempsey striking a pose in a shipyard with a workman's tool in his hands and patent leather shoes on his feet.

Dempsey was formally acquitted of draft evasion in 1920. From the time he lost the championship to Gene Tunney, in 1926, he was immensely popular in America and abroad. However, it was plain to anyone who knew him that he never forgot certain aspects of his public life between 1919 and 1926. He was commissioned, as a physical director, in the Coast Guard in the last war. I saw him during preparations for the Okinawa landing in 1945. He had obtained leave to go to Okinawa on a Coast Guard ship and could hardly control his excitement; in fact, it was almost necessary to gag him to maintain security before the operation began. He went ashore on the Marines' sector of the front shortly after D (or L) Day. He did not stay long, since he served no military purpose there, but it probably helped compensate him for an hour spent with a sharp-tongued crowd outside the wooden arena at Shelby in 1923. Shelby paid as it went for its attitude toward Dempsey, but, like Kearns, he was not an easy man to satisfy.